EXPLORING ORDINARY TI

This volume demonstrates how Ordinary Theology is rapidly becoming one of the most exciting and innovative areas in Practical Theology.

Pete Ward, King's College London, UK

This extraordinary collection of articles exploring Ordinary Theology is a must-read, showing the real significance of listening to what ordinary reflective Christians believe – consulting the faithful – in order to understand how diversely the tradition can be lived in and lived out.

Terrence W. Tilley, Fordham University, USA

'Ordinary theology' characterizes the reflective God-talk of the great majority of churchgoers, and others who remain largely untouched by the assumptions, concepts and arguments that academic theology takes for granted. Jeff Astley coined the phrase in his innovative study, *Ordinary Theology: Looking, Listening and Learning in Theology*, arguing that 'speaking statistically, ordinary theology is the theology of God's Church'.

A number of scholars have responded to this and related conceptualizations, exploring their theological implications. Other researchers have adopted the perspective in examining a range of Church practices and contexts of Christian discipleship, using the tools of empirical study. Ordinary theology research has proved to be key in uncovering people's everyday lay theology or ordinary dogmatics.

Exploring Ordinary Theology presents fresh contributions from a wide range of authors, who address the theological, empirical and practical dimensions of this central feature of ordinary Christian existence and the life of the Church.

Explorations in Practical, Pastoral and Empirical Theology

Series Editors

Leslie J. Francis, University of Warwick, UK
Jeff Astley, St Chad's College, Durham University, UK
Martyn Percy, Ripon College Cuddesdon and The Oxford Ministry Course, Oxford, UK

Theological reflection on the church's practice is now recognized as a significant element in theological studies in the academy and seminary. Ashgate's series in practical, pastoral and empirical theology seeks to foster this resurgence of interest and encourage new developments in practical and applied aspects of theology worldwide. This timely series draws together a wide range of disciplinary approaches and empirical studies to embrace contemporary developments including: the expansion of research in empirical theology, psychological theology, ministry studies, public theology, Christian education and faith development; key issues of contemporary society such as health, ethics and the environment; and more traditional areas of concern such as pastoral care and counselling.

Other titles in the series include:

Asylum-Seeking, Migration and Church
Susanna Snyder

How Survivors of Abuse Relate to God
The Authentic Spirituality of the Annihilated Soul
Susan Shooter

Ordinary Christology
Who Do You Say I Am? Answers From The Pews
Ann Christie

The Ecclesial Canopy
Faith, Hope, Charity
Martyn Percy

Ordinary Theology
Looking, Listening and Learning in Theology
Jeff Astley

Exploring Ordinary Theology
Everyday Christian Believing and the Church

Edited by

JEFF ASTLEY
Durham University, UK

LESLIE J. FRANCIS
University of Warwick, UK

ASHGATE

Published by
Ashgate Publishing Limited
Wey Court East
Union Road
Farnham
Surrey, GU9 7PT
England

Ashgate Publishing Company
110 Cherry Street
Suite 3-1
Burlington, VT 05401-3818
USA

www.ashgate.com

British Library Cataloguing in Publication Data
Astley, Jeff.
Exploring ordinary theology : everyday Christian believing and the Church. -- (Explorations in practical, pastoral and empirical theology)
1. Theology, Practical. 2. Commitment to the church.
3. Faith.
I. Title II. Series III. Francis, Leslie J.
234.2'3-dc23

The Library of Congress has cataloged the printed edition as follows:
Exploring ordinary theology : everyday Christian believing and the church / edited by Jeff Astley and Leslie J. Francis.
p. cm. -- (Explorations in practical, pastoral and empirical theology)
Includes index.
ISBN 978-1-4094-4256-1 (hbk) -- ISBN 978-1-4094-4257-8 (pbk) -- ISBN 978-1-4094-4258-5 (ebook) 1. Theology. I. Astley, Jeff. II. Francis, Leslie J.
BV3.E97 2013
230--dc23

2012031449

ISBN 9781409442561 (hbk)
ISBN 9781409442578 (pbk)
ISBN 9781409442585 (ebk – PDF)
ISBN 9781472401519 (ebk – ePUB)

Printed and bound in Great Britain by the MPG Books Group, UK.

Contents

PART II RESEARCHING AND SITUATING ORDINARY THEOLOGY: EMPIRICAL AND CONTEXTUAL PERSPECTIVES

Notes on Contributors

Dr Tania ap Siôn is Executive Director of the St Mary's Centre, Wales, Senior Research Fellow at the University of Warwick and Senior Lecturer at Glyndŵr University. Recent publications include articles on the study of prayer in a range of journals and chapters in the *International Handbook of Education for Spirituality, Care and Wellbeing* (Springer, 2009) and *The Public Significance of Religion* (Brill, 2011).

Revd Dr Michael Armstrong is a congregational minister. He recently completed doctoral research at Durham University focused on the views of his own congregation about life after death.

Revd Professor Jeff Astley was Director of the North of England Institute for Christian Education from 1981 to 2013. He is an honorary professor in Theology and Religion at Durham University, and visiting professor at Glyndŵr University and York St John University. He is the author or editor of over 35 books on Christian education, practical theology or religious faith, including *Ordinary Theology* (Ashgate, 2002) and the *SCM Studyguide to Christian Doctrine* (SCM, 2010).

Revd Dr Grant Barclay is a parish minister in the Church of Scotland. His doctoral research at Lancaster University was in the area of participation in adult Christian education with reference to multimedia resources. He is co-author of *Logon All Ye Faithful: Multimedia Courseware and Communication Within a Local Faith Community* (EDMEDIA, 2003).

Dr Matthew Barton did his doctoral research at the University of Leeds funded by the Arts and Humanities Research Council (AHRC), working on a theology and ethics of non-violence in relation to the response of the church and individual Christians to non-human animals. At an intersection between systematic theology, Christian ethics and qualitative research, his work involved interviews and ongoing interaction with Christian vegetarian laity and activists.

Dr Tom Beaudoin is Associate Professor of Theology at the Graduate School of Religion at Fordham University, New York. He is the author of several books, including *Witness to Dispossession: The Vocation of a Postmodern Theologian* (Orbis, 2008) and *Virtual Faith: The Irreverent Spiritual Quest of Generation X* (Sheed and Ward, 2003).

Revd Dr Mark J. Cartledge is Director of the Centre for Pentecostal and Charismatic Studies at Birmingham University. He is the author of several books in empirical theology, including *Testimony in the Spirit: Rescripting Ordinary Pentecostal Theology* (Ashgate, 2010).

Dr Ann Christie is Senior Lecturer in Theology and Ministry at York St John University. She is the co-author of *Taking Ordinary Theology Seriously* (Grove Books, 2007) and the author of *Ordinary Christology: Who Do You Say That I Am? Answers from the Pews* (Ashgate, 2012).

Revd Canon Professor Leslie J. Francis is Professor of Religions and Education within the Warwick Religions and Education Research Unit, University of Warwick, and Canon Theologian at Bangor Cathedral, Wales. He is the author or editor of over 50 books, and has authored or co-authored over 500 papers, mainly within empirical and practical theology, the psychology of religion and empirical psychology. Recent books include *Faith and Psychology* (Darton, Longman and Todd, 2005), *Preaching with all our Souls* (Continuum, 2008) and *Ordained Local Ministry in the Church of England* (Continuum, 2012).

Professor Nicholas M. Healy is Professor of Theology and Religious Studies at St John's University, New York. He is the author of *Church, World and the Christian Life* (Cambridge, 2000) and *Thomas Aquinas: Theologian of the Christian Life* (Ashgate, 2003).

Dr J. Patrick Hornbeck II is Assistant Professor of Theology and Medieval Studies and Associate Chair for Undergraduate Studies in the Department of Theology, Fordham University, New York. He is the author of *What Is a Lollard? Dissent and Belief in Late Medieval England* (Oxford, 2010) and co-editor of *Wycliffite Controversies* (Brepols, 2011) and *Wycliffite Spirituality* (Paulist, 2012).

Revd Anthony Lees-Smith is currently Vicar of Evington in the Diocese of Leicester.

Dr Rachel Muers is Senior Lecturer in Christian Studies at the University of Leeds. She is the author of *Keeping God's Silence: Towards a Theological Ethics of Communication* (Blackwell, 2004), *Living for the Future: Theological Ethics for Coming Generations* (T. & T. Clark, 2008) and, with David Grumett, *Theology on the Menu: Asceticism, Meat and Christian Diet* (Routledge, 2010).

Dr Bridget Nichols has taught at the Universities of the Witwatersrand, Sunderland and Durham, and at Sarum College. She has been Lay Chaplain and Research Assistant to the Bishop of Ely since 1998. Her publications on liturgy include *Liturgical Hermeneutics* (Peter Lang, 1996) and *The Collect in the Churches of the Reformation* (SCM, 2010); publications in theology and literature include *Literature in Christian Perspective* (Darton, Longman and Todd, 2000) and 'Liturgy as Literature' in *The Oxford Handbook of English Literature and Theology* (Oxford University Press, 2007). She is currently chair of the Society for Liturgical Study and a member of the Church of England Liturgical Commission.

Revd Canon Professor Martyn Percy is Principal of Ripon College Cuddesdon and the Oxford Ministry Course, Honorary Professor of Theological Education at King's College and Heythrop College, London and an Honorary Canon of Salisbury Cathedral. He writes on Christianity and contemporary culture, modern ecclesiology and practical theology. Recent books include *Engaging Contemporary Culture: Christianity and the Concrete Church* (Ashgate, 2005), *Shaping the Church: The Promise of Implicit Theology* (Ashgate, 2010) and *The Ecclesial Canopy: Faith, Hope, Charity* (Ashgate, 2012).

Dr Andrew Rogers is Senior Lecturer in Practical Theology at the University of Roehampton, London. His Bible Society work on a project to enrich biblical hermeneutics within UK churches led to the publication of the course *H+ Making Good Sense of the Bible* (Bible Society, 2011). He is the author of *Congregational Hermeneutics: How Do We Read?* (Ashgate, forthcoming).

Revd Dr Helen Savage is a writer and freelance adult educator. She was Vicar of Bedlington and Adult Education Adviser in the Diocese of Newcastle. She has published on adult education and music in Christian learning, and recently completed research on adult Christian learners for the Receptive Ecumenism Project (Department of Theology and Religion, Durham University).

Revd Canon Dr John B. Thomson was brought up in Uganda and educated in Scotland and England; he has lived and worked in South Africa and Yorkshire as a parish priest, theological educator and Director of Ministry. His most recent books are *DOXA: A Discipleship Course* (Darton, Longman and Todd, 2007) and *Living Holiness: Stanley Hauerwas and the Church* (Epworth, 2010).

Revd Dr Andrew Village is Reader in Practical and Empirical Theology at York St John University. Formerly an ecologist, he was a parish priest until 2004. His research publications include many journal articles and *The Bible and Lay People* (Ashgate, 2007), *Preaching With all our Souls* (Continuum, 2008) and *The Mind of the Anglican Clergy* (Mellen, 2009).

Rt Revd David Walker is Bishop of Dudley in the Anglican Diocese of Worcester, and a Senior Visiting Fellow at Glyndŵr University. Recent publications include articles in the *Journal of Anglican Studies* and *Rural Theology*, and a chapter in *Changing Rural Life* (Canterbury Press, 2004).

Revd Dr Roger L. Walton is currently Chair of the West Yorkshire Methodist District. He was Director of the Wesley Study Centre at St John's College, Durham for 11 years, before researching Christian discipleship formation and small group involvement as the William Leech Research Fellow at Durham University. Recent publications include *The Reflective Disciple* (Epworth Press, 2009) and *Learning for Ministry* (Church House Publishing, 2005).

Preface

The significance of the beliefs of lay churchgoers, and others who have received little or no academic theological education, has long been recognized by these believers themselves. Ten years ago the phrase 'ordinary theology' was applied to these beliefs, and served as the title of the first volume of Ashgate's series of Explorations in Practical, Pastoral and Empirical Theology.

The book was welcomed by many, including academic theologians, empirical researchers, clergy, theological educators and adult Christian educators. It also provoked some criticism and argument. The editors of the Ashgate series (all contributors to this volume) felt that the time was ripe to commission a collection of new essays to develop the idea of ordinary theology further, and to explore the important phenomenon that it labels both through empirical research and in its application to a range of contexts.

The division of the contents of this book into two parts, theoretical and empirical/contextual, is rather artificial (e.g., Chapter 5 might have been placed in either part). We do not mean to imply by this twofold separation that *real* reflection takes place in Part I, with some inferior form of thinking in Part II. Nor are the essays in Part I wholly independent of empirical realities, and each of them is surely rooted in some context or another. But it could have been worse. We originally intended to divide the material into three parts, devoted to 'reflecting on', 'researching' and 'contextualizing' ordinary theology, which would have been even less convincing.

We expect diversity in exploring the terrain of ordinary theology, and we have found plenty of it here. From the first, we also gladly embraced variety among its explorers. A wide span of perspectives is on offer in this volume from a group of researchers, scholars and practitioners with different styles, backgrounds, academic trades, pastoral vocations, theological positions and experiences of church. As editors, we welcome such a mix of voices, whether they be complementary or dissenting. Our attempt to impose a consistent house style is not meant to hide the diversity of these students of ordinary theology.

May there be many more of them.

Jeff Astley
Leslie J. Francis
November 2012

Acknowledgements

The authors and editors wish to thank all the 'ordinary theologians' who are the subjects of the empirical studies in this book, whether as individuals or churches. Names have been changed to preserve their anonymity. The editors are also most grateful to the contributors for writing essays for this volume and for bearing with the editorial process. They are especially grateful to Mrs Evelyn Jackson, Administrative Secretary of the North of England Institute for Christian Education for 17 years, for preparing our text for publication and assisting with the indexes.

The authors, editors and publisher are grateful to the following for permission to quote from previously published material: Faber and Faber Ltd and Alfred A. Knopf, a division of Random House Inc., for material from 'The Man with the Blue Guitar' from *The Collected Poems of Wallace Stevens* by Wallace Stevens, copyright 1954 by Wallace Stevens and renewed 1982 by Holly Stevens; Penguin Books Ltd for material from 'People' by Yevgeny Yevtushenko (*Yevtushenko: Selected Poems,* 2008); and Enitharmon Press for material from 'Patience Strong' by U.A. Fanthorpe (*New and Collected Poems*, 2010).

Quotations from the Bible are from the *New Revised Standard Version* Bible, Anglicized Edition, copyright © 1989, 1995, by the Division of Christian Education of the National Council of the Churches of Christ in the USA, and are used by permission.

Chapter 1

The Analysis, Investigation and Application of Ordinary Theology

Jeff Astley

Definition and Characterization

I have *defined* ordinary theology as 'the theological beliefs and processes of believing that find expression in the God-talk of those believers who have received no scholarly theological education' (Astley, 2002: 1, cf. 55–8, 64, 94). As not all such discourse can count as theology, I restrict the designation to 'reflective' God-talk (52–7). We should not automatically deny a reflective status to the theology of these believers, although the reflections of ordinary theologians are frequently less precise than the academy expects. This sort of theological reflection also involves more than can be mapped on to people's cognitive faculties alone (140–45). Along with its 'practical goal', this may allow us to describe such reflection as 'ultimately intended for every believer' rather than a 'theological speciality reserved only for experts' (Kinast, 2000: 64).

My *description* of the nature of ordinary theology (Astley, 2002: 57–95) treats it, to some extent, as an 'ideal type' in that it stresses, and sometimes simplifies and exaggerates, certain common elements and tends to focus on extreme cases. I hold that the difference between ordinary and academic theology is only a matter of degree – no pun intended. Even academics normally begin by doing theology in an ordinary way, and this ordinary theology often continues to underlie their more academic theological expressions. And, historically speaking, the academic mode of theology owes much of its origin to – and develops alongside – this less conceptual, technical or systematic form of theology, which begins as a 'cognitive disposition and orientation of the soul' that represents the 'wisdom proper to the life of the believer' (Farley, 1983: 35; 1988: 88) and becomes a personal, autobiographical and aphoristic 'irregular dogmatics' (Barth, 1975: 277–8).

Such a widespread – and, in that sense, 'common' and 'ordinary' – theology (Astley, 2002: 49–52) is learned and 'taught' in very different ways from those of the university or seminary. Much of this takes place through Christian prayer, worship and Bible reading, and Christian living and fellowship; through the life of the home, street or workplace; and in reflection on other, everyday life experiences and activities – and hardly at all through such 'out of the ordinary' things as lectures, academic seminars, tutorials or private study.

The *significance* of ordinary theology is twofold (144 62). There is an uncontroversial, pragmatic justification for its study, in that the church needs to know about the beliefs, and patterns and processes of believing, of those who receive its communicative and pastoral ministries.[1] The wider significance of ordinary theology, however, and the theological justification for its study, is that ordinary theology in some sense ‘works’ for those who own it. It fits their life experience and gives meaning to, and expresses the meaning they find within, their own lives. It is highly significant *for them* because it articulates a faith and a spirituality, and incorporates beliefs and ways of believing, that they find to be salvific – healing, saving, making them whole. Ordinary theology helps people spiritually and religiously.

This is not to say that every part of the unsystematic bricolage that makes up most Christians’ ordinary theology works in this way. People often find themselves holding beliefs that are not helpful to their spiritual life or sense of meaning, and may even get in the way of these things. I would argue, however, that the *whole* of their belief-(non)system – and some parts of it in particular – must be salvific for people if they are to continue to hold it.[2] Although there are other causes, this is one positive reason why religious learners are often so resistant to any change in their ordinary beliefs.[3]

Analogies

Does something like the ordinary/academic distinction in theology apply in other areas? The relationship between ordinary and academic theology and ordinary and academic physics or statistics (or social sciences such as economics) is not really analogous. For ordinary (‘folk’ or ‘naïve’) physics often fails us in negotiating the physical world, and our ‘informal mathematics’ is frequently misleading. Our natural misunderstandings in these areas are poor substitutes for empirically proven or logically secure beliefs. By contrast, even when our ordinary theology is wholly anecdotal, figurative, inconsistent or even logically confused, it may serve us as a personal expression of a self-involving religious response or relationship that works. Its salvific, meaning-making function involves a psychological/spiritual change in a person, which (theological realists insist) depends on transcendent facts about God’s structuring of the human heart

1 Including those outside the church (cf. Astley, 1996; Shag and Schweitzer, 2011).

2 This is an empirical hypothesis that requires testing, not something that is true by definition.

3 Neuroscience reveals a biological basis for our general resistance to changing our ideas, in the resilience of the ‘personal and individual’, pre-existent neural networks that code them. As learning and understanding comes through cumulative connections, teachers should build on people’s existing beliefs rather than ignoring them or sweeping them away (Zull, 2002: chs 6 and 7). Cf. Chapter 5 below.

through nature and grace, so that it is restless until it rests in him. Bad science or poor risk assessment do not help us in any similar way. Certainly, they do not spiritually heal people or make them whole.

We may speculate that ordinary theology more closely resembles our folk knowledge about human thinking, feeling and behaving, than it does our untutored understanding of the laws of physical things or numerical relationships. Some moral philosophers interpret their task as making sense of everyday or common morality, rather than imposing a more sophisticated notion to overwrite and replace it (e.g., Gert, 1998: preface and ch. 1). Our ordinary morality works in our social relationships and decision-making, and moral theories are often tested against widely held moral 'knowledge', 'ideals', 'experience' or 'insights'. Some psychologists argue similarly that the ideas of folk (naïve, common sense or vernacular) psychology embrace well-established constructs and assumptions, albeit expressed in aphoristic style, that academic psychologists should seek to extend rather than to eliminate (cf. Crane, 2003: ch. 2). Folk psychology also 'works', in human interaction and in predicting and even explaining everyday behaviour, even though it too is open to cognitive refinement and correction.

Study

Our characterization of ordinary theology needs to be earthed in – and adequate to – the empirical reality of people's beliefs and values. The content, and perhaps sometimes the form, of ordinary theology are likely to vary across cultures, churches, congregations and individuals. There is no one ordinary theology, as there is no one academic (or, in truth, normative ecclesiastical) theology. As the church is both many and varied, we should expect variety in ordinary Christian theology.

Empirical Study

The *descriptive task* of the study of ordinary theology requires us to engage in 'theological listening': listening out for it and attempting to portray it. This sort of description is always partly dependent on the listener's own theological presuppositions, if only because we won't hear another person's God-talk *as* theology unless we have some idea about what sort of thing a theology is. (And if we think that theology can only exist in the form of technical concepts and systematic arguments, we shall not hear much of it from the pews – or the pulpit, come to that.) So even at this stage, and certainly if they listen in detail, students of ordinary theology are engaged in a hermeneutical task in which 'continuing theological reflection, i.e., a process of ordering and interpretation, … [modifies] the perspective within which the "facts" are perceived' (van der Ven, 1993: 121).

This description, therefore, always 'takes place within a dialogue or conversation' (Browning, 1991: 64).[4]

Theological listening may take many different forms. In trying (often unsuccessfully, I fear) to encourage clergy and ordinands to take seriously the ordinary theology of churchgoers and others, I am sometimes accused of pressing them to become professional ethnographers or expert statisticians. This volume contains several examples of such time-consuming empirical studies, which report either rich qualitative data derived from small samples, or more representative analyses based on quantitative data from larger populations. We must welcome this work; the church needs much more of it. But with the necessary reflexivity (critical self-reflection on the enquirer's role and effect), normal pastoral conversations and alert, empathetic and intelligent observations can already tell us a great deal about what people believe, as some of the other essays here bear witness. The great value of more in-depth study through research interviews and questionnaires is that it allows us both to validate the anecdotal, and to explore behind it. But *all* theological listening will encourage people to think and speak (even write) about their theologies, and to feel that their beliefs are being taken seriously – because they are.

In this volume we are largely concerned with theological listening directed to what people are literally saying (or writing). This process takes seriously their feelings, relationships and actions, and especially their values, ideas, beliefs and understanding, as these are expressed in their words.

Studying Ordinary Theology in Practice Practical theology centres on the claims that *praxis*[5] is 'the fundamental locus of theology, the "place" where theology occurs' (Boff, 2009: xxi); that people's practice is 'its own proper "articulation" of theological conviction and insight' and has its own theological authority as the bearer of 'embodied theology' (Cameron et al., 2010: 51); and that theology is a 'performative discipline' whose task is to describe how a situation is already theology-in-practice (Graham, 1996: 7). Practice is here viewed as the performance, or acting out, of the 'text' of a person or group's beliefs, values, theories and theologies (Swinton and Mowat, 2006: 19–20). Other language that is used of this relationship between theological beliefs and practices (or communities

4 A purely phenomenological account is impossible; there can be no 'immaculate perception' (van Maanen, 1988: 74). An interpretative or hermeneutical-phenomenological framework will not naïvely ignore the role of the listener-interpreter. At its most basic, researchers perceive other people's words and beliefs as having theological significance and meaning for those people. But these categories of theological significance and meaning are partly dependent on the researchers' *own* theological comprehension and standpoint (see Astley, 2002: 108–14).

5 Reflective action, 'value-directed and value-laden action' or 'action and reflection working together' (Graham, 1996: 7; Green, 2009: 7).

of practice) includes 'embedding' and 'underpinning', and belief being 'within the act itself'. These are all potent and illuminating metaphors.

Unfortunately, it is often difficult to *infer* people's beliefs from their practice. Unless one defines beliefs in terms of behaviour,[6] there is rarely a one-to-one relationship between beliefs and their expression in actions, and sometimes only a weak empirical correlation. Disagreements over the metamechanics of sacramental theology and the metaphysics of divinity rarely map tidily onto the overt behaviour of Christians at their worship, or in their actions outside the church building. In this sense, different theologies may undergird the same practice, and we must be cautious about imputing to people's practice a theology that they would not themselves claim to hold (but see below).

This is why ordinary theology research normally concentrates on people's beliefs as they are expressed in their words: portraying the theology in what people say (or write) rather than the theology implicit in what they do. I want *literally to hear* the theological voice of those who call themselves 'just ordinary'. In taking their practices seriously, we must include in this category the speaking (or writing) of their reflective God-talk. However hesitant, inarticulate and unsystematic is a person's ordinary theology, it is easier literally to hear than is their practice. Practice speaks 'very loudly', of course, as we say; and often 'more loudly than words'. But it does not speak *in words*. Inferring people's theology from their practice may sometimes be our only recourse; but it is a rather different sort of activity from describing, understanding and analysing what they say.[7]

---

[6] Beliefs are introspectable states of a person, as well as dispositions to act in certain (outwardly observable) ways.

[7] Note further: (1) For Wittgenstein, action always comes first and is the context in which our language makes sense. He urged the philosopher not to speculate in an armchair what language means, but to go out into the world – back to the 'rough ground' of 'everyday thinking' and 'actual language' (1968: §§106–7) – in order to see how people really live there, because 'only in the stream of thought and life do words have meaning' (1967: §173). In analysing religious words, what matters is the difference they make in a person's life: '*practice* gives the words their sense' (1980: 85). This does not mean, however, that we can ignore the actual words people say. It means, rather, that we should be more sensitive to what these words mean to the people saying them, as shown (to them, as well as to us) in how they live and what they do – which includes their accounts of their living and doing, and their other linguistic practices; (2) The three aspects of human beings – our behaving or acting side; our cognitive, thinking or believing side; and our feeling or valuing side – are abstractions from a concrete unity. Action, like belief and affect, is a part of a greater whole; all human actions are the actions of a thinking-and-feeling person. So the faith expressed in Christian action is not *separate from* faith as Christian belief, or from faith as the attitude or orientation that constitutes Christian trust and commitment. Furthermore, practice doesn't come out of nowhere: it is brought to birth by our beliefs and feelings, and emerges alongside them. Each of these elements is in turn reinforced and changed by the other two. Research separates out parts that function and belong together in one integrated person. Although 'the concept of practice connotes doing', this is 'not just doing in and of itself.

I would argue that we should not only listen, but also (wherever possible and appropriate) *ask* people about what they believe, pressing them as to what they mean by what they say. Wittgenstein argued that to understand the believer we have to know the inferences that *the believer* draws.[8] As usual, the enemy is superficiality. Our earnest hope is that if we really 'listen up', and listen in depth, we shall find out what these ordinary theologians truly believe, in part 'based on the evidence of the *implications*, both implicit and explicit, that they actually draw and adopt in their discourse and their lives from the language they are using' (Astley, 2002: 121). (Please note: lives *and discourse*.) In descriptive ordinary theology, we must always strive to unveil the theology in the linguistic data, rather than impose our own theological categories onto that data (within the limits of n. 4).

There is a problem here, of course. If people are conscious that they are drawing these theological implications, then they will probably cheerfully accept the account we give of their theology. It will then become an *agreed* account of what they actually mean by what they say and do. But if they do not consciously recognize that they are drawing and accepting these implications from their own theology, they may not accept our account of it. On such occasions, and having reported this disagreement, we may be permitted to stick to our account. If at all possible, however, we should always give people the opportunity to disagree with our description of what it is they are 'really saying'.

Theological Study

There is a further, and wholly proper, way of studying ordinary theology that takes us beyond such empirical description-and-interpretation to a more evaluative and reflective, broadly *theological critique.*

Having first listened to what ordinary theologians say, and probed the theological inferences and connections that ordinary theologians themselves make, theologically-trained observers may then reflect theologically on this ordinary theology, presenting their own *theology of ordinary theology*. This will

... The process of engaging in practice always involves the whole person, both acting and knowing at once' (Wenger, 1998: 47–8). Thus 'practice is not inherently unreflective', as Wenger adds. (3) People's beliefs matter to them, even those that are not expressed in action (some cannot be). They especially affect how people feel. (4) But beliefs, unlike feelings and actions, are primarily cognitive states. Their linguistic expressions are therefore more directly open to analysis and critique, including evaluation in terms of their implications, coherence, evidence and justification (Astley, 2002: 72, 94–5). (5) None of this means that people's beliefs are more fundamental or important than their actions or lives; I do not believe that they are (see 32–3, 55; 2010: 18–20, 45–6).

[8] 'I don't want to say anything he himself wouldn't say. I want to say that he draws these conclusions.' We need to know whether 'eyebrows are going to be talked of, in connection with the Eye of God?' (1966: 71).

usually take the form of a 'critical practical theology' (see Kelsey, 1992: 206–7, 211; Heitink, 1999: 221), in which questions are raised about the truth of what ordinary theologians are saying, and the extent to which it is faithful to Christian norms.[9] This mode of studying ordinary theology can be appropriate within 'a *full* theological study *redirected* to the [beliefs] of the everyday believer' (Astley, 2002: 104).

There are examples of this critical theological study of ordinary theology in many of these essays (e.g., Chapter 8). Social scientific reflection is also of value (e.g., Chapter 9). The theological analysis and critique of ordinary theology is, however, a distinctive task and likely to be of most interest to academic theologians. But they, too, must distinguish this theological reflection *on* the words and the other practices of others, from the theological reflections *of* those others (those practitioners themselves): that is, their ordinary theology. And they must be open to letting this ordinary theology critique their own academic theology (cf. chapters 2 and 10).

Context, Content and Relevance

In the second part of this book certain contexts of church practice are explored in greater detail, including Christian learning, the use of the Bible, and prayer and worship. The application of the concept of ordinary theology to other situations may be equally illuminating. 'Denominational' contexts are also significant, and detailed consideration is given below to the ordinary theology of Anglicans, Congregationalists, Pentecostals, Roman Catholics and members of independent churches. Other groups and individuals from across the ecumenical spectrum are also studied. Taken together, these enquiries help to illustrate the variety of ordinary theology, from conservative to liberal.

Content cannot be easily separated from context, but some of the studies included here concentrate our attention on different examples or dimensions of the content of ordinary theology, in particular the ethical and the doctrinal (chiefly ecclesiology, soteriology and eschatology). Theology and practice often come together here, as they do in the chapters that direct the spotlight of ordinary theology research onto worship, prayer and mission, and in the broader studies included in this collection. The application of ordinary theology research and reflection to more specific Christian doctrines and activities, such as the doctrine of revelation and the concept of the church, is of particular significance.

In many of these areas, the very existence of an ordinary theology challenges certain assumptions of academic and ecclesiastical theology. The debates that need to follow from such challenges are of signal importance to Christianity. Once it has been uncovered, ordinary theology cannot be facilely ignored.

---

9 These norms are themselves not immune from the empirical facts about what ordinary theologians believe (cf. chapters 4 and 7).

References

Astley, Jeff (1996), 'Theology for the Untheological? Theology, Philosophy and the Classroom', in Jeff Astley and Leslie J. Francis (eds), *Christian Theology and Religious Education: Connections and Contradictions*, London: SPCK, pp. 60–77.

Astley, Jeff (2002), *Ordinary Theology: Looking, Listening and Learning in Theology*, Aldershot: Ashgate.

Astley, Jeff (2010), *SCM Studyguide to Christian Doctrine*, London: SCM Press.

Barth, Karl (1975), *Church Dogmatics*, I/1, Edinburgh: T. & T. Clark.

Boff, Clodovis, OSM (2009), *Theology and Praxis: Epistemological Foundations*, Eugene, Oreg.: Wipf & Stock.

Browning, Don (1991), *A Fundamental Practical Theology: Descriptive and Strategic Proposals*, Minneapolis, Minn.: Fortress.

Cameron, Helen et al. (2010), *Talking about God in Practice: Theological Action Research and Practical Theology*, London: SCM Press.

Crane, Tim (2003), *The Mechanical Mind: A Philosophical Introduction to Minds, Machines and Mental Representation*, London: Routledge.

Farley, Edward (1983), *Theologia: The Fragmentation and Unity of Theological Education*, Philadelphia: Fortress.

Farley, Edward (1988), *The Fragility of Knowledge: Theological Education in the Church and the University*, Philadelphia: Fortress.

Gert, Bernard (1998), *Morality: Its Nature and Justification*, New York: Oxford University Press.

Graham, Elaine L. (1996), *Transforming Practice: Pastoral Theology in an Age of Uncertainty*, London: Mowbray.

Green, Laurie (2009), *Let's Do Theology: Resources for Contextual Theology*, London: Mowbray.

Heitink, Gerben (1999), *Practical Theology: History, Theory, Action Domains*, Grand Rapids, Mich.: Eerdmans.

Kelsey, David H. (1992), *To Understand God Truly: What's Theological about a Theological School*, Louisville, Ky.: Westminster/John Knox.

Kinast, Rob L. (2000), *What Are They Saying About Theological Reflection?* New York: Paulist.

Shag, Thomas and Friedrich Schweitzer (2011), *Brauchen Jugendliche Theologie?* Neukirchen: Neukirchen-Vluyn.

Swinton, John and Harriet Mowat (2006), *Practical Theology and Qualitative Research*, London: SCM Press.

van der Ven, Johannes (1993), *Practical Theology: An Empirical Approach*, Kampen, Netherlands: Kok Pharos.

van Maanen, John (1988), *Tales from the Field: On Writing Ethnography*, Chicago: University of Chicago Press.

Wenger, Etienne (1998), *Communities of Practice: Learning, Meaning, and Identity*, Cambridge: Cambridge University Press.

Wittgenstein, Ludwig (1966), *Lectures and Conversations in Aesthetics, Psychology and Religious Belief*, Oxford: Blackwell.
Wittgenstein, Ludwig (1967), *Zettel*, Oxford: Blackwell.
Wittgenstein, Ludwig (1968), *Philosophical Investigations*, Oxford: Blackwell.
Wittgenstein, Ludwig (1980), *Culture and Value*, Oxford: Blackwell.
Zull, James E. (2002), *The Art of Changing the Brain: Enriching Teaching by Exploring the Biology of Learning*, Sterling, Va.: Stylus.

PART I
Reflecting on Ordinary Theology: Analytical and Theological Perspectives

Chapter 2
Ordinary Theology, Theological Method and Constructive Ecclesiology

Nicholas M. Healy

In this chapter I begin by considering the work of Friedrich Schleiermacher and Stanley Hauerwas, particularly their strong – and surprisingly similar – emphasis upon the church's communal identity and formative function. Ordinary theology – understood broadly as a reflective practice of non-academic and non-clerical Christians – is largely incompatible with their accounts of the church which, I argue, are inadequate and distorting. I conclude by briefly discussing how a more adequate ecclesiology encourages the practice of ordinary theology.

Schleiermacher's Account of Christian Identity Formation

Schleiermacher's *The Christian Faith* constitutes (amongst much else) an apologetics legitimating the practice of academic theological enquiry within the modern university. The book begins with a phenomenological account of religious communities in general, developed in relation to the essence of religion ('piety') as the universally available feeling of absolute dependence. The task of scientific academic theology is to study such religious communities. Thus, Christian theology studies the Christian church as a particular instance of a more widespread and diverse social form. With this methodology, Schleiermacher shifts the object of theological study in a fundamental way. Theology's object is no longer 'God and things in relation to God', to borrow the premodern formulation of Thomas Aquinas. Rather, it is 'the doctrine prevalent in a Christian church at a given time' (Schleiermacher, 1928: para. 19). Christian theology becomes the critical study of a particular form of human collective production: the beliefs and practices that constitute the church's distinctive communal identity.

The identity of a religious community is individuated by its specific understanding of piety (para. 10). In the case of the Christian church, this is the Idea of Christianity, which is 'the redemption accomplished by Jesus of Nazareth' (para. 11). The church's primary function is to form the God-consciousness of its members in relation to this Idea. This task is entrusted to its leadership, who are to be trained in academic theological enquiry, which is reserved to them. Academic theology is therefore fundamentally practical, designed to enable church leaders to discern what is consistent or not with the Idea of Christianity, and thereby to guide their flock by their preaching, teaching and example.

This conception of the church and the role within it of academic theology thus rules out ordinary theology except in a largely passive form whereby individual members mull over and interiorize what they have learned from their leaders (Schleiermacher, 1928: para. 133). Since they lack both the training and the appointment to leadership, they cannot engage in the kind of active theological enquiry that would issue in their own theological decisions, and even less can their decisions affect the shape of their church. Thus, while the religious philosophy of his early *Speeches* (Schleiermacher, 1958) may seem to advocate a kind of religious individualism, Schleiermacher's mature writings make clear that 'the life of each individual springs from that of the community, while the life of the community springs from no other individual life than that of the Redeemer' (Schleiermacher, 1928: para. 113).

Hauerwas's Account of Christian Identity Formation

Hauerwas's work differs, of course, from Schleiermacher's in important ways. He rejects the latter's religious philosophy; nor is his primary concern to show the reasonableness of theological enquiry within the academy. His position is, however, remarkably similar to Schleiermacher's in certain key respects that, to my knowledge, have not as yet been adequately analysed. Significantly, both sit rather lightly to doctrine. Besides shifting the object of theology, Schleiermacher, for example, treats the doctrine of the Trinity as an inference from other doctrines, perhaps in reaction to Protestant orthodoxy's tendency toward doctrinal extrinsicism. Hauerwas does not address doctrine much at all, perhaps as part of his own rejection of a doctrinal extrinsicism that views Christianity as a 'system of beliefs' that can be held without transforming the Christian's life (e.g., Hauerwas 1988: 10; 1998: 4–5). And while it would be inaccurate to say that Hauerwas changes the subject of theological enquiry in quite the same way as Schleiermacher, he does talk far more about the church and its members' formation than about God, as has been not infrequently noted.[1] For both men, the church's life is the starting point and the dominant concern.

Relatedly, Hauerwas's account of the church and of formation is, like Schleiermacher's, structured and governed by theories of social identity and formation that he appropriates with few, if any, directly theological considerations. Hauerwas moves from the general to the particular, from an understanding of what all communities are to the specific differences of the Christian ecclesial community. The 'basic methodological claim' is that 'every community and polity involves and requires a narrative. The distinctive character of the church's social ethics thus

[1] With typical openness and good humour, Hauerwas himself notes a remark to this effect by Nigel Biggar (Hauerwas, 1998: 37). See also Kerr, 2008: 93–126.

does not follow from the fact that it is a narrative-formed community, but rather from the *kind* of narrative that determines its life' (Hauerwas, 1981: 4), namely, the narrative of Jesus of Nazareth. As a community or *polis*, the church embodies its own distinctive narrative, so that it 'stands as a political alternative to every nation, witnessing to the kind of social life possible for those that have been formed by the story of Christ' (Hauerwas, 1981: 12). To witness to the gospel is thus to display our communal identity which, as distinctive, counters all alternatives, especially 'modernity and its bastard offspring postmodernity [which] are but reflections of the Christian attempt to make God a god available without the mediation of the church' (Hauerwas, 2000: 38).

Christian formation is obviously vital to such a programme. Christians are effective witnesses only insofar as they have been adequately formed by ecclesially sanctioned practices so as to acquire Christian virtues. The process of formation does not include active ordinary theology, however.[2] Instead, Hauerwas (probably with tongue at least partially in cheek) advocates a 'peasant Catholicism' – which has the church make 'one's body shaped, one's habits determined, in a manner that the worship of God is unavoidable. Of course beliefs and doctrines matter, but it is not the peasant's task to ensure they are rightly maintained. That is the task of the church located in the office of the bishop assisted by the theologian' (Hauerwas, 1998: 79). On the same page he directs a footnote against those educated professionals who 'assume what they know as a banker or lawyer or university professor gives them a critical perspective on Christianity'.[3]

Initial Questions

Hauerwas's account, like Schleiermacher's, thus indicates that, if ordinary members of the church find it difficult to believe or practice something accepted as correct by their leadership, it is they, the ordinary believers, who should change. Of course, an alternative would be to leave an uncongenial congregation or denomination for another that is more to one's liking. But the very possibility of that option raises a difficulty for such an account, since it must acknowledge the diversity and inconsistency of the churches' identities and ways of life, prompting the question: which church should we be let ourselves be formed by? Hauerwas is obviously aware of this, for in spite of his presumption that the church's practices and narrative constitute a largely settled and secure ecclesial identity, he also contends that, if we are formed within a community corrupted by liberalism or

2 Earlier, he seems to have thought quite differently (Hauerwas, 1974/1981: 60–62).

3 Latterly, Hauerwas often makes assertions about strong formation when arguing for a more 'Catholic' understanding of the church. In a forthcoming book-length treatment of Hauerwas, I argue that his understanding of the matters treated here is as much in line, methodologically and materially, with the liberal theological tradition initiated by Schleiermacher as it is with traditional Catholic theology.

other errors, our formation will distort us. Indeed, in a recent sermon, he insists that living in the wrong kind of church means that 'your salvation is in doubt' (Hauerwas, 2011: 116). It is difficult to see, though, on Hauerwas's theoretical account of the church, how I could figure out my community is distorting me since I am not permitted any critical distance from it.

More broadly, the social-theoretical aspects of these accounts of the church and its formative function rely upon some doubtful empirical assumptions. Limited space here means I can only note that, taken in the aggregate, sociological and ethnographic studies of church communities undermine such strong accounts of communal identity and formation.[4] Of course the churches form their members to some degree and it is reasonable to urge increased activity in this area. But the churches are usually not sufficiently central for and exclusive to their members' daily lives to counter the often far more intense formation that occurs within the family, at work, in school, from the media, amongst friends, and the like. Massive changes within Christianity would be required to make the churches the central community for a good majority of their members, as is indicated by the steps that must be taken by those who are exceptionally concerned to be well-formed. They must live for some time within a carefully structured ecclesial environment, such as programmes of formation for the priesthood, or the novitiate, or within a suitably isolated, highly-dedicated Christian community.

Yet even if such steps could be and were taken, it is doubtful this would lead to the settled church identity and consistency of formation required by Hauerwas's and Schleiermacher's accounts of Christian leadership and the role of the ordinary theologian. Well-formed Christian leaders, whether academic or ecclesiastical, do not necessarily agree with either of their accounts of the way we should live as Christians, and, of course, they usually disagree with one another. This cannot be explained merely as a lack of formation, or corruption by worldly intrusions, and certainly not by sin alone. It is hard to think of a more well-formed, dedicated Christian than Schleiermacher, rightly acknowledged as an extraordinary man of the church. Hauerwas is another exemplary Christian, in my view, and so are Karl Barth, William of St Thierry, Roger Haight, SJ, George Schner, SJ, Benedict XVI, and a couple of parish priests I know, to add a few of my favourites at random. All of these disagree with one another in substantive ways about how best to live as Christians. Strong formation and exemplary Christian living do not result in agreement about Christianity, nor about strong formation and sharply distinctive church identity.

So, given the real and arguably legitimate diversity amongst their leadership, plus the diversity of congregational identities, it cannot be enough for the average Christian to attend church once a week, listen attentively to the sermon, and be passively guided in Christian living by their priest or minister or congregational elders. Christians have little choice but to think things through for themselves at times if they are truthfully to 'embody' the narrative of Jesus. Each of us will need

[4] I note a few of these studies and their implications in Healy, 2012.

to engage – as we do – in an ongoing, ad hoc correlation between our personal experiences and knowledges, and what we know of Christianity.[5] This is necessary, furthermore, in view of the fact that our leaders cannot always effectively address the particular issues we face, since their range of experience is, like everyone's, limited in scope and depth.

Schleiermacher and Hauerwas in effect reify the church. They do not account for the way the churches actually are, especially their members' massively complex and diverse relationships with what is outside, as well as the churches' internal messiness and complexity. Acknowledging such realities questions both the opposition 'internal' and 'outside' as well as the reliance upon a secure and settled Christian communal identity, even as a project. Reification can be useful as a means to point up some significant issues, but beyond this it can lead astray if followed too far or too closely. Hauerwas has responded to something akin to this charge: 'The problem is not that the church [he describes] does not exist, but that we too often lack the vision to see the miracle that is the church. The problem is the blindness of our sight. To see truthfully we must be sanctified' (Hauerwas, 1998: 11). This would seem, however, only to add to the problems in his account of witness. For if seeing the church truthfully requires being sanctified by acquiring a Christian character and virtues, then we cannot expect those of goodwill outside the church, who have not been transformed, to have the vision to be able to see it.

Hauerwas has also remarked, more convincingly: 'I find I must think and write not only for the church that does exist but for the church that should exist if we were more courageous and faithful' (Hauerwas, 1981: 5). However, my argument here is that his account of the ideal church does not work well enough as it stands to provide a conception of the goal towards which to aim. Nor does it address adequately the means to get there, means which surely include 'courageous' and 'faithful' efforts by ordinary theologians to grapple with whatever life throws at them, and figure out a Christian response to it that they can believe is reasonable.

A Theological Account of the Church

These accounts reify the church in another, more significant, way. I remarked earlier that they are largely non-theological, constructed with little or no guidance from a description of its relation to God. Partial non-theological accounts are often useful, as both these two are, to be sure. They can, for example, help us root out ideological blind spots in the church's theological self-understanding. But taken as sufficient, they will distort. It is vital, then, to go beyond the church as 'a phenomenon of world history which can be grasped in historical and psychological and sociological terms like any other' (Barth, 1956: 651), to consider 'the third dimension, in which the church is what it is', a dimension which 'is completely

[5] Cardinal Newman's account of 'real assent' is helpful here; and see his examples of moves from 'notional' to real assent (Newman, 1979: 76–85), notably the third.

absent' in Schleiermacher (Barth, 1956: 656) and in Hauerwas. This 'third dimension' – the church's relation to God made possible and actual by God's active presence, by grace – is essential to any adequate description of the church. For it is only by God's grace that the church, the visible, concrete product of human actions, institutions and beliefs, is the church.

It is difficult for Schleiermacher to discuss grace as constitutive of the church. Doing so would render his account 'unscientific', because he would have to talk more directly about God's actions here and now. Perhaps this difficulty prompts him to blur the distinction between the spirit of the Christian community and the Holy Spirit (Schleiermacher, 1928: para. 123). Hauerwas also finds talking about grace difficult, for 'it too readily becomes a way to provide a generalized account of God's alleged relation to us' that undermines what he consider to be a more properly Catholic account of the church's mediation of salvation (Hauerwas, 1998: 13). He, too, undermines the distinction between the work of the church and that of Jesus Christ on the principle that 'there can be no separation of Christology from ecclesiology, that is, Jesus from the church' (Hauerwas, 1981: 37). Grace is also largely absent in his account of virtue and character, which is quite unlike that of, say, Thomas Aquinas, in that it lacks the infused virtues as the basis and form of any we acquire.

A strong emphasis on church identity and formation combined with an inadequate treatment of grace can result in an account in which, as Barth put it, Jesus Christ is 'absorbed and dissolved in practice into the Christian *kerygma*, Christian faith and the Christian community', so that he is 'replaced by Christianity' (Barth, 1962: 349). To counter this and the other form of reification, an ecclesiology needs to show how grace is the condition for the possibility of the church, and how a doctrine of grace can be developed so as to address the full range of the church's empirical realities.

We might argue that Barth's ecclesiology does much of that and could readily address these specific issues directly. After all, he engaged with Schleiermacher over the years, and shares with Hauerwas an emphasis on witness. Yet perhaps it would be better to draw only some guiding principles from him rather than appropriate his ecclesiology more or less *in toto*. For one thing, Hauerwas has accused him of undervaluing the historical mediation of salvation by the church (Hauerwas, 2001: 141–218). I have argued elsewhere that Hauerwas misconstrues Barth (Healy, 2004), but either way, matters of Barth interpretation are an unhelpful distraction. A related problem is Barth's tendency to over-separate God's action and ours, particularly with regard to the sacraments.

Barth does, however, indicate some of the necessary moves. He distinguishes between the work of the church, the vocation and task of the individual Christian, and the active presence of God in the individual, the church and the world. His emphasis upon the 'contemporary' prophetic activity of Jesus Christ (Barth, 1962: 497) not only underscores our need for grace in all three areas, it enables him to assign to God the final responsibility for the success of the church's witness. While the latter is necessary, only the self-witness of God is both necessary and sufficient. The church's task is not primarily to form a clear, distinctive cultural identity, since that is not the condition of the possibility of effective witness. Nor does effective witness require Christian individuals to be well-formed; they just have to be Christian. 'The Christian ethos does not allow itself to be understood as an end in itself' (Barth, 1962: 560). Our task as ordinary theologians is to attempt, cheerfully, prayerfully and in gratitude, to bring our lives into correspondence with our Lord. This we cannot achieve apart from the guidance and resources of the church, but each of us is called to our own particular vocation, so our response is our own, made possible in Christ.

Barth's ecclesiology may provide some guidance for developing a theological case for ordinary theology where it is perhaps most difficult to make. Only a century ago, Roman Catholicism advocated something very like Hauerwas's 'peasant catholicism'. Thus for Pius X the church is 'essentially an unequal society … comprising two categories of persons, the Pastors and the flock … So distinct are these categories that … the one duty of the multitude is to allow themselves to be led, and, like a docile flock, to follow the Pastors' (Pius X, 1906: para. 8). A year later, Pius rejected 'that most pernicious doctrine that would make of the laity a factor of progress in the church' (Pius X, 1907: para. 27).

The church's teaching has since developed significantly. The teachings of Vatican II favour a far more mutual and positive engagement between ordinary theologians (the 'laity') and the teaching authorities. A basic principle is that, while we all should pay 'careful attention' to the 'church's sacred and certain teaching', 'in the end everyone is bound to obey their own conscience' (Tanner and Norman, 1990: 1010, 1008). Beyond this, the Council acknowledged a special 'apostolate' for the laity – a task given specially to them by the Holy Spirit – which is 'to permeate the whole order of temporal things' (Tanner and Norman, 1990: 983, 985). Furthermore, the laity's work is to affect the church, too. Pastors are 'helped by the experience of the laity … to make clearer and more suitable decisions both in spiritual and in temporal affairs'. Indeed, the laity 'have the right and indeed sometimes the duty to make known their opinion on matters which concern the good of the church'. And pastors 'should willingly make use of their prudent counsel' and 'leave them freedom and space to act' (Tanner and Norman, 1990: 879).

Subsequent work indicates the 'reception' of church teaching by the laity is a kind of test of the truth of a magisterial decision. Where ordinary Christians generally fail to accept a decision, it may suggest, according to Cardinal Dulles, that the Pope may have 'exceeded his competence' (Granfield, 1987: 150). Reception is therefore not merely passive acceptance, perhaps taking some time to accomplish. Rather, it is a genuine test of a teaching's truthfulness; its liveability, as it were. This could be the case only if grace is at work for the good of the church amongst ordinary theologians. Sometimes reception has not occurred: for example, with regard to some of the teachings of Pius IX and Pius X concerning modernity and its institutions. And sometimes (not always, to be sure) it is ordinary lay people who collectively lead the way,[6] or even (exceptionally) maintain the true faith against errors among their leadership.[7]

This apostolate is impossible if the laity are to be passively formed by the church's leadership. It requires their grace-enabled, reflective and active self-formation as Christians who live within the world as well as the church. The active presence of Christ and the Spirit forms Christians through their personal experience and prayer, as well as through the church, and always with a view to bringing all things into correspondence with God's salvific will.

There are, then, some possible approaches within Catholicism to make a theological case for ordinary theology. A full-scale ecclesiology is needed to develop these and other possibilities, and to address, within the context of a doctrine of grace, the full range of empirical issues in relation to social theory and ethnographic studies.[8] I should note that I do not mean to propose that ordinary theology should necessarily have a formal role in the church's deliberations, nor do I advocate for a democratic church or wish to 'celebrate' the people in some kind of anti-elitist manner. My primary point, with Barth, is that human confusion does not hinder grace from achieving God's providential will in and through our confused efforts (*Dei providentia et hominum confusione*). Rather, the confusion should be acknowledged and addressed theologically. On that ground, an account of the concrete church can reckon with the Christianity of everyone, from the most insouciant to the most eager member of the church. The church can never do without its leadership and this, I would say, for practical as well as doctrinal reasons, must take the form of an official magisterium. We probably need academic theology, too. But they are not enough to make the church the church, if we consider the church as it really is, in its relation to God.

References

Barth, Karl (1956), *Church Dogmatics*, 4/1, Edinburgh: T. & T. Clark.

Barth, Karl (1962), *Church Dogmatics*, 4/3.2, Edinburgh: T. & T. Clark.

Granfield, Patrick (1987), *The Limits of the Papacy*, New York: Crossroad.

Hauerwas, Stanley (1974/1981), *Vision and Virtue*, Notre Dame, Ind.: Notre Dame Press, reprint of Fides edition.

Hauerwas, Stanley (1981), *A Community of Character: Toward a Constructive Christian Social Ethic*, Notre Dame, Ind.: University of Notre Dame Press.

Hauerwas, Stanley (1988), *Christian Existence Today*, Grand Rapids, Mich.: Brazos.

[6] For examples, see Noonan, 2005; especially his discussion of the role of 'empathy'.

[7] A classic example is the fourth-century Arian controversy discussed, classically, by Newman, 1961: 76–106.

[8] I am in the early stages of such a full-scale Catholic-yet-ecumenical ecclesiology along such lines, tentatively entitled *The Unsettled Church*.

Hauerwas, Stanley (1998), *Sanctify Them in the Truth: Holiness Exemplified*, Nashville, Tenn.: Abingdon.

Hauerwas, Stanley (2000), *A Better Hope: Resources for a Church Confronting Capitalism, Democracy, and Postmodernity*, Grand Rapids, Mich.: Brazos.

Hauerwas, Stanley (2001), *With the Grain of the Universe*, Grand Rapids, Mich.: Brazos.

Hauerwas, Stanley (2011), *Working With Words*, Eugene, Oreg.: Cascade Books.

Healy, Nicholas M. (2004), 'Karl Barth's Ecclesiology Reconsidered', *Scottish Journal of Theology*, 57, 3: 287–99.

Healy, Nicholas M. (2012), 'Ecclesiology, Ethnography, and God: An Interplay of Reality Descriptions', in Pete Ward (ed.), *Perspectives in Ecclesiology and Ethnography*, Grand Rapids, Mich.: Eerdmans, pp. 182–99.

Kerr, Nathan R. (2008), *Christ, History and Apocalyptic*, London: SCM Press.

Newman, John Henry (1961), *On Consulting the Faithful in Matters of Doctrine*, Lanham, Md.: Rowman and Littlefield.

Newman, John Henry (1979), *A Grammar of Assent*, Notre Dame, Ind.: University of Notre Dame Press.

Noonan, John T. (2005), *A Church That Can and Cannot Change: The Development of Catholic Moral Teaching*, Notre Dame, Ind.: University of Notre Dame Press.

Pius X (1906), *Vehementer Nos*, http://www.vatican.va/holy_father/pius_x/encyclicals/documents/hf_p-x_enc_11021906_vehementer-nos_en.html [accessed 1 September 2012].

Pius X (1907), *Pascendi Dominici Gregis*, http://www.vatican.va/holy_father/pius_x/encyclicals/documents/hf_p-x_enc_19070908_pascendi-dominici-gregis_en.html [accessed 1 September 2012].

Schleiermacher, Friedrich (1928), *The Christian Faith*, Edinburgh: T. & T. Clark.

Schleiermacher, Friedrich (1958), *On Religion: Speeches to its Cultured Despisers*, New York: Harper Torchbooks.

Tanner, S.J. and P. Norman (1990), *Decrees of the Ecumenical Councils*, London: Sheed and Ward.

Chapter 3
Ordinary Theology as 'Mother Tongue'

Anthony Lees-Smith

'Is ordinary theology, we may wonder, the theology of the mother tongue?' asks Astley, reflecting on Ursula Le Guin's distinction between two 'tongues' (Astley, 2002: 78). In this chapter we will explore how far it is possible to push the linguistic analogy in respect of ordinary theology. This will entail some critical discussion of where similarities have already been noted by others such as George Lindbeck and Don Cupitt. We will examine some of the more current research in language acquisition studies and draw on Dante Alighieri's study of the vernacular. This will lead us to a point where we can begin to explore the implications of the linguistic model for ordinary theology and Christian education more widely.

One way that Astley characterizes ordinary theology is by appropriating Ursula Le Guin's distinction between the 'father tongue' – a language of power and politics, a 'language of thought that seeks objectivity', and the 'mother tongue' – 'the vulgar tongue, common speech, colloquial, low, ordinary' (Le Guin, 1989: 147–60). The similarities between the 'father tongue' and academic theology are clear when the latter is stereotyped as a cold, formal, disinterested enterprise of the academy.[1] Le Guin's use of the word 'ordinary' in relation to the 'mother tongue' adds further weight to Astley's appropriation of this term for his own ordinary theology. Both are concerned with those who have not been educated in the 'father tongue' or academic theology. Both make use of 'common speech' and 'colloquial language'.[2] Astley defines the 'mother tongue' as 'the vulgar tongue of connections, of human communication and exchange, the language of relationship and conversation' (Astley, 2008: 202).

The 'vulgar tongue' is the focus of Dante Alighieri's study. He describes it as that language which is first learnt without rules as infants from a wet-nurse, whilst Latin or *gramatica* is acquired later through study (Alighieri, 1990: I.i). It is the noblest of languages, in preference to Latin, the ubiquitous language of medieval scholasticism. Such a distinction is remarkably close to that we have already begun to explore between ordinary and academic theology, but Dante goes on to identify what he calls an 'illustrious vernacular', a particular dialect, found in courts and palaces, which is 'found everywhere but belongs nowhere' and which can be used as a yardstick against which to measure all other dialects (Alighieri,

[1] Of course, such polarization is a long way from the truth, and the two are differentiated more by degree than kind, as Astley notes at 2002: 86.

[2] See, for example, Marie's God-talk (Clark-King, 2004: 70–71).

1990: I.xvi, 6). Furthermore, Dante goes as far as to identify the particular topics which it is appropriate to discuss in the 'illustrious vernacular': salvation, love and virtue (Alighieri, 1990: II.ii, 7). Ironically, it may be argued that in appointing a particular sophisticated form of the vernacular for such use, Dante was, in effect, creating another 'father tongue'. However, his desire to vindicate the vernacular as a worthy medium resonates with much of Astley's persuasive arguments for ordinary theology to be taken seriously.

Language Acquisition and the Development of Religious Belief

One of the striking things about both Le Guin's definition of 'mother tongue' and Dante's *volgare* is that they are described in terms of the language which is acquired in infancy. This reflects a key characteristic of ordinary theology in that it is acquired 'at our mother's knee', learnt through engagement with our environment and therefore inextricably bound up with autobiographical details and personal story. George Lindbeck uses this common characteristic of language and religion more widely to propose a 'cultural-linguistic' approach to conceptualizing religion (Lindbeck, 1984: 17–18). In doing so, he is strongly influenced by Wittgenstein's 'language-games' which call attention to the importance of cultural context in the acquisition and use of language. Each religious tradition in Lindbeck's view is a 'language-game' with its own commonly understood narratives, rituals and rules that help those who know the rules to interpret and structure human experience and language. In short, 'the meaning of a word is its use in the language' (Wittgenstein, 1967: 43). This means that words such as 'redemption' become intelligible 'not on the basis of private existential experience but on the basis of a public tradition of certain patterns of behaviour' (Thiselton, 1980: 382). Lindbeck takes this one step further by saying that 'to become religious – no less than to become culturally or linguistically competent – is to interiorize a set of skills by practice and training' (Lindbeck, 1984: 35). It is a question of learning the grammar or rules of the particular game in question.

Lindbeck is keen to reject the notion that there is a common universal experience of God which is simply interpreted differently in different contexts and cultures. He confidently asserts that religions are not 'diverse objectifications of the same basic experience' (Lindbeck, 1984: 41). Such universal claims might be compared in the linguistic analogy to Chomsky's 'universal grammar' and subsequent theories of a linguistic bioprogram or language faculty common to all human beings (Chomsky, 2004: 15–24; McMahon, 1994: 270–83; Pinker, 1994: 297–331). Such psycholinguistic theories are based on observations of grammatical similarities between human languages, together with the problem of the 'poverty of stimulus' which indicates that modelling and analogy alone do not account for the way in which children acquire and use their first language so creatively (Chomsky, 2004: 19). A similar argument could be formed against Lindbeck to account for the creative innovation seen in the development of religious traditions.

Growing interest in the area of sociolinguistics has led others to look more closely at the connections between language and the context in which it is used, highlighting levels of social and cultural awareness that are needed for language development. We find echoes of Wittgenstein in remarks such as 'the utterance has no meaning except in the context of situation' (Bronislaw Malinowski, cited in Foley and Thompson, 2003: 65). The theory of systemic functional linguistics developed by Halliday, for example, works with three metafunctions of adult language: ideational, interpersonal and textual (Halliday and Webster, 2009: 253). The second is particularly fascinating in this context given its focus on creating and maintaining relationships, echoing Le Guin's concept of a relational 'mother tongue'. For Halliday, language cannot be context-free, nor can it be free from the semiotic systems of the culture in which it occurs, including the prevailing traditions and values of that culture. 'It is through the processes of socialization, education and enculturation that young children learn to be communicatively competent within the speech community of their family, friends and neighbourhood' (Foley and Thompson, 2003: 69).

This is a view which ties in well with what we have seen of Lindbeck's 'cultural-linguistic' approach to religion. Halliday ultimately sees the whole experience of learning as a semiotic process: 'learning to mean … building up a potential' (Halliday, 2004: 40). Lindbeck similarly considers religions as 'idioms for dealing with whatever is most important – with ultimate questions of life and death, right and wrong, chaos and order, meaning and meaninglessness' (Lindbeck, 1984: 40). The centrality of meaning-making to both religious thinking and language learning suggests that Lindbeck was justified in identifying common ground.[3]

Don Cupitt also notes that language is bound up with the values and beliefs of the cultural context in which it occurs. Cupitt claims that idiomatic expressions and proverbs persist in our everyday speech because they express succinctly great philosophical or religious thoughts. 'By investigating the philosophy of life, the world-view and the religious outlook that is embedded in our ordinary language, we are finding out for the first time who we are and what we really believe' (Cupitt, 1999: 5). His approach has much to commend it in terms of his passion for 'ordinariness' and his desire for ordinary language and the beliefs of ordinary people to be taken seriously (Cupitt, 1999: 72). Such intentions resonate with Astley's own ideas about ordinary theology (Astley, 2002: 118–19).

However, Cupitt's methodology and conclusions are much more tenuous, inasmuch as they are based on arbitrary snapshot definitions of particular phrases largely from dictionaries (see 'Sources' in Cupitt, 1999), ignoring the semantic subtleties and indeed contextual variation of actual usage. If Wittgenstein was right about meaning then it becomes much harder to make simple like-for-like correlations between idiomatic expressions and their meaning without some

[3] Others have aligned Lindbeck's model with Chomsky's two-level generative grammar. See, for example, Heather, 2008: 462–3. However, contrary to Chomskyan thought, Lindbeck flatly denies any innate or universal experience, as we have seen.

consideration for context. It is also the case that some idiomatic expressions are more likely to be used in the way that Rowan Williams describes 'empty bromides' spoken at a bereavement visit (Williams, 2000: 91). This equates to the second metafunction of language, that of maintaining relationships. If idiomatic language is being used in this way on the whole, then Cupitt's study may provide fascinating insights into the history of the worldviews that led to the conscious creation of the idioms, but seems less reliable as far as current usage is concerned.

Cupitt's attempts to make generalizations about belief-systems based on aspects of language reflect a common view that thought is in some way dependent on language. This is expressed more strongly by Lindbeck, who says that 'it is necessary to have the means for expressing an experience in order to have it, and the richer our expressive or linguistic system, the more subtle, varied, and differentiated can be our experience' (Lindbeck, 1984: 37). However, many linguists and anthropologists have refuted the Sapir–Whorf hypothesis of linguistic determinism, the theory of direct correlation between cultural thought and language (Pinker, 1994: 59–67). It could be that Cupitt is in danger of falling into the same trap and making assumptions based on minimal evidence. For example, many of the expressions he quotes could be used innocently in casual conversation by those fundamentally opposed to the 'unmoralistic, radical humanism' which he claims is the worldview suggested by their etymology (Cupitt, 1999: 86).

So, we may ask, are Cupitt's idioms inherited from the surrounding and pre-existing culture, or formulated afresh by each new generation as a resource for dealing with the ups and downs of life? (Cupitt, 1999: 71). The first model tends to suggest a functional view based on social enculturation, the second an innate view of language or at least the innate capacity to generate new language. Perhaps the truth lies in what has been termed 'communicative competence', a continuing interaction between social and grammatical factors, enabling us to communicate meaningfully with one another (Romaine, 2000: 23–5, 30–31).

Le Guin's 'mother tongue' is defined in terms of its acquisition by enculturation and so may seem to resemble more closely the 'functional' model. It is distinguished from the 'father tongue' by the contexts in which it is used and by the purposes to which it is put. 'If you want to succeed in business, government, law, engineering, science, education, the media' you need to learn the 'father tongue' (Le Guin, 1989: 148). Dante's vernacular is similarly distinguished from Latin, which remains the language of the academy, law, ceremony and ritual. However, ordinary theology and academic theology are not just functionally different. They are different in essence, in the way that one's native language is essentially different from any second language one may learn.

Ordinary theology *is* therefore like a 'mother tongue', if by 'mother tongue' we assume a combination of innate capacity and acquired experience. It is, in one view, an attempt to make meaning out of a universal experience of life and the divine within the parameters of a particular tradition, whether religious or secular.

Academic theology, on the other hand, is like the 'father tongue'. Dante's view of Latin is particularly fitting here, since he too acknowledges the particular contexts in which it is to be used and the difficulty inherent in studying its rules (Alighieri, 1990: 1.i, 3). Despite some attempts to revive it, Latin is now a frozen language. Ordinary theology is, like the vernacular, essentially more fluid, evolving as we have seen through conversation, relationship and sociocultural context. Academic theology, although not as ossified as Latin, changes much more slowly by way of arguments, debates, articles, books and lectures. Academic theology not only serves a different purpose to ordinary theology, namely 'critical reflection on theological positions' (Astley, 2002: 75); it is also different in essence, being more formal, detached, impersonal and systematic. There are rules and doctrinal positions to be navigated, where ordinary theology, like a native language, is more instinctive. Implicit rules are being followed here, too, but in many cases the speaker only becomes aware of these through studying another language and comparing its patterns and rules with his or her 'mother tongue'. If this is also true of the ordinary theologian, then this will have a significant impact on our approach to Christian education.

Implications of the Linguistic Analogy

Reflection is central to Astley's concept of ordinary theology (Astley, 2002: 144). Without it, we have simply God-talk of the type Cupitt explores: words and phrases that may have some vestige of theological significance, but not explicit; 'empty bromides' used for the purposes of maintaining relationship through conversation rather than to make a theological point. It would seem unwise, then, to infer too much theologizing from the speaker's use of them. It may be, rather, that the Christian educator's approach to ordinary theology is that of a mirror, reflecting back the God-talk in order to raise awareness and prompt reflection. 'We need to stop telling people what the religious authorities think they ought to believe, and instead start to show people what they already *do* believe' (Cupitt, 1999: 4). Without an awareness of one's own position and the beliefs and values one has inherited, there can be minimal growth. The work of Robert Beckford and others has focused on 'the vernacular, the popular and the everyday as the vehicle through which people's theological aspirations achieve expression' (Graham, Walton and Ward, 2005: 224). If this is true, then reflection on popular culture will also help to reveal an underlying ordinary theology and both raise awareness and promote discussion around it.

Thomas Groome's 'shared praxis' model of education may provide an opportunity for such reflection (see Groome, 1991: 155–293). His process of 'theological listening' includes the willingness 'to acknowledge the theological content that resides below the surface of the often inarticulate, hesitant and confused, but also deeply-felt reflections' of the ordinary theologian (Astley, 2003: 8). Like second language acquisition, where our structures and knowledge of our first language can be used as a resource to create sentences in the new one, the dialectic proposed by Groome between Christian input and ordinary theological reflection is a two-way process. It should be possible, therefore, for ordinary theology to propose its own critique of the tradition, and this can be seen with ethical issues of the last century.[4]

The final movement within Groome's model is focused on a decision for action to be taken. There is the possibility for something new to be created out of the conversation which has taken place and this too is the hope for ordinary theology. An 'implicit theologian … knows and loves God, but she lacks the discourse to enable her to make this explicit' (Sadgrove, 2008: 102–3). It is Sadgrove's view that the priest brings the appropriate discourse so that only *together* can they become 'true theologians'. One of the difficulties encountered in Hay and Hunt's survey of adult spirituality was the absence in many cases of suitable language to talk about religious or spiritual matters. Where there is 'mutual reflection on praxis' by both interviewer and interviewee, Hay and Hunt believe it possible for a 'reconstruction of a common spiritual language' to occur (Hay and Hunt, 2000: 7.6.2).[5]

If we are to accept the analogy of 'mother tongue' for ordinary theology, then there are a number of implications. Not only does it help us to identify some of the characteristics of ordinary theology, as we have seen; but it could also help us acknowledge the 'marked local accent' in which even academic theology is done (Williams, 2000: 9). It may reveal more to us about the way in which our ordinary theology is acquired, the role of the Holy Spirit and the importance of cultural context as mediated by significant people in our upbringing, like Dante's wet-nurse who teaches a child the vernacular. There is much to be done to deepen our understanding of ordinary theology, but the church also needs to consider how it can respond sensitively to the ordinary theology of those in the pews and in the wider community.

Perhaps here the linguistic analogy will again bear fruit if we consider the impact of 'language death' as in the case of East Sutherland Gaelic, a vernacular dying because of the 'influx of another socially and politically dominant language' (Aitchison, 1991: 205–8). By contrast, we could consider the apparently successful attempts to restore the Welsh language through compulsory education and the nurture of a bilingual culture (see Williams and Morris, 2000). There is no doubt that Welsh is more widely used and esteemed, but standardization has created a somewhat artificial vernacular like Dante's 'illustrious vernacular' that is 'found everywhere and belongs nowhere'. Although it is arguably compulsory schooling that is having the greatest impact, in some areas it has proven harder to establish the more informal variety appropriate for use in the home and with peers. If we

4 See Astley's example of contraception in 2002: 159.

5 See also Heimbrock, 1987: 78–83. Inspired by the experience of the deaf in their use of non-verbal language, this author calls for a more 'affective approach' to religious education and the creation of 'new forms of religious language'. He argues for 'authentic forms of expression' rather than simply translating traditional theological language, all of which resonates with an ordinary theology expressed in a 'mother tongue'.

transfer this analogy to ordinary theology, we discover that there is a risk involved in analysing the situation as it stands. In the process, the inherent variety and unsystematic nature of ordinary theology could be lost. Some might see this as a positive step, but if a broad description is imposed, it will not necessarily be owned by those it claims to represent. On the other hand, the evidence from Wales is that it is possible to revive a vernacular through raising its status and encouraging its use in a variety of contexts. Perhaps this is a model which the churches could appropriate for their approach to ordinary theology.

All analogies have their limitations, but it seems that the linguistic analogy for ordinary theology is one which can provide us with much to reflect upon. It is not that we are dealing with a 'cultural-linguistic' system in the way Lindbeck suggests, or that ordinary everyday language will reveal our unspoken philosophy of life as Cupitt would have us believe. Rather, our ordinary theology may be the result of a complex interaction of cultural inheritance, contextual demands and an attempt to interpret our experience of God: just as our native language appears to develop as the combination of innate capacity and creativity together with immersion in a particular linguistic tradition.

We are not yet in a situation where the theological 'mother tongue' is considered on an equal footing with the 'father tongue', but the identification of ordinary theology is a helpful start. In Groome's terms, this is the naming of present action.

This chapter has been an attempt to reflect critically on the notion of ordinary theology as a 'mother tongue', but there has been insufficient space to move much beyond to a deeper engagement with the Christian tradition. A starting point for this could be found in the story of Pentecost. Here, we find that the Spirit comes to bring 'unity in diversity'. It is 'an affirmation of the movement of the Holy Spirit not through one authorized or prescribed official culture, but in its manifestation in the *vernacular* medium of all known languages' (Graham, Walton and Ward, 2005: 228). Could such an interpretation provide a biblical mandate for taking ordinary theology as 'mother tongue' more seriously?

References

Aitchison, Jean (1991), *Language Change: Progress or Decay?* Cambridge: Cambridge University Press.

Alighieri, Dante (1990), *De Vulgari Eloquentia*, translation and commentary in Italian by Claudio Marazzini and Concetto Del Popolo, Milan: Mondadori.

Astley, Jeff (2002), *Ordinary Theology: Looking, Listening and Learning in Theology*, Aldershot: Ashgate.

Astley, Jeff (2003), 'Ordinary Theology for Rural Theology and Rural Ministry', *Rural Theology*, 1, 1: 1–10.

Astley, Jeff (2008), 'Giving Voice to the Ordinary: Theological Listening and the Mother Tongue', in Natalie Watson and Stephen Burns (eds), *Exchanges of Grace: Essays in Honour of Ann Loades*, London: SCM Press, pp. 202–12.

Chomsky, Noam (2004), 'Knowledge of Language as a Focus of Inquiry', in Barbara Lust and Claire Foley (eds), *First Language Acquisition: The Essential Readings*, Oxford: Blackwell, pp. 15–24.

Clark-King, Ellen (2004), *Theology by Heart: Women, the Church and God*, Peterborough: Epworth.

Cupitt, Don, (1999), *The Meaning of It All in Everyday Speech*, London: SCM Press.

Foley, Joseph and Linda Thompson (2003), *Language Learning: A Lifelong Process*, London: Arnold.

Graham, Elaine, Heather Walton and Frances Ward (2005), *Theological Reflection: Methods*, London: SCM Press.

Groome, Thomas (1991), *Sharing Faith: A Comprehensive Approach to Religious Education and Pastoral Ministry*, San Francisco: HarperCollins.

Halliday, Michael (2004), 'Representing the Child as a Semiotic Being (One Who Means)', in Joseph Foley (ed.), *Language, Education and Discourse: Functional Approaches*, London: Continuum, pp. 19–42.

Halliday, Michael and Jonathan Webster (eds) (2009), *Continuum Companion to Systemic Functional Linguistics*, London: Continuum.

Hay, David and Kate Hunt (2000), *Understanding the Spirituality of People Who Don't Go to Church: A Report on the Findings of the Adults' Spirituality Project at the University of Nottingham*, Nottingham: University of Nottingham.

Heather, Noel (2008), 'Critical Postliberalism: Lindbeck's Cultural-Linguistic System and the Socially Extrasystemic', *Scottish Journal of Theology*, 61, 4: 462–76.

Heimbrock, Hans-Günter (1987), 'Life without Language? What Religious Education has to Learn From the Experience of the Hearing-Impaired', *British Journal of Religious Education*, 9, 2: 78–83.

Le Guin, Ursula (1989), *Dancing at the Edge of the World: Thoughts on Words, Women, Places*, New York: Grove.

Lindbeck, George (1984), *The Nature of Doctrine: Religion and Theology in a Postliberal Age*, London: SPCK.

McMahon, April (1994), *Understanding Language Change*, Cambridge: Cambridge University Press.

Pinker, Steven (1994), *The Language Instinct: The New Science of Language and Mind*, London: Penguin.

Romaine, Suzanne (2000), *Language in Society: An Introduction to Sociolinguistics*, Oxford: Oxford University Press.

Sadgrove, Michael (2008), *Wisdom and Ministry: The Call to Leadership*, London: SPCK.

Thiselton, Anthony (1980), *The Two Horizons: New Testament Hermeneutics and Philosophical Description with Special Reference to Heidegger, Bultmann, Gadamer and Wittgenstein*, Exeter: Paternoster.

Williams, Glyn and Delyth Morris (2000), *Language Planning and Language Use: Welsh in a Global Age*, Cardiff: University of Wales Press.

Williams, Rowan (2000), 'Making Moral Decisions', in Robin Gill (ed.), *The Cambridge Companion to Christian Ethics*, Cambridge: Cambridge University Press, pp. 3–15.
Wittgenstein, Ludwig (1967), *Philosophical Investigations*, Oxford: Blackwell.

Chapter 4

Deconversion and Ordinary Theology: A Catholic Study

Tom Beaudoin and J. Patrick Hornbeck II

Ordinary Catholicism: From Above and Below

Everyday Catholic life can appear to both outsiders and insiders as a bifurcated experience: desirous of satisfying the expectations from 'above' and/or honouring the needs emerging from 'below'.

On the one hand are attempts to live ordinary Catholic life, and accounts of that living, that prioritize the hierarchical character of the church, privileging the declarations of the magisterium and the deep meaning and joy to be found in surrender to an authoritative teacher who frees her students to love and suffer according to Christ's example. This kind of ordinary theology is fostered by lay movements and organizations that foster a connection to the hierarchical centre, such as the well-known Opus Dei and many secular institutes (Leahy, 2011). Communion is a key metaphor, authority a deep consideration, and the presentation of continuity through official ecclesial tradition highly valued. On the other hand are attempts and accounts that foreground social justice as an everyday Catholic anchor, taking such figures as Dorothy Day or Oscar Romero, and Catholic social teaching, as guides. Liberation is a key metaphor, context a deep consideration, and the spirit of Vatican II a common touchstone.[1]

To be sure, there are influential pastoral theological models for holding these dimensions together.[2] These models, however, have been most influential in pastoral ministry centres and have not made an impact on the larger Catholic theological agenda. Moreover, accounts of Catholic life that include theologically

[1] For a recent account of the ways Catholics hold together images for reclaiming their church, see Baggett, 2009. Timothy Radcliffe, former Master of the Dominican religious order, characterizes contemporary Catholicism as pulled toward two poles: 'Kingdom Catholics', primarily committed to the church's social mission, and 'Communion Catholics', primarily committed to the integrity of the whole faith – see Radcliffe, 2006.

[2] There is a literature grouped under the category 'theological reflection' in Catholic contexts that often draws from the following texts: Holland and Henriot, 1983; Killen and de Beer, 1994; Kinast, 1996; Whitehead and Whitehead, 1995.

significant discernments 'from below' have multiplied in recent years.[3] What is generally under-accounted, then – though far from under-lived – is precisely the sort of Catholic 'ordinary theology' along the lines that Jeff Astley articulates in his groundbreaking study (Astley, 2002). Beneath the push and pull that are two poles of a normative struggle in Catholicism – communion and liberation – there is a much more ambiguous everyday theological reality. This chapter underscores the newly recognized challenge that 'non-normative' belief and practice among US Catholics and former Catholics presents, and the openings it fosters, toward an ordinary theology of Catholicism.[4] The theological space to speak frankly and creatively about ordinary belief and practice among Catholics would make of ordinary theology an extraordinary phenomenon. It is not that all 'ordinary' Catholicism is out of sync with official expectations. But the fact that so much of it is, may be a clue – following Astley – to understanding the whole.[5]

Catholic Ideals, Catholic Realities

'Once a Catholic, always a Catholic.' While these words cannot be found in the *Catechism of the Catholic Church* or other official church documents, in many ways they sum up Roman Catholic teachings on church membership. According to the *Catechism*, the essential criterion for membership in the church is receipt of the sacrament of baptism, through which a person is permanently incorporated into the body of Christ and, thus, the church. 'Baptism seals the Christian with the indelible spiritual mark (*character*) of his belonging to Christ. No sin can erase this mark, even if sin prevents Baptism from bearing the fruits of salvation. Given once for all, Baptism cannot be repeated' (*Catechism of the Catholic Church*, 1993: para. 1272; see also paras 1262–74). With baptism comes a range of obligations: in their hearts and minds, Catholics are required by canon law to 'believe … all those things contained in the word of God … and at the same time proposed as divinely revealed either by the solemn magisterium of the Church or by its ordinary and universal magisterium'; in their actions, they are obligated to

[3] Some noteworthy recent examples include Dugan and Owens, 2009; Orsi, 1996; Seitz, 2011; Stevenson, 2000; Trevino, 2006.

[4] By 'non-normative' we mean two discursive dimensions at once: ways of belief and practice that diverge from those specified as important for Catholic life by official Catholic teaching, and ways of belief and practice that diverge from what baptized Catholics take to be specified as important for Catholic life by official Catholic teaching.

[5] In *Ordinary Theology*, Astley suggests that the ways that ordinary theologies operate may illuminate the ways that official or academic theologies actually work. We believe that part of the theological value of studying normatively problematic Catholicisms is the contribution to a rethinking of the generation of orthodox and normative stances in Catholicism, to look for similarities in style between them that are occluded by the long-standing rhetorical division between 'good/practising' and 'bad/lapsed' Catholics.

receive the sacraments, learn Catholic doctrine and lead holy lives (*The Code of Canon Law*, 1983: c. 750, §1; see also cc. 208–31).

Belief in the irreversibility of baptism informs the rhetoric that many official Catholic documents employ to describe the church's relationship to those whom it seeks to discipline or who reject its teachings. In particular, neither the *Catechism* nor the *Code of Canon Law* proposes that a person can be stripped of church membership; persons subject to excommunication, for instance, are prohibited from receiving the sacraments and exercising ministerial functions but are not, as in some other Christian denominations, expelled from the church (ibid.: c. 1331; cf., for instance, General Conference of Seventh-Day Adventists, 2005: 196–200, which provides guidelines for removing and reinstating erring members). Likewise, since the sacramental character of baptism is permanent, neither the *Catechism* nor the canon law code presently envisions that a person can voluntarily give up her or his membership in the church. In this connection, it is worth noting that such an action was at one time canonically possible: three sections of the revision of canon law promulgated in 1983 envisioned that a person could 'defect' from the church 'by a formal act' (ibid.: cc. 1086, §§1, 1117, 1124).[6] While these canons did not indicate what such a formal act might entail, a 2006 statement by the Pontifical Council for Legislative Texts enumerated specific requirements for the 'formal act' (Pontifical Council for Legislative Texts, 2006). In 2009, however, Pope Benedict XVI issued a legal document, called a *motu proprio*, which eliminated from Catholic canon law all mention of the formal act of defection (Benedict XVI, 2009).

The requirements of canon law notwithstanding, millions of individuals *do* describe themselves as 'former', 'ex-', 'post-' or 'recovering' Catholics. Millions more do not describe themselves as outside Catholicism but rather as inhabiting some marginal relationship to it: 'bad', 'lapsed' or 'non-practising' Catholics. In 2008, the Pew Forum on Religion and Public Life reported that, in the United States, people who were raised as Catholics but no longer identify themselves as Catholic comprise 10.1% of the overall adult population. If this group were treated as a denomination of its own, it would be the third largest in the nation (The Pew Forum on Religion and Public Life, 2008: 25). A website created by three former Catholics in Ireland to assist others in the process of completing a formal act of defection received more than 12,000 enquiries before it suspended its operations in the wake of the Pope's 2009 *motu proprio*.[7] In the Catholic press, news articles and opinion pieces describing the departure of Catholics from the church, as well as the psychological and spiritual struggles of those who are contemplating leaving, have routinely received substantial attention from readers and commentators (see, for instance, Roberts, 2010; Byron, 2011). Finally, according to the statistics

[6] The history of the notion of ecclesial 'defection' remains to be written; the word may be a modern canonical neologism.

[7] The website is www.countmeout.ie; the figure of 12,007 completed 'Declarations of Defection' can be found at http://www.countmeout.ie/faq/ [accessed 23 November 2011].

reported in the annual *Official Catholic Directory*, proportionally fewer Catholics are seeking church marriages, or baptism or confirmation for their children; the number of Catholic funerals per capita has declined as well.[8] More examples could be outlined, but it should be evident that the everyday practices of many American Catholics depart substantially from what are taken to be orthodox positions on the nature and obligations of membership.[9]

When considering departures from that orthodoxy, we observe that Catholic ecclesial teaching and academic Catholic theology have put forward renditions of Catholic identity in the generation since the Second Vatican Council. We focus here on two central aspects of that identity that are problematized by the present practice of US Catholics. These two aspects are so commonly accepted on the ecclesial landscape, including the training of pastoral workers and theologians, that they have attained something like the status of informal doctrines.

One is the centrality, in Catholic teaching, of eucharistic reception for Catholic life. The Second Vatican Council and the *Catechism of the Catholic Church* place eucharist as utterly central to life in the Church, the 'source and summit of the Christian life', the 'sum and summary' of Christian faith (*Lumen Gentium*: para. 11, in Flannery, 1996; *Catechism of the Catholic Church*, 1993: paras 1324, 1327). The theological idea is that the real presence of Christ in the eucharist grounds, sustains and symbolizes Christian life. At issue in regular reception of the eucharist is spiritual growth by way of a deeper incorporation into the church. Receiving Christ's body makes one more fully one with the body. In an often-cited formulation attributed to Augustine, 'Become what you receive.' But to turn that quote around, or rather to concretize it, to use it as an index and not a commandment: if most Catholics become what they receive, given that we know that most Catholics in the United States do not attend mass frequently or regularly, then their reception of something else on the weekends (family, work, television, sex, sports, sleep) is what is helping them become something other than the sort of Catholics official teaching envisions. It seems to us that Catholic theology has not been curious enough about what sorts of people those who are baptized Catholic are becoming through their ordinary practices, through what they regularly desire to receive. Nor has Catholic ecclesial teaching or academic theology (at least in the USA) attempted seriously to integrate a range of receptions of the eucharist, from daily to occasionally to rarely to never, into a theology of Catholic life; despite the fact that, in the United States, this is how most of those who were baptized Catholic choose to relate to the eucharist. 'Source and summit' risks becoming a slogan or tagline unless it be reinterpreted to mean something new.

---

8 The *Official Catholic Directory* has been published annually, since 1817, by P.J. Kenedy and Sons of Berkeley Heights, NJ.

9 We are not claiming that this situation is novel in modern Catholic history. The important question of the history of Catholic deconversion, defection and/or disaffiliation is one we hope to address in a separate work.

We think 'eucharist' as 'source and summit' ought to be treated theologically along the lines that John D. Caputo treats 'God' and 'love'. Caputo argues that the equivalence of God and love in the Johannine tradition positions these foundational concepts in a sliding relationship to each other, wherein one cannot finally know if one has cornered (or been cornered by) God or love. 'Notice how easily saying "God is love" slides over into saying "love is God." This slippage is provocative and it provides us with an exceedingly important and productive ambiguity, opening up a kind of endless substitutability and translatability between "love" and "God"' (Caputo, 2001: 5). If 'God' is to 'love' as 'eucharist' is to 'source and summit', then what we have as an alleged anchor for Catholic identity is not a fixed node, but rather an unsteady conceptual field for organizing Catholic experience in which 'eucharist' and 'source and summit' are mobile in relation to each other. What through ordinary life becomes the source and summit is being counted as eucharist as much as eucharist is being counted source and summit. Caputo's point is not that one finally positions the other, but that from within these theological categories themselves, one can never know for certain or finally which is which. This is the kind of conceptual circle that, as Caputo suggests, 'makes bishops everywhere nervous' (25).

For our second example, we turn to a major theme in academic Catholic theology. While most Catholic theologians affirm this centrality of eucharist for Christian life, it is frequently placed in Catholic theology in relation to a larger construal of the life of faith. This larger construal is known as the 'analogical imagination' or 'sacramental imagination'. Put into theological discourse influentially by David Tracy in *The Analogical Imagination*; elaborated social-scientifically and literarily by Andrew Greeley; and instantiated in Catholic education by inclusion as the coda to Richard McBrien's widely read compendium *Catholicism*, this imagination comes to reside in Catholics by way of participation in Catholicism's liturgical, intellectual and justice traditions, confirmed and concretized through innumerable, everyday minor sacraments, or 'sacramentals'. The theological idea is that the sacred is seen to be present in the everyday: the material world manifests the transcendent, the finite shows forth the infinite.

This notion quickly became something like the skeleton key by which most Catholic theologians interpret ordinary Catholicism. We see this notion as successful not because it so completely characterizes ordinary Catholicism, but because it aggregates various data in a way that creates a positive space for continued affiliation for questioning Catholics in secularizing cultures, and at the same time is impossible to falsify. The notion of the sacramental imagination can positively incorporate endless amounts of contradictory and potentially contrary data. There is substantial data to justify a more robustly ambiguous construal of this 'imagination'. For example, there is the destructive character of an all-male compulsorily celibate clerical culture, the profound history of white privilege in American Catholicism, and the inability of such a deeply rooted 'imagination' to keep large numbers of baptized Catholics affiliated with this imagination's purported home base, the Roman Catholic Church. These can easily enough be assimilated to 'sacramental imagination' by a negative mechanism: they are often taken to be evidence for the incomplete hold that this imagination has on Catholics.

Indeed, from the perspective of deconversion, that is, the vantage of those who have changed their faith-mind about their spiritual or religious identities, beliefs or practices, away from what is taken to be normative Catholicism, the analogical imagination appears to have been a failed attempt to create an adherence structure in relationship to the institution and the tradition on the part of Catholic intellectuals and pastors. Through this discourse, we have the fomentation of a Catholic soul with mediation as its essence, which is another way of saying, with a sense for mediation – a respect for it, a connatural responsiveness to the exhortation to the mediation – being who a Catholic *is*. In this construction of Catholic sensibility, one sees how it is possible that so many 'believers' are supposed to be able to stay in the Church and recognize each other as Catholics – even, and often particularly, through the struggles over Catholic identity. To be Catholic within these influential rhetorics or discourses is to live with the exhortation to mediation, to desire the mediation.

This is what helps structure the scene, so confusing to outsiders, of liberal Catholics who can occupy a church with a patriarchal authority structure, who are typically deferential to Catholic authority, and who develop elaborate hermeneutics of authority and call those hermeneutics central to Catholicism itself. From this vantage, mediation seems to us to be a Catholic theodicy of practice.

Deconversion in Scholarly Perspective

In the past four decades, people who choose to leave the religious traditions and communities to which they formerly belonged have become increasingly frequent subjects of academic study (see Hornbeck, 2010). In the 1970s and 1980s, greatest attention focused on 'new religious movements' such as the Unification Church ('the Moonies') and Hare Krishna; the possibility of 'deprogramming' former members of such movements was of interest to families who believed that they had lost their relatives to cults. Norman Skonovd, who wrote an influential doctoral dissertation on the process by which individuals depart totalizing religious movements, proposed in 1981 that those who choose to leave mainstream religious groups undergo a parallel, though usually less traumatic, process (Skonovd, 1981). Skonovd departed from the scholarly methodologies dominant in his day by focusing on the question of *how* a person experienced changing her or his religious affiliation, rather than on *who* among a population was likely to do so (see also Hoge, 1981). Skonovd was also among the earliest to employ the value-neutral term 'deconversion', rather than the potentially pejorative language of 'apostasy', 'defection' or 'falling away from the faith', to describe the experiences of those who have left a formerly cherished religious path (see Brinkerhoff and Burke, 1980).

While some continue to investigate the demographic factors that may predict which people are most likely to disaffiliate themselves from their religious communities, other researchers have begun to hone in, qualitatively, on the experiences of such individuals. In the 1990s and early 2000s, pastors and sociologists in evangelical Christian communities took the lead in producing research in this area (see, especially, Jamieson, 2002; Jamieson et al., 2006; cf. Richter and Francis, 1998). A milestone came with the publication of the results of the Bielefeld-Based Cross-Cultural Study of Deconversion, which reported on more than 1,100 questionnaires administered to former church members and their peers in the United States and Germany (Streib, Hood et al., 2009).

Few of the studies we have been describing, however, specifically address the experience of leaving the Roman Catholic Church. Scholars who have made Catholics their primary population have often focused more on explaining to church leaders the departure of former Roman Catholics than on chronicling the processes of departure that such individuals had undergone (see, e.g., Hoge, 1981). Other writers have produced books that explicitly or implicitly urge former Catholics to take some action vis-à-vis their former community: either to reconcile, or never even to consider reconciling, with the church (including Larsen and Parnegg, 1992; Meehl, 1995). What have almost always been missing from these and other studies are accounts of the personal theological negotiations that lead individuals to reconceive their relationship to Catholicism in ways that cause them either to disaffiliate from the church or to problematize through their practices the church's official account of the nature and duties of membership.

Catholic Deconversion as a Theological Question

It is somewhat unusual for a contemporary theological study of Catholic identity and practice to allow itself the latitude toward official teaching on Catholic life as to include such personal (and commonly experienced) theological negotiations. Indeed, one hallmark of the Catholic theologian has been her extraordinary discretion in dealing with official teaching in the formulation of theological stances (Sullivan, 1996). Our attention to official teaching on church affiliation, above, shows that style of generating theology in Catholic contexts. But that style has often been retained at the expense of allowing ordinary Catholic theologies their voices. As Bradford Hinze has argued, Catholic theology and tradition have not been able adequately to include the laments of those who have Catholic experience (Hinze, 2006; on laments in theology, see also Hinze, 2010). There are parallels here with the struggle of Latino/a theologians to get 'popular religion' taken seriously as a source of and mode for theologizing. One difference from the present project is that much of Latino/a theology of popular religion tries to show why popular religion fulfils deep Catholic commitments rather than contradicting them or, more subtly, being heterogeneous to them. That is why we are intrigued by the stance taken by Latina theologian Michelle Gonzalez, who until recently identified as a Catholic theologian. Her inability to place the experience of local Catholic practice in Guatemala on the theological maps she had been taught was a factor in the dispossession of her identity as a Catholic theologian. Moving beyond her earlier attempts to corral the experience of Latino/a Catholics under broad categories of ethnicity and Catholicity, her recent work shows how local Guatemalan practice is heterogeneous to normative Catholicism (Maldonado, 2011a, 2011b). In Astley's terms, it was her willingness to confront more fully the ordinariness of theology that helped activate her own distance from practices of normativity in Catholicism. We think this is the kind of disposition that the study of ordinary theologies of Catholicism encourages.

As Mary McClintock Fulkerson has argued for practical theology, theological reflection on practice starts from the scene of a wound and proceeds to assemble intellectual resources to care for that wound (Fulkerson, 2007: 12–18). One of theology's central questions is what people do with what they take to be at stake in the functional authorities in their lives. It is more helpful theologically to focus on what appeals to normativity do, than on what normativity is: for all rhetorics about what is normative are also ways of making things happen (or in post-colonial terms, trying to negotiate a performance of power) for those who experience themselves as subject to those normative terms. That is why we think that theologies of ordinary Catholicism should theorize normativity in two ways. First, as an institutional discourse that circulates through a network of faith-managers (including, but not limited to, bishops, theologians and pastoral workers) who through their actions make orthodoxy to be something real and central for Catholic faith – that is, they make normativity normative through ways of teaching and governing that contribute to fashioning the level of Catholic subjectivity in 'ordinary', lay Catholics. Second, normativity is not just what the managers take to be normative, but also what lay Catholics actually take to be normative, out of their own religio-cultural formation and personal psychology. As Astley argues, what is effective in people's lives for their faith decisions, consolations and desolations are those considerations that may or may not be considered central by the designated religious authorities, considerations like one's emotional history, one's mentors and peers, and more. These are the operationally 'normative' factors. Given the character of faith as historical, practice-based and contextual, it will not do to wish the first and second definitions to coincide. Religious subjectivity is ever a project, a work in and of transition in the cultural and psychological particularities of individual and social life. To appreciate this rich ordinary theological landscape will require the development of practice-based theological attention to the lives of baptized Catholics, whether they are 'practising' or 'non-practising'.

New Directions for Catholic Theological Research

With what ordinary theologies about church membership, affiliation, and disaffiliation are contemporary American Roman Catholics operating? Many more data on lived religious experience wait to be gathered, but the extant literature suggests some hypotheses.

First, the perspective of ordinary theology problematizes any attempt to map onto individuals' lives and actions formal teachings about church membership. Qualitative accounts and quantitative data reveal that many individuals who identify themselves as Catholic engage in practices proscribed by official documents: attending and participating in the services of other Christian denominations, or even of other religions; participating in self-described Catholic communities (such as the American Catholic Church, the Old Catholic Church, and perhaps especially communities presided over by Catholic women priests) not endorsed by Rome; and, perhaps most commonly, electing not to follow church teachings on matters of personal morality.

Second, studies of ordinary theology should pursue the clues in the literature that some individuals have described their practices of disaffiliating or disengaging from the Catholic Church as a working out of the values that they learned from Catholicism itself. It may be the case that some trajectories of deconversion represent attempts to attain a kind of moral authenticity in the face of church teachings and practices that individuals perceive as irrelevant, unworkable, destructive or even evil.

Third, an ordinary theology that takes seriously Catholic deconversion will need to deepen the exploration of the question that faith-managers have succeeded in placing close to the centre of many Catholics' lives and certainly of ecclesial discourse: who is and is not a Catholic?

In pursuing these future directions in theological research, it will help to bring emerging research in lived religion (often placed curricularly under 'Catholic studies' or 'religious studies') into much closer relationship to theology in and for Catholic contexts. In terms of the current divisions of knowledge in Catholic theological education, this will probably necessitate a deeper consideration of the place of practice-based theologies in the theological curriculum. But if Catholicism integrates practice-based theologies more foundationally in its research, practical theologies will need to relax their historically Protestant predilections toward 'discipleship' and toward integrating people more deeply into Christianity. Such a bias will be unhelpful for Catholicism, insofar as it plays into the ecclesial management of orthodoxy that has occluded so much ordinary theology from being recognized in Catholicism. On the horizon may lie much more 'polydoxy' and multiplicity in faith identity (see Keller and Schneider, 2010; Cataldo, 2008).

References

Astley, Jeff (2002), *Ordinary Theology: Looking, Listening, and Learning in Theology*, Burlington, Vt.: Ashgate.

Baggett, Jerome (2009), *Sense of the Faithful: How American Catholics Live Their Faith*, New York: Oxford University Press.

Benedict XVI, Pope (2009), *Omnium in Mentem*, 26 October, http://www.vatican.va/holy_father/benedict_xvi/apost_letters/documents/hf_ben-xvi_apl_20091026_codex-iuris-canonici_lt.html [accessed 23 November 2011].

Brinkerhoff, Merlin B. and Kathryn L. Burke (1980), 'Disaffiliation: Some Notes on "Falling from the Faith"', *Sociological Analysis*, 41: 41–54.

Byron, William J. (2011), 'On Their Way Out: What Exit Interviews Could Teach Us about Lapsed Catholics', *America*, 3 January, 2011, http://www.americamagazine.org/content/article.cfm?article_id=12642 [accessed 5 January 2011].

Caputo, John D. (2001), *On Religion*, New York: Routledge.

Cataldo, Lisa (2008), 'Multiple Selves, Multiple Gods? Functional Polytheism and the Postmodern Religious Patient', *Pastoral Psychology*, 57, 1–2: 45–58.

Catechism of the Catholic Church (1993), Rome: Libreria Editrice Vaticana.

Dugan, Kate and Jennifer Owens (eds) (2009), *From the Pews in the Back: Young Women and Catholicism*, Collegeville, Minn.: Liturgical Press.

Flannery, Austin (ed.) (1996), *Vatican Council II: The Conciliar and Post Conciliar Documents*, Northport, NY: Costello.

Fulkerson, Mary McClintock (2007), *Places of Redemption: Theology for a Worldly Church*, New York: Oxford University Press.

General Conference of Seventh-Day Adventists (2005), *Seventh-Day Adventist Church Manual*, 17th ed., Hagerstown, Md.: The Secretariat, General Conference.

Hinze, Bradford E. (2006), *Practices of Dialogue in the Roman Catholic Church: Aims and Obstacles, Lessons and Laments*, New York: Continuum.

Hinze, Bradford E. (2010), 'A Decade of Disciplining Theologians', *Horizons*, 37: 92–126.

Hoge, Dean R. (1981), *Converts, Dropouts, Returnees: A Study of Religious Change Among Catholics*, New York: Pilgrim.

Holland, Joe and Peter Henriot (1983), *Social Analysis: Linking Faith and Justice*, Maryknoll, NY: Orbis.

Hornbeck II, J. Patrick (2010), 'Deconversion from Roman Catholicism: Mapping a Fertile Field', *American Catholic Studies*, 122: 1–29.

Jamieson, Alan (2002), *A Churchless Faith: Faith Journeys Beyond the Churches*, London: SPCK.

Jamieson, Alan et al. (2006), *Church Leavers: Faith Journeys Five Years On*, London: SPCK.

Keller, Catherine and Laurel Schneider (eds) (2010), *Polydoxy: Theology of Multiplicity and Relation*, New York: Routledge.

Killen, Patricia O'Connell and John de Beer (1994), *The Art of Theological Reflection*, New York: Crossroad.

Kinast, Robert L. (1996), *Let Ministry Teach: A Guide to Theological Reflection*, Collegeville, Minn.: Liturgical Press.

Larsen, Earnie and Janee Parnegg (1992), *Recovering Catholic: What To Do When Religion Comes between You and God*, San Francisco: HarperSanFrancisco.

Leahy, Brendan (2011), *Ecclesial Movements and Communities: Origins, Significance, and Issues*, Hyde Park, NY: New City Press.

Maldonado, Michelle Gonzalez (2011a), 'A Response to Paul Lakeland', in Jonathan Y. Tan (ed.), *The Catholic Theological Society of America: Proceedings of the Sixty-Sixth Annual Convention*, Omaha, Nebr.: Catholic Theological Society of America, pp. 29–32.

Maldonado, Michelle Gonzalez (2011b), 'Expanding Our Academic Publics: Latino/a Theology, Religious Studies, and Latin American Studies', in Harold Recinos (ed.), *Wading Through Many Voices: Toward a Theology of Public Conversation*, Lanham, Md.: Rowman and Littlefield, pp. 17–32.

Meehl, Joanne H. (1995), *The Recovering Catholic: Personal Journeys of Women Who Left the Church*, Amherst, NY: Prometheus Books.

Orsi, Robert A. (1996), *Thank You, St Jude: Women's Devotion to the Patron Saint of Hopeless Causes*, New Haven, Conn.: Yale University Press.

Pontifical Council for Legislative Texts (2006), 'Actus formalis defectionis ab ecclesia catholica', 13 March, 2006, http://www.vatican.va/roman_curia/pontifical_councils/intrptxt/documents/rc_pc_intrptxt_doc_20060313_actus-formalis_en.html [accessed 23 November 2011].

Radcliffe, Timothy (2006), 'Overcoming Discord in the Church', *National Catholic Reporter*, 5 May 2006, http://natcath.org/NCR_Online/archives2/2006b/050506/050506a.php [accessed 13 February 2012].

Richter, Philip and Leslie J. Francis (1998), *Gone But Not Forgotten: Church Leaving and Returning*, London: Darton, Longman and Todd.

Roberts, Tom (2010), 'The "Had It" Catholics', *National Catholic Reporter*, 11 October 2010, http://ncronline.org/news/faith-parish/had-it-catholics [accessed 9 November 2010].

Seitz, John C. (2011), *No Closure: Catholic Practice and Boston's Parish Shutdowns*, Cambridge, Mass.: Harvard University Press.

Skonovd, L. Norman (1981), *Apostasy: The Process of Defection from Religious Totalism*, PhD diss., University of California, Davis.

Stevenson, Thomas (2006), *Sons of the Church: The Witnessing of Gay Catholic Men*, New York: Routledge.

Streib, Heinz, Ralph W. Hood, Jr et al. (2009), *Deconversion: Qualitative and Quantitative Results from Cross-Cultural Research in Germany and the United States of America*, Göttingen: Vandenhoeck and Ruprecht.

Sullivan, Francis A. (1996), *Creative Fidelity: Weighing and Interpreting Documents of the Magisterium*, New York: Paulist.

The Code of Canon Law: Latin-English Edition (1983), Washington, DC: Canon Law Society of America.

The Pew Forum on Religion and Public Life (2008), *US Religious Landscape Survey: Religious Affiliation: Diverse and Dynamic*, Washington, DC: Pew Forum.

Treviño, Roberto R. (2006), *The Church in the Barrio: Mexican-American Ethno-Catholicism in Houston*, Chapel Hill, NC: University of North Carolina Press.

Whitehead, James D. and Evelyn Eaton Whitehead (1995), *Method in Ministry: Theological Reflection and Christian Ministry*, Kansas City, Mo.: Sheed and Ward.

Chapter 5
Ordinary Theology and the Learning Conversation with Academic Theology

Jeff Astley

Conversation and Correlation

The metaphor of a conversation is integral to many accounts of practical theology, theological reflection and Christian education, as well as hermeneutics. It is used of a particular way of doing theology.

Theology as conversation depends on the idea of a 'mutual critical correlation' that relates one thing (human life experience, often of a particular contemporary practice or concern, and the reflections it engenders) with another, very different, thing (the Christian heritage of faith, which is itself in part a product of past, reflective theological dialogue). This process of 'structuring a correlation' is frequently expressed in metaphors of juxtaposition. We bring our experience and our practice 'alongside' the scriptures and reflections of other Christians, 'deliberately connecting our reflection on life to our religious heritage' (Killen and de Beer, 1995: 68; Green, 2009: 77). Educators encourage people through an appropriate pedagogy 'to bring their lives to their Faith and their Faith to their lives', so as to 'help to bridge the gap that Christians maintain between their lives and their faith' (Groome, 2011: 262, 283).

The foundations of this approach lie in Paul Tillich and David Tracy. Tillich advocated making Christianity comprehensible to modern culture through a 'dialectical theology' in which the Christian tradition offers answers in response to contemporary questions, a process best achieved by those whose broken lives or thinking opens them to respond in existential depth to the gospel. In Tillich's answering or apologetic type of theology, the form – though not the content – of the answer is determined by the nature of the question, and by the analysis of the human situation to which it is a response (Tillich, 1968: Introduction).

In Tracy's 'revisionist' pursuit of open-ended theological enquiry, all Christian theology is an attempt to correlate 'the meaning and truth of an interpretation of the Christian fact and the meaning and truth of an interpretation of the contemporary situation' (Tracy, 1983: 62; cf. 1975: 43).[1] Tracy accuses Tillich

---

1 In the humanities a correlation – a mutual relationship of interdependence between two things – is construed as a relationship of meaning, rather than one that implies cause and effect (as in empirical studies).

of overemphasizing Christianity's contribution to these answers, and insists on seeing the two conversation partners as equal; although some critics argue that human experience has too much priority on Tracy's account.

Thomas Groome describes his own approach as 'very close to' Tracy's critical correlation (Groome, 1980: 232 n. 9), while preferring 'integration' to correlation (2011: 283, 300, cf. 152, 282). Groome equates Tracy's Christian fact with his preferred, 'more open ended' metaphorical term, 'Christian Story', which designates 'the whole faith tradition of the Christian people'. He also adopts the term 'Christian vision' as a metaphor for 'the lived response' that this Story invites and the 'promise it offers' (1980: 29 n. 16, 192, 202 n. 13). For both authors, Groome contends, the main concern is that present praxis and the Christian tradition should be engaged, critiqued and brought into correlation with each other.

In Tracy, as in Groome, this correlation of meaning is most often described through the metaphor of a conversation (cf. Tracy, 1975: chs 3 and 4; 1981: 255, cf. 101, 167, 452). Groome normally employs the adjective 'dialectical' to characterize relating learners' reflections on their 'present action' (engagement with the world) to the Christian Story and Vision. This is largely because the process ideally involves, in Hegelian fashion, affirming and appropriating the truth in part of the Christian tradition (the thesis), but questioning and refusing other aspects of that tradition (antithesis), and then moving beyond it in creating a new understanding that modifies and carries that truth forward (synthesis); while allowing the tradition to do the same with our present action (see, e.g., 1980: 217–18, cf. 113, 179 n. 46; 1991: 145, 251, cf. 101, 475 n. 380). In this 'movement' of 'dialectical hermeneutics', therefore, the learners ask themselves *both* 'How does this Christian Story/Vision affirm, question, and call us beyond present praxis?', *and* 'How does present praxis affirm and critically appropriate' this version of the Christian Story/Vision? – so that they may move on to 'live more faithfully toward the Vision of God's reign' by choosing 'a personal faith response for the future' (1980: 208; 1991: 147).

Ordinary Theology in Conversation

The correlation and conversation I wish to highlight in this chapter, however, is somewhat different. It is the conversation between the learner's ordinary theology and the contributions of a more 'extraordinary' theology, largely derived from the academy but sometimes taking the form of an ecclesiastical theology defined by church councils or other formal authorities. How far does *this* conversation parallel the above account?

The learners' own theology begins by being quite untouched by academic theological study. In certain forms of adult Christian education and in those university and seminary settings where students learn to *do* theology and not solely to study the theology of others, however, their ordinary theology will interact with the academic or ecclesiastical theology they are learning.[2]

Learners never enter into any task of theological learning with empty minds or hearts; they always come with something to contribute themselves – something to say on their own account. In this conversational dialogue, it is unlikely that the new theology they are being taught will wholly erase the students' own ideas and imprint its own (any more than will the broader Christian tradition). And when students do 'take over' or 'take up' a piece of teaching, it will be subtly changed in becoming part of their own set of beliefs or values. As the ideas of another converse with the learners' own ideas, the two sets will interact and eventually transmute into something that may be rather different from either – in a way that is often as individual and personal as the ordinary theology from which it began (Astley, 2010: 7–13). Educators must therefore accept that 'people are not to repeat our word but to speak their own; that may well be a "new" word for both' (Groome, 1991: 263, cf. 251–2). Here, correlation truly leads to an 'appropriation' or 'integration' of Christian faith with the learner's life: with her identity and agency, and her own lived faith. This is 'learning from religion' with a vengeance (cf. Groome, 1991: 3, 250, 254; 2011: 91–2; 2012: 8–9).

Although this learning is never a monologue in which academic theology (or the Christian tradition) speaks and the learners silently record what it says; neither should it be a monologue in which they only speak about their own point of view, without ever hearing it being challenged or allowing it to be transformed. It should be a true 'fusion of horizons' (Gadamer, 1982: 350), and one in which the tension between the two remains.

However, my main point is that educators should *begin with ordinary theology*. The educationalist's mantra of acknowledging the centrality of the learner, and taking her contribution to the learning process seriously, takes on an ethnographical and a theological significance when we stress the necessity of knowing about and beginning with people's ordinary theology. 'The only

[2] In most of their 'ordinary learning', by contrast, Christians develop their ordinary theology with little input from academic theology (see Chapter 20). But the *ordinary/academic conversation* is: (1) essential for the *full* critical development of theology as a mode of understanding, although it may not improve its salvific power as an expression of (and possible influence on) people's salvific religion; (2) crucial to those whose cognitive and spiritual make-up means that they really want or need this sort of conversation with academic theology; (3) important in the training of ministers, who (a) ought to be capable of it; (b) are likely to come across lay people who want/need it or who may receive an academic theological education; and (c) must be made aware how academic theology generates many debates both outside and within the church. As a personal aside, *I* cannot make do with religion and my ordinary theology alone, both because I cannot help pressing the metaphors and stories of ordinary theology further, and because academic reflection has in my case proved to be a positive spiritual and religious resource. But my Christian education ministry is not about me, and most people (thank God) are not identical to me.

place that authentic theology can begin is with the real beliefs of real Christians' (Cobb, 1993: 41; cf. 1994: 4, 71–2).

I argue further – unlike John Cobb? – that if these beliefs have been found to sustain Christian learners when tested against the vicissitudes of their own lives, we may say that they are already 'adequate' or 'appropriate' in the sense that they work for them (see Chapter 1). The centrality of the learner also means that the Christian or theological educator often needs to occupy the mediatory role of a *translator*, fluent in both languages, whose primary task is to convey the sense of academic theology (or of the broader Christian tradition and its several 'languages') in a tongue that is 'understanded of the people'.

Imaginative Seeing

Laurie Green writes of the learner's central hermeneutical concern:

> Our task is to find some way of bridging this cultural gap and seeing connections between the Christian heritage on one side and our present experience on the other. … From one side of this gap to the other, we will hear resonances, sense similarities and challenges, eventually building up a whole range of sensitivities to the Christian treasure store of tradition. (Green, 2009: 82)

Although 'resonance' is an auditory analogy, I prefer to think of this as a kind of seeing involving spiritual (or theological) *imagination*. While this noun is usually used of having ideas, in particular creative and resourceful ideas, its etymology in the Latin *imaginare* allows me to indulge my predilection for metaphors of vision in religion.

Imagination's function is 'to see more in [something] than meets the regular eye of sense' (Warnock, 1986: 148). Having the eyes to see clearly and in depth is of the essence of religion; as is spotting connections and possessing insight, and recognizing something *as* being something else, by looking on it in a certain way (for example, seeing this alien, impoverished, damaged or sinful person as 'a child of God'). Visual language is also used with respect to discovering the significance of a human activity or religious text, discerning or 'seeing' its meaning. This may involve seeing the same thing ('theological situation') differently, by seeing 'the truth of what was really there all along', 'disclosed in its true meaning' (Cottingham, 2009: 98, 123; cf. Perkins, 1990: 60; Astley, 2007: 4–7, 11–18). However it is understood, some new form of vision is often taken to be a proper outcome of theological reflection (Killen and de Beer, 1995: 71; Cameron et al., 2010: 14), and as central to the act of discernment within much Christian experience. Such religious vision is not discursive, inferential thinking; it is more 'immediate' and requires wisdom rather than intellectual cleverness (cf. Hodgson, 1999: 7).

The imaginative vision that the Christian learner in general, and the theological learner in particular, requires is a matter of picturing life through theological or spiritual eyes. She needs to see with the eyes of faith, if faith is 'the means of divine teaching that allows theologians … to begin to see things as God does, to understand things by means of God's ideas about them' (McIntosh, 2007: 28). This is 'theology as spectacles for interpreting the world rather than simply "knowledge about" [it]' (Heywood, 2009: 171).

There are at least two aspects to this. One is discerning what is of religious, spiritual and theological *value* and *importance*. We can fail to see what a theology is all about if we lack the wisdom and insight to get to the heart of it, to see the purpose and value of it (cf. Astley, 1999). The Pharisees knew a great deal about God and scripture, and religion and morality; but Jesus thought that some of them had missed the point entirely. With their values, it was not salvific to them. With the eyes of their faith, they could hardly see it.

Is this part of what Charles Wood means when he writes of 'imaginative grasp', 'attention' and 'sensitivity' in theological judgement? (Wood, 1996: 350, 355). Would Basil Mitchell include it in the 'qualities of imagination and judgement in spiritual matters' required of the theologian (Mitchell, 1991: 19)? If learners see something in scripture, worship, doctrine or ethics that they take to have intrinsic worth – especially something of supreme value – they will surely embrace it, esteem it and use it. Even theology may then work for them, spiritually and salvifically. This discernment of value requires a form of *affective evaluation* involving attitudes and feelings (see Cottingham, 2009: chs 5 and 6; Astley, 2012).

Another aspect of spiritual imagination involves a different species of insight that is more of a *skill*. It is *seeing connections*, a function of 'imaginative intelligence'. A large part of this is spotting significant similarities, likenesses and relevances. Our ability to know God 'through imaginative analogy' rests on the tendency of the human mind 'to spring from likeness to likeness' (Headley, 2008: 5, 58).

Within the hermeneutical conversation, spiritual imagination involves an 'intuitive hunch' or 'imaginative leap' (Green, 2009: 81–2; Heywood, 2009: 168–9), in which we 'see' this particular juxtaposition as relevant, fertile, 'insightful'. Green describes the connectivity required for the tradition and our situation 'to fit together', by way of this intuitive recognition of similarities, as a 'liberation of the imagination' (2009: 82) – appending a reference to Ian Ramsey's 'disclosure situations' (Ramsey, 1957: ch. I; cf. Hick: 1973, ch. 3; Astley, 1984, 1994: 202–4). However, Green insists that these 'imaginative connections' must be checked out against reason and theological scholarship through a secondary cycle of reflection, to discover whether the intuition is 'an authoritative witness from the tradition' – thus bringing theological scholars 'more into the service of the active mission of the Church' (Green, 2009: 96, 102–3).

Groome sees a need for creative imagination, along with reason and memory, in the learners' critical reflection on their present action: 'without it we end up … with only negative criticism' (1980: 188). He avers that 'so much of our educational efforts stifle the imagination of the participants, telling them what to think and how to think it' (187; cf. 1991: 261, 263). He also finds a place for imagination in seeing the future consequences of our actions, discerning how the world might be other than it is, opening us to the otherness of other people, and even in 'enabling us to recognize and understand what "is"' (1991: 96, cf. 105, 196, 205–8, 287; 2011: 314).

Most significantly, Groome allows that 'revelation comes to meet us first in our imaginations', accepting imagination's role in mediating the dialectical encounter and appropriation by serving as a channel for the fusion of horizons (1991: 197, 253, 506 n. 5). This depends on the learners' '"natural" capacity to see the revelatory correlation' between, on the one hand, their present praxis and the stories and visions that express it; and, on the other, 'the resonant truth' in the received 'Story/Vision of Christian faith' (1991: 254–5; cf. 2011: 276). This ability to 'recognize the resonance between the truth in each source' relies in part on imagination.

Metaphor

The creation of metaphors also depends on seeing connections. We know what something is when we know what it is like. Spotting this imaginative resemblance allows us to 'carry over' a word or phrase between one application and another. Two networks of associations are thereby brought together, so that Jesus is seen as a 'shepherd' or God as a 'rock'. Metaphors thus give 'new possibilities of vision' (Soskice, 1985: 57–8): helping us see a new depth through a form of stereoscopic vision, in which not only two words but 'two worlds' are seen together and we are jolted into spotting similarities that we had not previously noticed, so that we 'see one thing in terms of another' (cf. Astley, 2004: ch. 4).[3] In doing so, *both* elements may be changed or 'reframed': 'it may be that shepherds are viewed with greater consideration after being related to God' (Stiver, 1996: 116; see also Gunton, 1988: 78–9, on the 'victory' of the cross).

Figures of speech can help my imagination leap the gap between my own story and experience, and the stories, histories and beliefs I hear from my theological teachers. Some Christian educators suggest that we ask ourselves first, 'What is my life *like*?'; then see what picture, poem or story comes to mind to illuminate or illustrate that experience, before entering into and exploring this metaphorical world. After these reflections, we may ask, 'Do these mediating images connect with anything in scripture, worship or Christian doctrine?' The characteristic process of the 'Education for Ministry' (EFM) programme encourages the adult learner (or group) first to 'generate a metaphor' that 'captures the human experience on which they are focusing', and then to explore the world of that metaphor before using it to identify relevant parts of the Christian tradition that 'are called to mind by the metaphor' (Bairnwick Center Staff, 1984: IR-7–IR-12). Patricia O'Connell Killen and John de Beer advocate a similar method, in which

[3] Much the same can be said of parables, which are similes rather than metaphors.

an 'image' that emerges from an incident from one's life is expected to suggest something about God's purposes, and thus to mediate between a person's own lived narrative and the resources of tradition (Killen and de Beer, 1995: 70–71).

Educating Vision

In their essay, 'Disciplined Seeing', Stanley Hauerwas and Brian Goldstone suggest that 'the vocabularies by which the objects of our inquiries are conceived and apprehended are themselves manifestations of historically specific pedagogies connected … to "how one sees things" – and, in seeing them, intuiting how properly to live with them.' Significantly, they also write that 'to "see something *as something*" is, in large measure, already to have been made by it' (2011: 37, 60).

Christian learning is partly *ophthalmic*. It involves a correction of vision, a change in people's ways of seeing, by forming the skills, attitudes and framework of belief that enable them to see the point of Christianity, and to see beyond the appearances so as to perceive physical and human nature in depth – the universe as God's world, other people as God's children, the church as the body of Christ. And especially to see Jesus as Lord and to see with his eyes, through the refractive power of the kingship of God (cf. Astley, 2007: 11–14, 16–18, 69, 85, 112–17). Nonna Verna Harrison argues that such 'spiritual perception' is a facet of the divine image in human beings. It is 'a kind of double vision': seeing human beings and the natural world as themselves, as they are; but also 'seeing through to the presence of God, who is within them and beyond them' (Harrison, 2010: 53, 192). The Greek fathers, however, often spoke of the fall as a turning away, or even a closing, of one's eyes. Even our imagination may fail us (cf. Chapter 4). 'As a man is, so he sees', as William Blake wrote.

He added, 'As the eye is formed, such are its powers' (Keynes, 1961: 835). Much spiritual vision is down to Christian nurture or formation – Christian 'nourishing' and 'moulding', in more overtly metaphorical language. In the 'Enculturation' or 'Faith Community Approach' to Christian education, the church teaches itself to be Christian and inducts new members into its faith primarily through speaking the Christian language and beliefs, expressing the Christian attitudes and affections, and practising the Christian behaviours in its worship, witness and service. (And only secondarily by *talking about* these things, through specific forms of instruction.)

But this needs to be supplemented by an 'Interpretation Approach', in which individuals or (preferably) small groups *self-consciously* and *explicitly* seek to relate the Christian tradition to their own perceived beliefs, and their reflections on their own practices and situations. This is our conversational, hermeneutical process, which begins with the learner and her concerns and needs, rather than with the Christian tradition; but explicitly relates the former to the latter through specific educational interventions.[4] I have argued that this conversation itself depends on nurturing the character and capacities of spiritual vision and imagination, in order that these wider connections may be seen. Perhaps this will be easier for certain personality types (see Chapter 9).

Unfortunately, accounts of the Interpretation Approach often seem to advocate a first stage of reflection on present experience that is wilfully non-theological, recommending its exploration using the tools of the social sciences (in particular sociology) alongside moral and political evaluations (Groome, 1991: ch. 7; Green, 2009: ch. 4). Theological criteria are only occasionally invoked. Explicit theology is mostly reserved for the later stage of the dialectical hermeneutic between life (and these *non*-theological explorations) and the Christian tradition (Groome, 1991: ch. 9, cf. 189–93; Green, 2009: ch. 5, cf. 69). But most Christians are already reflecting theologically on their practice and experience; their theology goes all the way down. It is this ordinary theological reflection that Christian educators should mainly seek to build on, linking it with the wider resources of the Christian tradition.

Despite appearances, in the particular hermeneutical conversation between ordinary theology *and academic or ecclesiastical theology*, a metaphorical bridge to facilitate this link is already in place. For ordinary theology tends to be very rich in figurative language and autobiographical stories; and the concepts of academic theology are themselves founded and funded by metaphors, models, analogies and narratives (including the 'story-metaphors' of myths), and work best when they keep in touch with their origins (McFague, 1983: 26). Hence, experience gives rise to an ordinary theology voiced in metaphor and story; and academic theology is undergirded by very similar linguistic forms. The hermeneutical conversation envisaged here, therefore, primarily begins and develops on the bridge between the metaphors and stories of the conversation partners on *both* sides of the gap. Like speaks to like.

Or at least it could. Much Christian and academic theological teaching, however, seeks wholly to raze people's pre-existing theological fabrications to the ground, trampling their personal narratives and imaginative images, before attempting (often unsuccessfully) to build something entirely new and unrelated on the bulldozed site.

We need to try harder, beginning where – and with what – people already are.

References

Astley, Jeff (1984), 'Ian Ramsey and the Problem of Religious Knowledge', *Journal of Theological Studies*, 35, 2: 157–67.

4 On these approaches to Christian education, see Seymour and Miller, 1982: chs 3 and 6; 1990: 27–62, 83–101, 216–38; cf. Astley, 2000: ch. 1.

Astley, Jeff (1994), *The Philosophy of Christian Religious Education*, Birmingham, Ala.: Religious Education Press.

Astley, Jeff (1999), 'Learning Moral and Spiritual Wisdom', in Stephen C. Barton (ed.), *Where Shall Wisdom be Found? Wisdom in the Bible, the Church and the Contemporary World*, Edinburgh: T. & T. Clark, pp. 321–34.

Astley, Jeff (2004), *Exploring God-Talk: Using Language in Religion*, London: Darton, Longman and Todd.

Astley, Jeff (2007), *Christ of the Everyday*, London: SPCK.

Astley, Jeff (2010), *SCM Studyguide to Christian Doctrine*, London, SCM Press.

Astley, Jeff (2012), 'A Theological Reflection on the Nature of Religious Truth', in Jeff Astley, Leslie J. Francis, Mandy Robbins and Mualla Selçuk (eds), *Teaching Religion, Teaching Truth: Theoretical and Empirical Perspectives*, Bern: Peter Lang, pp. 241–62.

Astley, Jeff (ed.) (2000), *Learning in the Way: Research and Reflection on Adult Christian Education*, Leominster: Gracewing.

Bairnwick Center Staff (1984), *Manual for Mentors* (Education for Ministry Handbook), Sewanee, Tenn.: University of the South.

Cameron, Helen et al. (2010), *Talking About God in Practice: Theological Action Research and Practical Theology*, London: SCM Press.

Cobb, John B., Jr (1993), *Becoming a Thinking Christian*, Nashville, Tenn.: Abingdon.

Cobb, John B., Jr (1994), *Lay Theology*, St Louise, Mo.: Chalice Press.

Cottingham, John (2009), *Why Believe?* London: Continuum.

Gadamer, Hans-Georg (1982), *Truth and Method*, New York: Crossroad.

Green, Laurie (2009), *Let's Do Theology: Resources for Contextual Theology*, London: Mowbray.

Groome, Thomas H. (1980), *Christian Religious Education: Sharing Our Story and Vision*, New York: Harper & Row.

Groome, Thomas H. (1991), *Sharing Faith: A Comprehensive Approach to Religious Education and Pastoral Ministry*, New York: HarperSanFrancisco.

Groome, Thomas H. (2011), *Will There Be Faith? Depends on Every Christian*, Dublin: Veritas.

Groome, Thomas H. (2012), 'From Life to Faith to Life: Some Traces', *Journal of Adult Theological Education*, 8, 1: 8–23.

Gunton, Colin (1988), *The Actuality of Atonement: A Study of Metaphor, Rationality and the Christian Tradition*, Edinburgh: T. & T. Clark.

Harrison, Nonna Verna (2010), *God's Many-Splendored Image: Theological Anthropology for Christian Formation*, Grand Rapids, Mich.: Baker Academic.

Hauerwas, Stanley with Brian Goldstone (2011), 'Disciplined Seeing: Forms of Christianity and Forms of Life', in Stanley Hauerwas, *Learning to Speak Christian*, London: SCM Press, pp. 33–60.

Headley, Douglas (2008), *Living Forms of the Imagination*, London: Continuum.

Heywood, David (2009), 'Learning How to Learn: Theological Reflection at Cuddesdon', *Journal of Adult Theological Education*, 6, 2: 164–75.

Hick, John (1973), *God and the Universe of Faiths*, London: Macmillan.

Hodgson, Peter C. (1999), *God's Wisdom: Toward a Theology of Education*, Louisville, Ky.: Westminster John Knox Press.

Keynes, G. (ed.) (1961), *The Poetry and Prose of William Blake*, London: Nonesuch.

Killen, Patricia O'Connell and John de Beer (1995), *The Art of Theological Reflection*, New York: Crossroad.

McFague, Sally (1983), *Metaphorical Theology: Models of God in Religious Language*, London: SCM Press.

McIntosh, Mark A. (2007), *Divine Teaching: An Introduction to Christian Theology*, Oxford: Blackwell.

Mitchell, Basil (1991), 'Philosophy and Theology', in Ann Loades and Loyal D. Rue (eds), *Contemporary Classics in Philosophy of Religion*, La Salle, Ill.: Open Court, pp. 7–20.

Perkins, Pheme (1990), *Jesus as Teacher*, Cambridge: Cambridge University Press.

Ramsey, Ian T. (1957), *Religious Language*, London: SCM Press.

Seymour, Jack and Donald E. Miller (eds) (1982), *Contemporary Approaches to Christian Education*, Nashville, Tenn.: Abingdon.

Seymour, Jack and Donald E. Miller (eds) (1990), *Theological Approaches to Christian Education*, Nashville, Tenn.: Abingdon.

Soskice, Janet Martin (1985), *Metaphor and Religious Language*, Oxford: Oxford University Press.

Stiver, Dan (1996), *The Philosophy of Religious Language: Sign, Symbol and Story*, Oxford: Blackwell.

Tillich, Paul (1968), *Systematic Theology: Combined Volume*, London: Nisbet.

Tracy, David (1975), *Blessed Rage for Order*, New York: Seabury.

Tracy, David (1981), *The Analogical Imagination: Christian Theology and the Culture of Pluralism*, London: SCM Press.

Tracy, David (1983), 'The Foundations of Practical Theology', in Don S. Browning (ed.), *Practical Theology*, San Francisco: Harper & Row, pp. 61–82.

Warnock, Mary (1986), 'Religious Imagination', in James P. Mackey (ed.), *Religious Imagination*, Edinburgh: Edinburgh University Press, pp. 142–57.

Wood, Charles (1996), 'Theological Inquiry and Theological Education', in Jeff Astley, Leslie J. Francis and Colin Crowder (eds), *Theological Perspectives on Christian Formation: A Reader in Theology and Christian Education*, Leominster: Gracewing and Grand Rapids, Mich.: Eerdmans, pp. 342–58.

Chapter 6
Power in the Local Church: Locating the Implicit

Martyn Percy

Generally, one problem that faces many theological colleges and seminaries is the unspoken assumption that most of the churches in which clergy will serve are essentially similar in character, and only different in form. Thus, principles, ideas and visions are taught and offered as though what might work in one place can be easily transferred to another. Formulae for church growth particularly come to mind. Yet, as one educationalist cautions (Grierson, 1985: 18),

> the 'church' so talked about in seminary is neat, tidy, and generally civilised. A particular congregation is never neat, sometimes barely Christian and only rarely civilised. Part of the 'culture shock' is due to the changed status of the student. There is a world of difference between being a member of a congregation, and carrying the weight of its symbolic meaning in the institutionalised role of 'priest', whether that word is understood in a high or low sense. In addition, the student emerging from theological college is a different person from the one who entered.
>
> Again what appears to be the case upon the surface is not necessarily the case. In one parish a prolonged conflict occurred over the practice of the ladies' guild of placing a vase of flowers on the communion table. The new minister on the basis of sound theological principles and an impeccable liturgical viewpoint well supported in theological college, made strenuous efforts to remove them.
>
> The conflict proved to be an illustration of two world views passing each other. The practice had arisen in the particular congregation positively as a confession of God's grace in renewing the world daily, and negatively because of the attempt of a former minister to close the women's group down. A vase of flowers was to the women's group, symbol both of their identity as a group and a confession of their faith as Christians. The new minister saw only a custom he could not affirm with integrity. That was all he saw, and before his outlook had become informed much damage had been done to the life of the parish. Similar stories can be told about attempts to remove national flags from churches, or to change the arrangement of church furniture bearing brass plates in honour of deceased parents and grandparents …

Power in religious institutions can be as inevitable and ubiquitous as anywhere else. It can be the power of virtue or vice. Equally, it can be a power that drives a morally ambiguous potency, or the naked assertion of a particular fecundity. Power can be seen gorgeously vested; splendidly arrayed in ritual, material and organization. But it can also be disguised in the apparently ordinary and insignificant, only erupting as problematic when a synergy of events causes the hidden face of power to be revealed.

An understanding of power, then, is a crucial hermeneutical key for arriving at an understanding of the local church, and in specific congregations. To understand the nature of power in churches, it is not necessary to be engaged in a reductive sociological or psychological task. It is, rather, to recognize that any social body (and this includes churches) can benefit from a form of 'deep literacy' (to coin a phrase of Paulo Freire: 1972 and 1973) that readily faces up to the myriad of ways in which power is present, distributed, wielded and transformative. Furthermore, and perhaps inevitably, attention to the phenomenon of power as a primary motif within congregations can provide a degree of illumination that leads to transformative self-critical praxis within a congregation. In seeking to understand the local church, attention to the dynamics of power can go some considerable way to providing some causal explanations related to organization, mission, identity and worship.

Because the nature of power is essentially contested – either within any one individual discipline, or in dialogue between the disciplines – there is no common analytic or explanatory language that uniquely commends itself to the study of congregations or the local church. Theologically, it is commonplace to speak of the power of God. In turn, most denominations will have a conceptualization of how that power typically is expressed or reified (i.e., materially manifested) in the midst of a congregation. Put another way, the 'pure' power of God is known through particular and given 'agents' which (or who) are deemed to most faithfully express that power, and the nature of the giver (God). Thus, for some denominations, the power of God is made known in the celebration of the mass; or in a particular individual; or in the exposition of an inerrant Bible; or in the faithful gathering that witnesses miracles, signs and wonders; or in debate and dialogue, where fresh vistas of perception are reached through new patterns of communion.

What is interesting about 'mapping' theological conceptualizations of power in this way, is noting how conflated the giver and the gift become. Critics of the traditions mentioned above will often remark on how the mass is raised to a level of apotheosis or how the Bible is almost worshipped; or comment upon the exalted status given to ministers who are gifted in thaumaturgy; or on how democracy can sometimes be paraded as the eleventh commandment. These preliminary critiques are all linked, insofar as they have identified one of the most pressing problems in expressions of theological and ecclesiological power: it is the problem of conflation. In other words, the inability to distinguish between the power of God, and the power of the agencies or channels through which such power is deemed to flow. This is an acute issue in the study of congregations, and in coming to terms with implicit and explicit theologies in churches.

Typically, attention to power in local congregations focuses on abuse and the problematic. High-profile cases are often reported in the media: clergy who sexually abuse adults or minors; arguments over money and trust; disputes about promises made, and then broken. But it is a pity to become fixated on the pitfalls of power and to overly problematize it, since a deeper appreciation of the dynamics of power can reveal the hidden governance, resources and untapped potential in a congregation. Too often, it is the fear of power and its potential for harm that prevents many congregations from coming to a more assured appreciation of how they (as a body) might symbolize that power to the wider community. Understanding power is essential for mission, organization and transformation; its dynamics need ownership, not shunning.

Conventional Thoughts on Power

To help us think a little more about the study of power in the local church, it can be helpful to begin by focusing on different types of leadership, which in turn tend to embody different views of power. Consider, for example, three different caricatures of how Church of England bishops might operate within a diocese. One may see their role and task as primarily *executive*: being a hands-on manager, making key strategic decisions on a day-to-day basis. This view of pastoral power thrusts the bishop into the contentious realm of management, efficiency and rationalization, where they operate as a kind of chief executive officer in a large organization. This is a form of *rationalized* authority, and it will typically empathize with reviews, strategies and appraisals.

Another may take a different approach, and see their power in primarily *monarchical* terms. There are two faces to monarchical power. One is to rule by divine right: like a monarch, the bishop's word is law. But the second and more common manifestation of monarchical law is manifested in aloofness. Like most monarchs, bishops seldom intervene in any dispute decisively, and choose to remain 'neutral' and 'above' any divisive opinions or decisions. This is not an abrogation of power. Rather, the adoption of the second type of monarchical model proceeds from an understanding that others ('subjects') invest mystique and meaning in the power of the ruler, which in turn leads many monarchs and bishops to be 'officially silent' on most issues that have any immediacy, or are potentially divisive. Their symbolic power is maintained through mystique, and ultimately reticence. This is a form of *traditional* authority, where the power is primarily constituted in the office rather than in the individual charisms of the person holding it.

Another model is more *distributive*, and is concerned with facilitation and amplification. In this vision for embodying power in any office, the bishop becomes an enabler, helping to generate various kinds of powers (i.e., independent, related, etc.) within an organization. He or she will simply see to it that the growth of power is directed towards common goals, and is ultimately for the common good. But in this case, power is valued for its enabling capacities and its generative reticulation (i.e., the energy derived from and through networking, making connections, etc.); it is primarily verified through its connecting and non-directional capacities. To a point, such leadership requires a degree of *charismatic* authority, since the organization constantly requires a form of leadership that is connectional and innovative.

To be sure, most bishops will move between these models of power (and their associated types of authority), according to each case, and with each situation dictating which mode of power is deployed. But most bishops will naturally favour one kind of model over another. The advantage of looking at power through models of leadership, though, is that it illuminates other issues. For example, how is power 'conceptualized' in this situation or place? Who is said to have any ownership of power? How is power shared or dispersed in a congregation or denomination?

These issues are important when one considers the perpetual puzzling that often persists in relation to the status of charismatic leaders. For power is at its most obvious when it is at its most concentrated, and is intensely experienced. For this reason, an understanding of the complexities of power in relation to the local church is an essential element within the study of congregations. There are at last three ways of 'mapping' the power as it is encountered.

In one sense (as theorists of power in organizations argue: see Percy, 1996, 2006), power can be understood as *dispositional*. This refers to the habits and worldview of a congregation, and will closely correspond to their normative 'grammar of assent'. Appeals to an almighty God and Lord will have direct social consequences in terms of the expectations set upon obedience and compliance. On the other hand, *facilitative* power describes the agents or points of access through which such power is accessed. Here, the status of those agencies will normally match the power that they are connected to. Then again, *episodic* power refers to those events or moments in the life of a congregation that produce surges of energy, challenge or opportunity.

Putting this together – with a charismatic congregation serving as an example – one could say that the worship is dispositional, the leaders are facilitative, and the invocation of the Holy Spirit a cue for episodic manifestations of power that are unleashed. This sequence, of course, quickly becomes a dynamic cycle: the episodic confirms the validity of the facilitative and dispositional, and in so doing creates further expectations of episodic manifestations of power, and the strengthening of other kinds. There is a real sense in which the local church is a 'circuit of power', replete with connections, adaptors, converters and charges of energy. The local church is a complex ecology of power, where energy of various types can flow in different ways, be subject to increase and decrease, and be converted and adapted for a variety of purposes.

Closely related to power is the question of authority. All Christian denominations evolve over time, and their patterning of power and arrangements for agreeing on normative sources of authority are also subject to change. Again, given proper scrutiny, excavating models of authority and power can reveal much about the structure of a church or congregation. Following Paula Nesbitt's sociological observations (Nesbitt, 2001), we might note that in the first evolutionary phase of denominationalism, or in specific congregational evolution (which can currently be seen in the early history of new house churches), institutional relations usually can be governed through obedience and, if necessary, punishment. We might describe this as the exercise of *traditional* authority, where power over another can be nakedly asserted.

However, in the second phase, interpersonal contracts emerge between congregations, regions and individuals. Here 'ecclesial citizenship' is born, and law and order develop into agreed rather than imposed rule. We might call this *rational* authority: it has to be argued for and defended in the face of disputes and questioning. Again, a number of new churches are now at the point where their power and authority needs explaining in relation to their context and other relations. In the third phase (postmodern, etc.), more complex social contracts emerge between parties, which require a deeper articulation of a shared ethos and an agreement about the nature of a shared moral community. To retain unity and cohesive power, authority must be *negotiated.* It is here that the denomination effectively crosses the bridge from childhood to adulthood. Congregations learn to live with the differences between themselves.

Finally, there is *symbolic* authority. This states that authority and power are constituted in ways of being or dogma that are not easily apprehensible. Networks of congregations may choose a particular office ('chief pastor'), event ('synod') or artefact of tradition ('Bible') and position as having supreme governance. However, the weakness of symbolic authority is often comparable to the dilemma faced by those who prefer monarchical power. By positing power in an office that seldom intervenes in a decisive way, symbolic authority normally has to justify its substance. If it can't, it loses its power and authority. And no amount of assertion can make up for the imprecision which people vest in symbolic or monarchical power. Attempts to compensate for this dilemma often end with accusations of capriciousness.

Unconventional Thoughts on Power

Locating instances of power and abuse of power is a fairly obvious way of studying the shape and cadence of a congregation. However, some attention to apparently 'neutral' phenomena is also useful when trying to sketch or map the power dynamics of the local church. At least one of Paulo Freire's aspirations was to help people achieve 'deep literacy' – to be aware of the far from innocent forces which can shape lives and institutions. Freire (1972) argued that deep literacy came through dialogue. It is in conversation and reflection that we become aware of how we are *determined* by our cultural inheritance and the powers within them.

For example, the power of a building, and the mystique invested in its capacity to mould and inspire, is a form of power that may operate restrictively in a certain context.

Equally, one must also pay attention to the numerous instances of power relations that continually construct and reconstruct power relations in a congregation. Silence on the part of individuals or groups within a congregation, and in the midst of a dispute or debate, can be interpreted in a variety of ways: as defeat – they have nothing more to say in this argument; as withdrawal – a refusal to participate; as 'wisdom' – they are waiting for you to see their point of view; as an act of defiance or disapproval; as a spiritual rejoinder to too much discussion. Silence, then, even in its informal guise, is seldom innocent. It is a form of power that needs to be 'read', understood and interpreted.

Another example of what educationalists term the 'hidden curriculum' in relation to power can also be detected in apparently ordinary phenomena, such as dress codes and manners. I have often remarked that an important hermeneutical key for understanding Anglican congregations is to appreciate that, at a deeper level, Anglicanism could be said to be a sacralized system of manners. In other words, any disagreements must be moderated by a quality of civility. The means usually matter more than the ends: better to chair a good, but ultimately inconclusive discussion, than to arrive prematurely at a (correct) decision.

Similarly, codes of dress in church can also carry theological meaning that is related to dynamics of power. For some, dressing in a relaxed style connotes disrespect, a lack of formality and, ultimately, is unacceptable. It is not that a congregation will necessarily have any hard or written rules about how to dress (e.g., gentlemen must wear ties and jackets, etc.). The codes and expectations evolve over a period of time, and in their own way act as a sieve within the congregation. Conformity in uniformity indicates a degree of acquiescence in the pattern of belonging. To 'not dress right' is not only to rebel against the prevailing code; it is also to question the formal or informal ascriptions of God that are symbolized in those dress codes. Thus, in the relaxed gathering of a house church, where God is deemed to be immediate, friendly and even neighbourly, relaxed dress codes will tend to 'fit' and symbolize the theological outlook. Where God is deemed to be more formal and distant, with worship to complement this, it is likely that (like the worship itself) the dress code will be much more 'buttoned up'.

To be sure, one would have to exercise considerable caution in pushing these observations too far. But my point is that by paying simple and close attention to what the laity chooses to wear when they come to church, one can begin to gain some understanding of how power relations and expectations are constructed locally, and how they, in turn, reflect upon the congregation's (often unarticulated) theological priorities. Furthermore, this is an area that can be rich with conflict.

For example, in a North American church with which I was briefly involved some years ago, the pastor presented the following problem. One of the newest additions to the team of twelve elders, elected by the congregation, was refusing to wear a suit and tie for Sunday worship as the others did. (The elders were all male by custom rather than rule.) The new elder was also late for weekly meetings, and sometimes failed to turn up at all. The other elders petitioned their pastor to have the errant elder removed or 'brought into line', claiming that the casual mode of dress signified disrespect (to God), and was mirrored in 'sloppy attendance habits'. The pastor made enquiries of the dissenter, and discovered that he had his reasons for 'dressing down'. He wanted the church to be more relaxed and less stuffy; he thought that formal attire inhibited worship and also suggested a stern, somewhat formal God. The dissenting elder added that he thought that God was more mellow and relaxed, and he was merely expressing this. It was to this God that he was committed – or at least thinking about being committed. So he did not miss meetings to be rude, or to make an obvious point; he simply didn't think it that it mattered that much, *theologically* and in the wider scheme of things. And that, of course, is itself theologically significant.

This story leads me to conclude by underlining the importance of reflecting on stories. James Hopewell's alert and prescient study of congregations (Hopewell, 1987) discusses the extent to which congregations are 'storied dwellings'. By this Hopewell means that congregations are frequently in the grip of myths and narratives that reflect worldviews, which in turn determine theological priorities. Congregations seldom understand that they are often owned or 'performed' by these 'dramatic scripts', but the stories do shape a congregation, nonetheless. His book is too rich and complex to be discussed further here, but the agenda he sets is a teasing one for the subject that we are concerned with. More often than not, what makes a congregation are the powerful narratives and stories it collects, that then go on to construct and constitute its inner life. These may be heroic stories, or they may be tales of triumph over adversity. Equally, however, the preferred stories can be centred on struggle, or on the value of coping.

But in focusing on stories, Hopewell has understood that power in the local church is more than a matter of studying the obvious or official lines of authority, or the authorized power constructions and relations. True, there is value in paying proper attention to what we might term 'formal' religious structures and apparatus. Who is pastor or vicar, and how does their style mediate their authority and power? In what ways do people regard the clergy? And how do the laity perceive themselves – as passive receptors of power, or as generators of empowerment? This is important, to be sure.

But there is also value in paying attention to the seemingly less formal, 'operant' faith of a congregation. For example, this might be the kind of language and expectations that perhaps emerge in lay-led prayer meetings or home-based Bible-study groups, where more 'domestic' expectations of God might be at variance with what is proclaimed by 'professional' Christians (i.e., clergy). So, what is the scale of the gap between the 'official' teaching of a church, and the actual 'concrete' discipleship of a congregation and its individuals? What does that gap tell us about power relations between the macro denomination and the micro congregation? Quite independent of what congregations are supposed to affirm, what kinds of stories of faith do they commonly tell? Where does the congregation think power lies? With the clergyperson? Or perhaps with a committee or Governing Body? Or perhaps with named individuals who wield different kinds of power (e.g., 'a pillar of the church' – perhaps through patronage, age, skill, charisma or experience)? Or perhaps with an individual or group who may have an alternative theological and spiritual agenda that attracts a significant part of the congregation?

Ultimately, stories have power because they give us a kind of knowledge that abstract reasoning usually cannot deliver. One of the advantages of 'story knowledge', as a conveyor of power, lies in its sheer concreteness and specificity. Stories give us individualized people in specific times and places doing actual things: so they speak to congregations with a force and a power that dogma sometimes lacks. Rationality and theological formulae can tend to sidestep the messy particulars of life; stories, however, immerse us in life. So, if Hopewell is right, it is the narratives we tell each other that build and make the church what it is, and determine its sense of power. In imagining that the local church is a 'storied dwelling', we are invited to contemplate the many different ways in which we become what we speak, as churches. It is the stories that churches tell – much like personal testimonies – that turn out to be reliable reservoirs of power and authority. Such vignettes can be midrash: creeds-in-waiting.

Conclusion

Whilst it is commonplace to pay attention to abuses or collapses of power in churches, the purpose of this chapter has been to show that there are deeper reasons why a focus on power is important for the study of the local church. First, the contested nature of power means that its study is essential if one is to clarify the culture, theology or anatomy of the local church. Second, there are conventional understandings of power that can illuminate ecclesiological analysis. Third, there are unconventional ways of understanding the identity and location of power that also merit attention. Simply to study 'official' authority in the church is only to undertake half the task, since there are hundreds of subtle and unofficial forms of power and authority that are no less significant. Ultimately, it is only by immersing oneself in a local church that one can begin to understand the complex range of implicit dynamics that make and shape a congregation. And in the act of immersion, the scholar needs to develop a deeper literacy that is attentive to the multifarious dynamics of power.

References

Freire, Paulo (1972), *Pedagogy of the Oppressed*, Harmondsworth: Penguin.

Freire, Paulo (1973), *Education for Critical Consciousness*, New York: Seabury.

Grierson, Denham (1985), *Transforming a People of God*, Melbourne: Joint Board of Christian Education of Australia and New Zealand.

Hopewell, James F. (1987), *Congregation: Stories and Structures*, London: SCM Press.
Nesbitt, P. (2001), *Religion and Social Policy*, Lanham, Md.: AltaMira Press.
Percy, Martyn (1996), *Power in the Church: Ecclesiology in an Age of Transition*, London: Cassell.
Percy, Martyn (2006), *Engaging with Contemporary Culture: Christianity and the Concrete Church*, Aldershot: Ashgate.

Chapter 7

Ordinary Theologians as Signal Processors of the Spirit

Michael Armstrong

Ordinary theology must be more than contemporary social opinion if it is to be *theology* at all. Jeff Astley accepts that, although ordinary theology is non-scholarly and non-academic, ordinary theologians 'are inevitably engaged in doing their own theology if and when they speak and think about God, or at all events when they do so *with any seriousness*' (Astley, 2002: 56, emphasis added). If the views and opinions of ordinary theologians are to be regarded as 'theology', then, there must be evidence of reflection on and evaluation of their own beliefs. What ordinary believers say about their faith is of value and potentially important for the wider faith community only if such talk about God is the result of some critical reflection, and not simply idle thoughts or unreflective opinion.

Ann Christie found that this was not to be the case with all the subjects she interviewed in her study of 'ordinary Christology'. Some were 'highly resistant to any kind of critical reflection and evaluation of their faith' (Christie, 2005: 209). Christie utilizes the affective dimension of ordinary theology in defence of the claim that her interviewees are 'doing' Christology, but nevertheless recognizes that 'affective Christology that only entertains warm feelings is superficial'. So ordinary theology's subjective pole of affective response (the necessary complement to the objective pole of formal theology and doctrine) must 'lead to volitional action, or to transformation of the person in any other way' (214). Voas and Crocket make a similar point in the context of seeking to assess what 'believing without belonging' can actually mean. 'It is not enough to find that people accept one statement of belief or another; unless these beliefs make a substantial difference in their lives, religion may consist of little more than opinions to be gathered by pollsters' (Voas and Crockett, 2005: 14).

There are, then, two complementary criteria for confirming whether or not ordinary *theology* is actually being done. On the 'objective-cognitive' side, the ordinary theologian must *demonstrate sufficient critical reflection*. This does not mean that the evaluative (critical) element of reflection must be up to the standards of the academy, but the ordinary theologian must show a serious attempt to engage with the cognitive issues of her beliefs (Astley, 2002: 138–45). On the 'subjective affective-volitional' side, the ordinary theologian must also *demonstrate sufficient evidence of personal appropriation of her beliefs*. In other words, there must be a clear indication of an effect on their spirituality, feelings and therefore their behaviour as a result of holding these beliefs; for example, a commitment or action. There is no simple way to measure such things. However, the key thing to be identified is absence of such criteria rather than an accurate measure of the extent to which they are present.

For Astley, ordinary theology represents an enormous untapped resource within the church: a 'huge living experiment of people struggling to find and make meaning in their lives', a 'vast user-base' which allows us to check the latest releases of 'theological code' (148). Ordinary theologians have to live their theology; it has to work for them. It is their footwear, to be tested against the pathways and weather of real life. It is in the experience of ordinary theologians that theology is put to the test. Believers are 'the people who decide what *in fact* will count as falsifying evidence for their own beliefs' (150). But it is not just the practical 'workability' of theology that is tested in the lived experience of ordinary theologians; it is theology itself as the formal statement of church and tradition.

The Action Research: Church and Society (ARCS) Project argues that the value of Christian practice, in theological terms, is clear. 'Our theological method is based on the assumption that the practices we are exploring … are themselves already the bearers of theology; they express the contemporary living tradition of the Christian faith' (ARCS, 2008: 25). The notion of a 'living Christian tradition' is crucial here. The authors point to the Second Vatican Council's *Dei Verbum* (8) as an illustration of this idea, and claim that similar views can be seen within other 'established theologies of tradition and revelation' (Cameron et al., 2005: 51–2). The embodied ('espoused' and 'operant') theologies of Christians who practice their faith are not only challenged by formal and normative theologies, but *they can also challenge and change* the normative and formal. This is how tradition actually develops, 'from the theological wisdom of practice'. A central conviction of Theological Action Research (TAR) is that 'the forms of theology articulated by practices have a crucial role in informing and forming both formal and, ultimately, normative theologies' (56). Tradition is seen as 'more than a discrete body of knowledge or a history which we seek to bring into contact with contemporary practice'. It is also:

> the living embodiment of faith unfolding in and through these faith practices. There is a complex relationship of continuity and change here which requires discernment as to what can be regarded as truly authoritative tradition. What characterises contemporary, or living, tradition is that it has yet to be discerned by the Church as a whole. It is tradition in tentative, growing mode, whose authority, whilst real, is different from that of the already discerned (and continually re-discerned) tradition of Christian history. (ARCS, 2008: 41)

So ordinary theology expresses the living tradition of the church, which is a key indicator in how far the normative tradition can and should change. Furthermore, the key driver in this is the work of the Holy Spirit. It is important to realize that this kind of challenging and re-formulation of doctrine and tradition has always been taking place. This is one of the primary claims of practical theology. Practical theology is not a new way of doing theology, but rather 'has constituted Christian "talk about God" since the very beginning'. Theological reflection 'developed out of specific circumstances and historically came to birth in order to resolve particular demands experienced by the earliest Christian communities' (Graham, Walton and Ward, 2005: 4, 15). Elaine Graham argues that practical theologians are increasingly concerned to 'interrogate how theology as more formal, logical discourse is actually *done*: why doctrine emerges, and how theological claims are constructed out of the streams of Scripture, tradition, reason and experience'. All theology is 'practical', and practical theologians 'are concerned with nothing less than the *recontextualisation* of Christian doctrine' (Graham, 2011: 334).

Astley suggests that ordinary theology can help us regain the traditional idea of the 'consensus of the faithful' (the *consensus fidelium*, reaffirmed by the Second Vatican Council – *Lumen Gentium* 12). He argues that 'a strain, if not a paradox, is created when theology identifies as "Christian doctrine" or a "doctrine of the church" beliefs that many ordinary Christians do *not* share' (Astley, 2002: 158). It is possible, of course, to argue orthodoxy on the grounds of appeal to scripture or tradition alone, but the voice of ordinary Christians surely has a key role. Ordinary believers are those who are most open to the influences of a changing world, because they live in it and reflect their faith in it and are therefore the best placed theologians to judge and respond to such changes. Ordinary theology '*is the church's front line*. … And whatever we make of it theologically, speaking statistically ordinary theology *is* the theology of God's church' (162).

I wish to extend Astley's arguments in order to suggest that a key role that ordinary theologians can play is in acting as 'signal processors of the Spirit'. In other words, ordinary theology can be an important mechanism for discerning the continuing guidance of the Holy Spirit for the Christian community. Ordinary theologians are those best placed to notice when theology goes astray at a fundamental level, because they are the community of practice and belief where theology is accepted or rejected, tested and judged.

This metaphor of signal processor is taken from the device used in electrical engineering for the extraction of information from complex signals in the presence of noise. Ordinary theologians, I would argue, act as aerials or receivers for the Spirit. As people seeking to put into practice their Christian faith they are ideally placed to undertake this function. However, this is not sufficient. It implies that the Spirit-signal is clear and simple, requiring only its reception by someone. This is rarely if ever the case, for individual believers or church communities. God communicates with us in and through our complex, and often confusing, human condition and context. What we believe we understand as the prompting of the Spirit requires a degree of filtering and clarification. There is a great deal of theological noise in the 'Spirit-ether', but complexity can sometimes be turned into clarity by appropriate signal processing.

As a Congregationalist, this claim is somewhat easier for me to make than may be the case within other Christian denominations. The independence of local congregations is foundational to our understanding of how the Spirit operates. The church meeting is key; it is 'the governing body of the Church, which meets … under the guidance and power of the Holy Spirit'.[1] As a Congregationalist, my basic assumption is that the community of believers is the place where God's guidance is sought and the promptings of the Spirit discerned.

However, I am fully aware from long experience that even this apparently simple mechanism for discernment of the Spirit is by no means straightforward or foolproof. I am also aware that the equivalent mechanism in other denominations can be a far more complicated process. In addition, claims to spiritual discernment can be closely associated with power and authority within any church (or sect) structure. David Martin argues that 'from the point of view of ecclesiastical authority, "the Spirit" is an all-purpose legitimator' (Martin, 1984: 60). However, I only want to indicate the basis upon which ordinary theologians can be signal processors of the Spirit, particularly with regard to doctrine.

'Doctrine' and 'theology' are very different. In Alister McGrath's words, the former 'implies reference to a tradition and a community', while the latter 'more properly designates the views of individuals, not necessarily within the community or tradition, who seek to explore ideas without any necessary commitment to them'. So, 'one could suggest that doctrine is essentially the prevailing expression of the faith of the Christian community with reference to the content of the Christian revelation'. The community can accept or reject the views of theologians, and doctrinal development is *not* due entirely to the speculation of theologians; for instance, McGrath believes that the doctrine of original sin came from the sacramental life of the Christian community, and the assumption of Mary from popular piety (McGrath, 1997: 10–11).

I wish to argue that the judgement of the community relies on the correct discernment of the promptings of the Holy Spirit. In his remarkable 1859 essay, Cardinal Newman argued for just such a key role for the ordinary faithful. The reason for this is clear: 'because the body of the faithful is one of the witnesses to the fact of the tradition of revealed doctrine, and because their *consensus* through Christendom is the voice of the Infallible Church'. Newman lays great stress on the *consensus fidelium*. It may be relied upon by the Pope as the judgement of the infallible church. Yet this does not mean 'that infallibility is in the "consensus fidelium," but that that "consensus" is an *indicium* or *instrumentum* to us of the judgement of that Church which is infallible'. One way that the consensus of the faithful has been regarded by theologians of the church is 'as a direction of the Holy Ghost'. Newman gives historical instances of where this consensus has been influential, including the Arian controversy of the fourth century. The Nicene dogma was maintained not by bishops, councils or Pope, but by the ordinary people of the church (Newman, 1992).

---

[1] *Congregational Way*: http://www.congregational.org.uk/content.aspx?id=3758 [accessed 30 June 2011].

David Brown has provided a compelling view of continuing revelation and the value of a dynamic tradition informed by changing human experience, which also explains why the views of ordinary theologians have been and continue to be of great significance. Brown shows that tradition is not secondary to revelation, but is actually 'the motor that sustains revelation both within Scripture and beyond'. Christians should, therefore, 'disabuse themselves of the habit of contrasting biblical revelation and later tradition, and instead see the hand of God in a continuing process that encompasses both'. The incarnation itself 'reveals a God who took with maximum seriousness the limitations of a specific cultural context' (Brown, 1999: 1). We thus need to see how the story develops; how God has continued to be involved in the history of the community of faith in a way that takes seriously their human context. Within Christianity the primary focus of reflection on that interaction must be the Bible, because at root Christianity rests on the specific historical claim of the incarnation. The biblical text is not unchanging, however, rather it 'becomes part of a living tradition that is constantly subject to change, and that includes change in the perceived content of the biblical narratives: new insights are generated as different social conditions open up new possibilities and perspectives' (107–8).

If a doctrine of the church (or indeed a position within academic theology that claims to be normative) says one thing, but ordinary theologians say something quite different, then there is reason to re-examine the former.[2] This is not to claim any simple relationship between the views of ordinary theologians and any new doctrinal claim; one cannot just 'read off' from ordinary theology a new doctrine, or even a correction to existing doctrine. To push the analogy to near breaking point, the 'signal processing' may be incomplete or distorted by too much interference, or the signal may simply be too complex to process. However, if the expected signal cannot be processed with the expected degree of clarity, then that in itself is worthy of attention.

The 'rule' concept of doctrine from George Lindbeck (and others) provides a more nuanced understanding of the relationship between normative doctrine/theology and ordinary theologians. On Lindbeck's cultural-linguistic understanding, religions are viewed 'as a kind of cultural and/or linguistic framework or medium that shapes the entirety of life and thought'. To become a Christian is to know the Christian 'story' well enough so as to be able to interpret one's experience by it. However, although the story is important, this is not to say that belief in propositions is vital. 'A comprehensive scheme or story used to structure all dimensions of existence is not primarily a set of propositions to be believed, but is rather the medium in which one moves, a set of skills that one employs in living one's life.' Religion is thus not about choosing to believe certain propositions; but rather to become religious is to interiorize a set of skills through practice and education. 'The primary knowledge is not *about* the religion, nor *that*

---

[2] I find just such a dislocation with respect to Christian views of life after death: see Chapter 10.

the religion teaches such and such, but rather *how* to be religious in such and such ways.' According to Lindbeck, these interiorized skills manifest themselves in an ability to make intuitive judgements about authenticity within the religion, which is quite unlike the reflective and theological knowledge of the trained theologian (Lindbeck, 1984: 32–6).

Lindbeck proposes a regulative or 'rule' theory of doctrine, in which doctrines are seen as 'communally authoritative rules of discourse, attitude, and action', rather than as 'expressive symbols or truth claims' (18). Propositional truths do not reside in doctrine, because doctrines are actually the grammatical rules of the language of the religion. So 'propositional truth and falsity characterise ordinary religious language when it is used to mould lives through prayer, praise, preaching, and exhortation' (69). Lindbeck recognizes that these 'rules' can remain constant as the unchanging core of the doctrine, while the propositions which follow from them can and do change in different historical and cultural situations. For example, in the case of trinitarian doctrine it is not the creeds themselves which are doctrinal, but rather the three 'regulative principles' that Lindbeck detects as underlying the emergence of the various propositional statements about the Trinity.[3] Nicaea and Chalcedon were about setting limits on how we could speak about Jesus and God, not about unchanging first-order propositions.

In similar vein, Gerard Loughlin claims that doctrine 'resists closure'; it is both complete and yet never complete, and it is always possible to supplement what has already been said. The *story* of Jesus Christ (his person) 'is the non-doctrinal basis upon which doctrine rests'. Knowledge of this person and story comes only through practice, and doctrine 'is simply the rule and discipline of the practice. … We can thus think of doctrine as the grammar of Christian discourse; the stage directions for the church's performance of the gospel.' Loughlin stresses, therefore, that 'doctrine is always secondary to that which it informs – the church's performance of the gospel – which alone is its basis or foundation. … There is thus no legitimation of doctrine, in history or experience, outside of Christian practice itself' (Loughlin, 1997: 52–8).

The key question is, though, how do we know which changed form of doctrinal expression is faithful to the religious roots? Lindbeck claims that 'those who are best able to judge in these matters … are those who have effectively interiorised a religion' (Lindbeck, 1984: 79). Applying a rule theory of doctrine gives infallibility a partly empirical meaning. 'It suggests explanations … for how the Holy Spirit operates in preserving the church from error.' The most nearly infallible 'is what the theological tradition calls the *consensus fidelium* or *consensus ecclesiae*'. Just as a linguist would test grammar by seeing if it makes sense to competent speakers

[3] The first is a monotheistic principle; the second is the principle of historic specificity (Jesus was actually born, lived and died in real human history); and the third is 'Christological maximalism' (ascribe every possible importance to Jesus that does not contradict the other two principles). Lindbeck, 1984: 94.

of the language, 'so the student of religion submits the consequences of doctrinal formulations to the judgement of competent practitioners of that religion' (99).

But who are these competent practitioners and how do we recognize them? Are they the mass of ordinary theologians? Here, Lindbeck takes a more robust view than Astley, arguing that Christian membership does not guarantee religious competence. Indeed, 'most Christians through most of Christian history have spoken their own official tongue very poorly'. Such lack of competence means 'they cannot, from the cultural-linguistic perspective, be part of that *consensus fidelium* against which doctrinal proposals are tested'. Religious competence, for Lindbeck, 'is the empirical equivalent of insisting on the Spirit as one of the tests of doctrine'. The competent must be mainstream and orthodox, and (even without formal theological training) 'likely to be saturated with the language of Scripture and/or liturgy'. They are 'flexibly devout', for, 'they have so interiorised the grammar of their religion that they are reliable judges, not directly of the doctrinal formulations (for these may be too technical for them to understand), but of the acceptability or unacceptability of the consequences of these formulations in ordinary religious life and language'. The agreement of such people, Lindbeck suggests, can be described as infallible. A very high level of certitude is possible with regard to religious doctrines because, given a cultural-linguistic approach, they 'are matters of empirical knowledge' – although this means they are 'Christian' rather than that they are ontologically true (100–101).

However, Lindbeck seems to soften this view somewhat in later work concerning the reform of clerical training. He now identifies a kind of 'passive [theological] competence in which the saintly excel', which does not need theological expertise. Such spiritually mature people 'may have only the most meagre ability to articulate and describe their patterns of belief and practice, but they can recognise misdescriptions. They may have no talent in assessing differences between the second-order accounts which theologians formulate, but they can sense … when the usages authorised by these accounts violate the deep grammar of the faith' (Lindbeck, 1996: 288). The potential importance and ordinariness of ordinary theologians is thus recognized by Lindbeck, albeit in a more restricted way than Astley has suggested (Astley, 2002: 153–4).

Lindbeck is concerned to ensure that adequate theological and spiritual discipline and expertise is maintained by those responsible for the grammar of faith, a view which ultimately conflicts with Astley's view of ordinary theologians. But these positions may at least partly be reconciled by a clear articulation and application of the two essential criteria outlined above (pp. 65–6). Furthermore, Lindbeck's concept of underlying 'regulative principles' of doctrine is still highly relevant to ordinary theology because it is in the *practice* of faith that the articulation of underlying regulative principles of doctrine, as propositional statements, is tested.

Ordinary theology remains the expression by ordinary theologians of their practice of faith. The views of ordinary theologians are well placed to indicate when current propositional doctrinal or academic expressions are at odds with the underlying regulative principles.[4] In other words, ordinary theology may still challenge current expressions of doctrine.

References

ARCS (2008), *Living Church in the Global City: Theology in Practice*, http://www.rcc.ac.uk/downloads/pdf_files/ARCS%2520Report%25202008.pdf [accessed 21 February 2011].

Astley, Jeff (2002), *Ordinary Theology: Looking, Listening and Learning in Theology*, Aldershot: Ashgate.

Brown, David (1999), *Tradition and Imagination: Revelation and Change*, Oxford: Oxford University Press.

Cameron, Helen et al. (2005), *Studying Local Churches: A Handbook*, London: SCM Press.

Christie, Ann (2005), 'Ordinary Christology: A Qualitative Study and Theological Appraisal', PhD thesis, University of Durham.

Graham, Elaine (2011), 'Frailty and Flourishing: Good News for Humanity – Response to Alister McGrath', *Practical Theology*, 4, 3: 333–8.

Graham, E., H. Walton and F. Ward (2005), *Theological Reflection: Methods*, London: SCM Press.

Lindbeck, George A. (1984), *The Nature of Doctrine: Religion and Theology in a Postliberal Age*, London: SPCK.

Lindbeck, George (1996), 'Spiritual Formation and Theological Education', in Jeff Astley, Leslie J. Francis and Colin Crowder (eds), *Theological Perspectives on Christian Formation: A Reader in Theology and Christian Education*, Grand Rapids, Mich.: Eerdmans, pp. 285–302.

Loughlin, Gerard (1997), 'The Basis and Authority of Doctrine', in Colin E. Gunton (ed.), *The Cambridge Companion to Christian Doctrine*, Cambridge: Cambridge University Press, pp. 41–64.

Martin, David (1984), 'The Political Economy of the Holy Ghost', in David Martin and Peter Mullen (eds), *Strange Gifts? A Guide to Charismatic Renewal*, Oxford: Blackwell, pp. 54–71.

McGrath, Alister (1997), *The Genesis of Doctrine: A Study in the Foundations of Doctrinal Criticism*, Grand Rapids, Mich.: Eerdmans.

Newman, John Henry (1992), 'On Consulting the Faithful in Matters of Doctrine', *The Rambler*, July 1859, reproduced in John Henry Newman, *Conscience, Consensus and the Development of Doctrine: Revolutionary Texts by John*

[4] It is not necessary to identify these principles in order to know that they are at odds with current doctrinal expression. Lindbeck recognizes that the judgement of ordinary theologians is intuitive, based on their experience of seeking to practise this aspect of their religion. Lindbeck, 1984: 32–6.

Henry Cardinal Newman, ed. James Gaffney, New York: Image/Doubleday, pp. 392–428.

Voas, David and Alasdair Crockett (2005), 'Religion in Britain: Neither Believing nor Belonging', *Sociology*, 39, 1: 11–28.

PART II
Researching and Situating Ordinary Theology: Empirical and Contextual Perspectives

Chapter 8
Jesus as Exemplar

Ann Christie

My qualitative research into ordinary theologians' views about the person and work of Jesus Christ, using in-depth interviews with 45 regular churchgoers from four Anglican churches in rural North Yorkshire, UK, has been published in Christie, 2007, 2012; Christie and Astley, 2009; and Astley and Christie, 2007. The aim of this chapter is to explore in more detail the dominant soteriology of this research sample – namely Jesus as exemplar.

The main soteriological aim of the interview was to investigate ordinary theologians' understanding of the death of Jesus, and in particular the idea that we are saved through Jesus' atoning death. However, many had great difficulty understanding how the death of Jesus could be said to save us, and tended to circumvent atonement. This was an unexpected finding, since in academic theology it is nearly always the cross and atonement that dominate soteriological discussion.

For well over half of the sample, Jesus is saviour because 'he shows us how to live'. For them, Jesus as exemplar is *the* dominant soteriological theme, the default position. When asked about Jesus' function and significance, they would reply by saying:

> [Jesus'] purpose was to show us what it is to follow God and how to be a good person.

> [Jesus was] God's way of getting through to us humans how we should conduct ourselves.

> He set out by his example the way we should all live.

> [Jesus was] sent from God to teach us how to live.

> [Jesus] gives us the rules for living.

> He came to get us all back on track.

Jesus as Moral Exemplar

The data show that when people say 'Jesus shows us how to live' they are primarily casting Jesus in the role of moral exemplar: Jesus is the model for moral behaviour (because he was morally 'totally perfect' and 'never did anything wrong') whom they 'should always aspire and strive to be like'. For most of these Christians that means 'helping others', 'doing good acts' , 'being nice', 'not doing bad and wrong things through your life', 'following the code of conduct', 'being public-spirited'. In sum, it means 'being a good person', someone who follows certain lines of conduct (they do not 'do bad and wrong things') and is characterized by certain virtues (they are 'kind and good').

These findings chime with other studies. Thus, Richard Hoggart's study of working-class culture in the 1950s shows an identification of Christianity with morals – doing your best to be an 'ordinary decent' person is what Christianity really means (Hoggart, 1958: 87–94); and more recent studies of English folk religion reveal 'Christianity' as 'a way of life that is readily (if anachronistically) summarized as "the Ten Commandments", or "the golden rule" or (now, only occasionally) as "the Sermon on the Mount", or by the oft-repeated paradigm of "helping a little old lady across the road"' (Bailey, 1989: 155). This identification of Christianity with 'a rather undemanding type of kindness' may be a particularly English form of Christianity (Astley, 1997: 101; cf. Towler, 1984: 22; Woodhead, 2004: 5). But it is obviously prevalent in America, too, according to a sociological study by Nancy Ammerman. She characterizes American Christians as 'Activist', 'Golden Rule' or 'Evangelical'. Activists define the Christian life in terms of social action and working for justice; Golden Rule Christians in terms of doing good and caring for others; and Evangelical Christians in terms of being saved. Golden Rule Christianity may be the dominant form of religiosity among middle class, suburban Americans (Ammerman, 1997: 196–216), as it appears to be here among these mainly middle class, rural members of the Church of England.

One consequence of identifying Christianity with morality is that 'you can be a Christian without going to church', since 'being Christian' means 'being good'. Anecdotal evidence suggests that there are many living in these geographical parishes who consider themselves to be Christian but do not go to church, and my data show that some churchgoers do not consider churchgoing to be an essential part of being a Christian either.[1] 'It is how you live your live is being a Christian.' What matters is 'being morally a good person … that is much more important than how often you go to church'. 'Going to church is nothing.'

When Christianity is detached from churchgoing and reduced to morality like this, Jesus is effectively made superfluous and morality loses its connection with him. In this type of exemplarism the emphasis is on personal, as opposed to any form of sociopolitical, morality. Most interviewees consider Jesus to have given

---

1 Richter and Francis's study (1998: 12) shows that well over two-thirds of their church leavers believed that churchgoing was unnecessary for Christians.

a code of conduct for personal morality; moral priorities are seen to rest with the local community and 'doing good' there. The four churches with which we are concerned here are not preoccupied with a concern for social justice, or social or political radicalism. Several talked about the importance of Jesus' concern for the poor and the outcast, 'the lowly in society'; but when asked how they saw this impacting on their own behaviour, their replies were not generally of a sociopolitical nature, targeted at oppressive social structures. Their practice is Golden Rule rather than Activist. It involves 'helping those who are worse off than yourself' and 'helping people when you can', not changing the whole political system.

The Rule of Love

Most of the exemplarists go along with the thesis that the principle underlying Jesus' teaching is the principle to love, taking the commandment 'love God and love your neighbour' to be the central and all-embracing principle of Jesus' ethical teaching. This is perhaps not surprising, as the commandment to love is singled out as the major theme of Jesus' ethical teaching in all three synoptics (Mk 12:28–34; Mt 22:34–40; Lk 10:25–28) and expounded at length in the final meditational text in John's Gospel (chapters 13–17). However, perhaps the primary reason why people appeal to love as the principle underlying Jesus' teaching is that Jesus' commandment to love both God and neighbour is part and parcel of the weekly eucharistic liturgy that these ordinary believers use.

Most exemplarists also appear to take it for granted that their idea of love coincides with that espoused by Jesus. But does it? The distinctive feature of Jesus' ethical teaching is often said to be the way it radicalized common morality. Jesus' ethic goes beyond 'natural' morality, and is very different from the everyday ethic of reciprocity – doing good turns to those who do good turns to you (see Preston, 1993: 94–100; cf. Astley, 2000: 27–8). Jesus' teachings and ministerial practice concretize the abstract notion of love and give it material content, showing what Christian love is (should or could be). The parable of the Good Samaritan, for example, enlarges the view of who is one's neighbour. Other stories, sayings and actions of Jesus also demonstrate the radical nature of his love, such as its exceeding generosity and unlimited forgiveness. Only by becoming familiar with these stories, sayings and actions can Christians begin to learn what Jesus' model of loving is. If there is no engagement with the Gospels, then the principle of love loses the radicality Jesus brought to it. Following the Golden Rule – do to others as you would have them do to you – is not the same as modelling one's life on the radical ethic of Jesus and his pattern of self-giving love.

Beyond the commandment to love, many appear to have no clear idea about the main thrust of Jesus' teaching. They are not clear what the New Testament has to say about ethical matters and are unsure about the meaning of key concepts such as 'the kingdom of God' (although scholars cannot agree about the meaning of this concept either!). What these Christians have are snippets of the story: remembered fragments to which they struggle to give meaning. Churchgoing over the years has furnished them with a memory bank of stories and aphorisms, such as 'turn the other cheek', 'go the extra mile', 'the last will be first'; together with certain images of Jesus as the man for others, the man who went about doing good, the one who laid down his life for his friends. They have a 'bits-and-pieces' theology, not unlike Jesus' teaching itself, at least as recorded in the synoptics – or, rather, as it existed in the oral tradition prior to the evangelists' redactions. This was a theology and ethics conveyed in an ad hoc fashion, by means of unconnected snippets, more like ordinary theology than academic theology (see Keck, 2000: 157–8).

Jesus as the Norm for Moral Life?

The statement 'Jesus shows us how to live' implies that Jesus is a norm for the moral life. But is he? As I have already hinted, *if* Jesus is to function as a norm for Christian moral life, then there must be an ongoing critical conversation between the stories of Jesus as portrayed in the Gospels and the unfolding story of the believer. Only by engaging with the story of Jesus are possibilities opened up for the story to shape the moral life of the believer. A commitment to certain spiritual practices (such as meditative Bible study) is therefore desirable, if not essential (see Spohn, 2003).

However, the majority of our exemplarists display no evidence of entering into an engaged reading with the text. They listen (maybe) to two Bible readings when they come to church on a Sunday (one of the interviewees admits that the time when she 'switches off most' is when the scriptures are read). Personal or group study of the scriptures is not part of their spiritual practice. Strictly speaking, Jesus only becomes a moral exemplar when his story is determinative of moral life. Miroslav Volf argues that practices (e.g., hospitality) are *Christian* 'only insofar as Christ serves as the model for its practitioners, and Christ is available as a model only through … beliefs about who Christ is and what Christ did, expressed in the form of narratives, ritual actions, or propositions'. The way in which Jesus' life is exemplary has to be carefully specified, says Volf, but in an appropriately qualified way. Christian practices should have an 'as-so' structure: 'As Christ, so we' (Volf, 2002: 250–51). On this view, much so-called exemplarism is not really exemplarism at all.[2] If there is no engagement with the Gospels, then there is very little that we may identify as *specifically Christian content* to the concept of love or the practice of hospitality. For these to be Christian they have to be animated by the Gospel stories and attention paid to the actual practice of Jesus. Without this, the concept of love risks turning out to be little more than the projection of cultural

---

2 This is perhaps particularly the case for exemplarism among 'the great body of the unchurched' (Towler, 1984: 22–5).

assumptions. Love becomes a guiding principle whose content is filled, not by direct reference to the Gospels, but by reference to other (Golden Rule) norms.

The present data show that Jesus is clearly not the only norm or source of moral guidance. People live by a range of norms, standards, principles or rules: some derived directly or indirectly from the Christian tradition and others not. People learn their morality from a variety of sources and in a variety of ways; their moral formation is often implicit and 'unacknowledged as a learning process' (Astley, 2000: 102). These data show that this sample draws on various aspects of the tradition; while many appeal directly to the New Testament commandments to 'love God and love your neighbour', others prefer a Ten Commandment morality.

> *Ben*: I mean if you have got the Ten Commandments in front of you and the Lord's Prayer, you can do an awful lot worse in life. I try to have those guiding lights in front of me. It doesn't always work, but you can make the effort.

> *Tom*: We have the Ten Commandments as a code of conduct that we ought to do.

> *Richard*: We also have the guidance of the Ten Commandments as a sort of good benchmark as to how we should behave. And I think it is a very, very applicable and a very relevant benchmark as to how we should behave.

Tom Deidun writes, 'nearly all Christians, more or less consciously and more or less selectively, subscribe to [divine command] morality, having been brought up on it; and the mainstream churches have traditionally made a carefully selective use of it (e.g., when focussing on "the Ten Commandments" or Jesus' prohibition of divorce)' (Deidun, 1998: 22).

> *Bruce*: Jesus has actually changed the way that we live … that is how you end up with the Christian ethos and the so-called Christian country. I know it is probably a bit different now, but it is still very much the Christian ethos that drives our way of life and our idea of fair play and justice.

The norms of 'fair play and justice' may be said to derive from the late flourishing of the Christian tradition or from Jesus himself, but they are values to which many atheists are also committed (perhaps more so than many Christians), independently of Jesus (or religion). While it is widely acknowledged that 'you do have to be good to be a Christian', it is also recognized that 'you don't have to be a Christian to be good'. 'Doing good' is not a specifically Christian practice.

It must be clear by now that the simplicity of the claim 'Jesus shows us how to live' belies its complexity: it is by no means obvious in what ways or to what extent Jesus does 'show us how to live'. It may be that for some, and almost certainly for those who never attend church or engage in any kind of Christian spiritual practice, Jesus does not actually play a large part in their moral life. This is not to say, of course, that these people are not highly moral, they probably are, only that their morality may not be influenced to any great extent by the figure of Jesus. When ethical principles such as love or justice become disconnected from the actual story of Jesus, then Jesus has little direct import for ethics other than as the author of the moral principle. When Jesus is reduced to a formula, then his lived teaching is largely irrelevant to ethics. Jesus may look as if he plays a large part in ethics, but I suggest that in reality he does not.

It is not, therefore, strictly accurate to say that Jesus is an *exemplar*, unless through familiarity with his story, life, death, teachings and ministerial practice one begins to work out what following him might actually mean. Leander Keck asserts that Jesus cannot be the authorizer of the moral life 'if externally he is a stranger or a casual acquaintance about whom one knows a few stories and sayings'.

> What such knowledge is more likely to produce is a caricature instead of a trustworthy image. Not only must one acquire true familiarity with the gospels, but one must also be left alone with them in order to ponder the figure they portray. Internalizing Jesus requires steady exposure; a sudden impulse to 'look it up' in the gospels will not suffice. (Keck, 2000: 167)

Richard Jones asserts, 'Much Christian decision-making occurs somewhat naturally in the ongoing stream of a life that is orientated towards God; within it roles and rules all have a place, as do the advice and example of others and the background of the church's life and traditions' (Jones, 1995: 96). These data suggest that the story of Jesus is very much *in the background* when people make moral decisions. In English folk religion as characterized by Edward Bailey, God and Jesus are similarly located. 'God plays a part akin to the part played in the theatre by the backcloth, or the actual floor of the stage' (Bailey, 1989: 154).

However, for regular churchgoers, the Gospels will have played *some* role in the nurturing of a basic orientation and in the generating of particular attitudes and intentions, as the data clearly show.

> *Jan*: He brought a new way of living that isn't condemnatory. I know the history of Christianity doesn't bear out what I am saying, but at its best it is not condemnatory of other faiths; it is not condemnatory of other races; it is not condemnatory of other ways of living … 'go thou and sin no more' … it is a kind of generosity of forgiving and by living it out, in what seems to have been a modest lifestyle, that opens up possibilities for us.

> *Bruce*: [Jesus] dealt in a goodly and kindly way with many people who in society at that time were really looked down upon or ignored. And I think that is really the crux of it. It doesn't mean to say that people who may be down at a low level through circumstances, that you should give up on them or that they were beyond help and redemption.

> *Jill*: I suppose it moves me very much the way he dealt with people who were unacceptable in society. Because that is one of the things that annoys and moves and irritates me in the world today …

Some exemplarists clearly desired, therefore, as Richard puts it, 'to measure my behaviour and the way I conduct myself in everyday life against what has been happening in the various stories and activities of the Gospels'. Jesus *is* the moral exemplar of some. However, what the data do not show is whether the values that are selected and admired (such as the way Jesus related to people) are values which the interviewees would otherwise have always valued, or whether it was through exposure to the story of Jesus that they came to value them.

There is also evidence to suggest that the morality of some of these exemplarists is motivated and shaped by beliefs concerning the character and activity of God, rather than through any striving to be like Jesus (which is acknowledged to be impossible). The story of Jesus is only part of the story of Christianity; Jesus' story is embedded 'in the larger story of God with Israel and the nations, and this larger story is framed by the narratives of God's creation and final consummation'. It is this 'nexus of stories' which provide 'the normative space in which human beings exist as agents of Christian practices' (Volf, 2002: 251). So Christian moral action can flow from other beliefs, such as 'we are all made in the image of God', 'all things come from God' and 'God is the giver of life'. These beliefs all have implications for how we should behave. They all 'entail practical commitments' (Volf, 2002: 253). Moral behaviour can also flow from gratitude for who God is (dependable, caring, loving) and what God has done and is doing through God's creating and saving activity. For some exemplarists, 'doing good' may be motivated more by a desire to love and serve the Creator-Father God, than through any self-conscious attempt to follow Jesus. As I have demonstrated elsewhere (see Christie, 2012), exemplarists' faith is usually theocentric and Jesus may not be that important. For many, therefore, it may be that belief in God is what primarily makes a difference to moral life rather than Jesus as exemplar.

Having said this, it must be remembered that Jesus as exemplar cannot be circumscribed by his role as *moral* exemplar. It may be that Jesus plays a part in morality through his role as spiritual or even theological exemplar. Thus, Jesus' example as a man of faith may have more direct import for believers' moral lives than his radical love ethic. Ian Wallis contends that being a Christian is primarily about practising Jesus' faith and that action flows from this (Wallis, 2000). Imitation of Jesus' habitus of faith, such as trust in God, can have profound ethical effects as morality flows from learning the 'mind of Christ' (1 Cor 2:14–16).

> Such a morality does not consist in conformity to any stereotyped pattern; it consists rather in learning from Jesus an attitude of mind which comprises sensitivity to the presence of God and to the will of God which is the only authority, a constant submission of personal interest to the pursuit of that will in the well-being of others, and a confidence that, whatever the immediate

> consequences may appear to be, the outcome can safely be left in God's hands. (Caird, 1994: 203)

Finally, it is important to note that exemplarists also talk about Jesus as 'the conduit', 'the bridge' or 'the link' to God; and of Jesus 'showing us what God is like', 'acting as God' and 'assisting belief in God'. Jesus may be more important as a revealer of God than as an exemplar of human existence.

All of this shows that we should not be misled by the set soteriological answer 'Jesus shows us how to live'. People may speak of Jesus as their exemplar, but this claim has to be interrogated further if false conclusions are not to be drawn. *Listening* to ordinary theology is clearly not enough. It is also necessary to look and see 'what people do as well as what they say' (Astley 2002: 121). In other words, attention must be paid to people's practices as well as their speech. Only then can we begin to see if Jesus really is their exemplar and, more importantly, what kind of exemplar he is – one who sacralizes 'the British way of life' ensuring conformism and conservatism, or one who 'brings a new way of living' that constantly 'challenges the status quo'? Uncovering the depth grammar of people's speech – including its real significance in their lives – has to be one of the key tasks of any ordinary theology research.

References

Ammerman, Nancy T. (1997), 'Golden Rule Christianity: Lived Religion in the American Mainstream', in David D. Hall (ed.), *Lived Religion in America: Toward a History of Practice*, Princeton, NJ: Princeton University Press, pp. 196–216.

Astley, Jeff (1997), 'Non-Realism for Beginners?', in Colin Crowder (ed.), *God and Reality: Essays on Christian Non-Realism*, London: Mowbray, pp. 100–113.

Astley, Jeff (2000), *Choosing Life? Christianity and Moral Problems*, London: Darton, Longman and Todd.

Astley, Jeff (2002), *Ordinary Theology: Looking, Listening and Learning in Theology*, Aldershot: Ashgate.

Astley, Jeff and Ann Christie (2007), *Taking Ordinary Theology Seriously*, Cambridge: Grove Books.

Bailey, Edward (1989), 'The Folk Religion of the English People', in Paul Badham (ed.), *Religion, State and Society in Modern Britain*, Lampeter: Edwin Mellen, pp. 145–58.

Caird, G.B. (1994), *New Testament Theology*, Oxford: Clarendon Press.

Christie, Ann (2007), 'Who Do You Say I Am? Answers From the Pews', *Journal of Adult Theological Education*, 4, 2: 181–94.

Christie, Ann (2012), *Ordinary Christology: Who Do You Say I Am? Answers From the Pews*, Farnham: Ashgate.

Christie, Ann and Jeff Astley (2009), 'Ordinary Soteriology: A Qualitative Study', in Leslie J. Francis, Jeff Astley and Mandy Robbins (eds), *Texts and Tables: Explorations in Empirical Theology*, Leiden: Brill, pp. 177–96.

Deidun, Tom (1998), 'The Bible and Christian Ethics', in Bernard Hoose (ed.), *Christian Ethics: An Introduction*, London: Cassell, pp. 3–46.

Hoggart, Richard (1958), *The Uses of Literacy*, Harmondsworth: Penguin.

Jones, Richard G. (1995), 'How Christians Actually Arrive at Ethical Decisions', in Cyril S. Rodd (ed.), *New Occasions Teach New Duties? Christian Ethics for Today*, Edinburgh: T. & T. Clark, pp. 85–96.

Keck, Leander E. (2000), *Who is Jesus? History in Perfect Tense*, Columbia, SC: University of South Carolina Press.

Preston, Ronald (1993), 'Christian Ethics', in Peter Singer (ed.), *A Companion to Ethics*, Oxford: Blackwell, pp. 91–105.

Richter, Philip and Leslie J. Francis (1998), *Gone But Not Forgotten: Church Leaving and Returning*, London: Darton, Longman and Todd.

Spohn, William C. (2003), *Go and Do Likewise: Jesus and Ethics*, New York: Continuum.

Towler, Robert (1984), *The Need for Certainty: A Sociological Study of Conventional Religion*, London: Routledge and Kegan Paul.

Volf, Miroslav (2002), 'Theology for a Way of Life', in Miroslav Volf and Dorothy C. Bass (eds), *Practicing Theology: Beliefs and Practices in Christian Life*, Grand Rapids, Mich.: Eerdmans, pp. 245–63.

Wallis, Ian G. (2000), *Holy Saturday Faith: Rediscovering the Legacy of Jesus*, London: SPCK.

Woodhead, Linda (2004), 'Should Churches Look Inward, Not Outward?', *The Church Times*, 31 December, p. 5.

Chapter 9

Ordinary Readers and Reader Perspectives on Sacred Texts: Drawing on Empirical Theology and Jungian Psychology

Leslie J. Francis

Introduction

Jeff Astley understands the study of ordinary theology as a way of looking, listening and learning in theology: taking seriously the empirical challenge to observe ordinary theologians at work, to listen to what they have to say and to learn from the insights of their reflective God-talk. In this sense, Astley's ordinary theology can be situated within the broader traditions of empirical theology as modelled by van der Ven (1998) and explored in a disciplined way through a variety of qualitative and quantitative techniques pioneered by the social sciences to bring rigour to the challenges of looking at and listening to human behaviours (see Francis, Robbins and Astley, 2009).

The present study proposes to listen to ordinary theologians as they explore the meaning of sacred text. This form of listening offers coherent connections between ordinary theology and the broader field of reader perspectives in biblical hermeneutics (see Francis and Village, 2008). What this broader field offers is a range of conceptual frameworks within which to analyse and interpret the reflective God-talk of ordinary theologians as they explore the meaning of sacred text.

Reader perspectives in biblical hermeneutics have for a long time drawn on sociological categories and theories to interpret distinctive voices among readers. Such categories include sex (feminist reading of sacred text), race (Black reading of sacred text) and social position (liberation reading of sacred text). More recently, reader perspectives in biblical hermeneutics has also drawn on psychological categories and theories to interpret distinctive voices among readers (Rollins and Kille, 2007), and the SIFT method of biblical hermeneutics and liturgical preaching belongs to this tradition. It is rooted in psychological type theory as originally proposed by Jung (1971), and as developed, clarified and popularized by a series of type indicators, including the Myers-Briggs Type Indicator (Myers and McCaulley, 1985) and the Francis Psychological Type Scales (Francis, 2005).

Psychological type theory conceptualizes core individual differences in terms of two orientations (introversion and extraversion), two perceiving functions (sensing and intuition), two judging functions (thinking and feeling) and two attitudes (judging and perceiving). Francis and Village (2008) argued that, while the two orientations and the two attitudes may be relevant for shaping the context in which and the manner through which the reading and interpretation of scripture take place, the two perceiving functions and the two judging functions are inextricably involved in the hermeneutical process itself that shapes the content of what is seen in the text and proclaimed from the pulpit.

According to Jungian theory, the two perceiving functions are concerned with distinctive ways in which information is gathered and processed. Sensing types (S) prefer to process the realities of a situation as perceived by their five senses. They attend to specific details rather than the wider picture. They are concerned with practical matters. They are down-to-earth and matter-of-fact. Intuitive types (N) prefer to process the possibilities of a situation as perceived by their imagination or their sixth sense. They attend to wider patterns and relationships rather than to specific details. They are stimulated by abstract theories. They are typically imaginative and innovative.

According to Jungian theory, the two judging functions are concerned with distinctive ways in which information is assessed and evaluated. Thinking types (T) assess and evaluate information objectively, using logic and abstract principles rather than concern for their personal values and relationships. They prize integrity and justice. They tend to be truthful and fair, even at the expense of upsetting others. Feeling types (F) process information subjectively using their personal values and their concern for relationships rather than abstract principles. They prize compassion and mercy. They tend to be tactful and empathetic even at the expense of fairness and consistency.

Francis and Village (2008) extrapolate from psychological type theory to suggest that type preferences influence the way in which sacred text is read and proclaimed. For sensing types, interpreting a text may be largely about attending to what is actually there. They will value interpretations that highlight the details in the text, especially those that draw on sensory information. Interpretations that begin with a repetition of the text and draw attention to details will appeal to sensing types, who will be reluctant to speculate too widely about hidden or metaphorical meanings. The sensing function draws attention to factual details, so sensing types will be likely to interpret biblical passages literally rather than symbolically or metaphorically.

For intuitive types, interpreting a text may be largely about using the text as a springboard for imaginative ideas. They will be inspired by interpretations that fire the imagination and raise new possibilities and challenges. Interpretations that raise wider questions and that look for overarching or underlying concepts will appeal to intuitive types, who may find the plain or literal sense rather uninteresting. Intuitives find it natural to make links between analogous ideas and concepts, and they will be likely to interpret passages symbolically or metaphorically, rather than literally.

For feeling types, interpreting a text may be largely about applying the human dimensions to present day issues of compassion, harmony and trust. They will be drawn to empathizing with the characters in a narrative, and will want to understand their thoughts, motives and emotions. Interpretations that try to understand what it was like to be there will appeal to feeling types, who may be less interested in the abstract theological ideas that might be drawn from the text.

For thinking types, interpreting a text may largely be about seeing what the text means in terms of evidence, moral principles or theology. They will be drawn to using rationality and logic to identify the ideas and truth-claims in a text. Interpretations that highlight the theological claims in a text will appeal to thinking types, who may be less interested in trying to understand the characters described by the text.

Drawing on this extrapolation from psychological type theory, the SIFT method of biblical hermeneutics and liturgical preaching commends approaching both the study of the text and the construction of sermons through the disciplined application of four psychological functions in the order of sensing (S), intuition (I), feeling (F) and thinking (T). In a series of three books, Francis and Atkins (2000, 2001, 2002) applied this method in a systematic approach to the principle Sunday Gospel readings proposed by the Revised Common Lectionary.

A small but growing body of empirical research has begun to interrogate and to underpin this approach, drawing on both quantitative and qualitative research traditions. Support for this approach is provided by studies using quantitative approaches reported by Village and Francis (2005), Francis, Robbins and Village (2009) and Village (2010), and by studies using qualitative approaches reported by Francis (2010), Francis and Jones (2011), Francis (in press) and Francis and Smith (in press). It is these qualitative studies that provide the research context for the new study reported in this chapter.

In the first qualitative study, Francis (2010) invited two groups of Anglican preachers (24 licensed readers in England and 22 licensed clergy in Northern Ireland) to work in groups defined by their dominant psychological type preferences (dominant sensers, dominant intuitives, dominant thinkers and dominant feelers). Within these dominant type groups they were asked to prepare a presentation on Mark 6:34–44 (the feeding of the five thousand). In his analysis of their presentations, Francis distinguished and displayed the four clear voices of the dominant type perspectives.

In the second qualitative study, Francis and Jones (2011) focused on Mark 16:1–8 and Matthew 28:1–15 (resurrection narratives), working with two different groups (26 ministry training candidates, and 21 Anglican clergy and readers). On this occasion Francis and Jones developed a two-stage process. In stage one, the participants were divided according to the perceiving process (sensing and intuition) and invited to discuss the Marcan narrative. In stage two, the participants were divided according to the judging process (thinking and feeling) and invited to discuss the Matthean narrative. In their analysis of the presentations made by the different groups, Francis and Jones distinguished and displayed the four clear voices of sensing, intuition, thinking and feeling.

In the third qualitative study, Francis (in press) focused on Mark 11:11–21 (the cleansing of the temple and the incident of the fig tree), working with three different groups (31 Anglican clergy, a group of 14 clergy and lay preachers, and a mixed group of 47 lay people and clergy). Instead of inviting the participants to work in dominant type groups, on this occasion Francis invited the participants to discuss the passage in two stages. For stage one, the participants were divided according to the perceiving process, distinguishing between groups of sensing types and groups of intuitive types. For stage two, the participants were divided according to the evaluating or judging process, distinguishing between groups of feeling types and groups of thinking types. In his analysis of the presentations made by different groups, Francis distinguished and displayed the four clear voices of sensing, intuition, thinking and feeling.

In the fourth qualitative study, Francis and Smith (in press) focused on Matthew 2:13–20 and Luke 2:8–16 (birth narratives), working with a group of 12 training incumbents and 11 recently ordained curates (8 women and 15 men). First, the narrative of the shepherds from Luke was discussed by three groups organized according to scores on the perceiving process. In accordance with the theory, sensing types focused on details in the passage, but could reach no consensus on the larger picture; and intuitive types quickly identified an imaginative, integrative theme, but showed little interest in the details. Second, the narrative of the massacre of the infants from Matthew was discussed by three groups organized according to scores on the judging process. In accordance with the theory, the thinking types identified and analysed the big themes raised by the passage (political power, theodicy, obedience), while the feeling types placed much more emphasis on the impact that the passage may have on members of the congregation mourning the death of their child or grandchild.

The empirical studies that have analysed the interpretation of sacred text through the lens of the SIFT method of biblical hermeneutics have up to now drawn exclusively on data generated by people who have been trained to read and to proclaim sacred text. As professional theologians these people are quite different from Astley's ordinary theologians, who are innocent of academic theological education. Against this background, the originality of the present study resides in the intention to employ the theoretical framework offered by the SIFT approach to the interpretation of scripture offered by ordinary theologians. Since the empirical investigation was conducted during Advent the biblical narrative chosen for interpretation concerned John the Baptist. The Marcan narrative was chosen for the exercise exploring the perceiving functions (sensing and intuition) in light of its rich narrative. The Lucan narrative was chosen for the exercise exploring the evaluating function (thinking and feeling) in light of the challenges offered by the passage.

Method

A small group of eight people associated with their local church and attending a church-based study group came to two Monday seminars during December 2011 (lasting 90 minutes each) to explore the theme of studying and interpreting scripture. In the first session they were given a brief introduction to the principles of the SIFT approach, an opportunity to recall awareness of their psychological type profile from previous encounters with the theory, and a copy of the Francis Psychological Type Scales to complete.

Participants

Eight people attended both sessions, three women and five men. There were four sensing types and four intuitive types; five feeling types and three thinking types; six introverts and two extraverts; seven judging types and one perceiving type.

Results

Perceiving Process

Following a brief presentation on the characteristics of the sensing function and of the intuitive function, the participants were invited to organize themselves into a horseshoe, with the most extreme sensing person at one end and the most extreme intuitive person at the other end. After an appropriate period of negotiation (while individuals tested their position in relation to others), a division emerged between the four sensing types and the four intuitive types. At this stage the Marcan narrative of John the Baptist was read (Mk 1: 2–8). The two separate groups (sensing types and intuitive types), meeting in different rooms, were simply asked to discuss what they saw and perceived in the passage drawing on both their sensing and intuitive functions.

Sensing The group of sensing types began by using their preferred sensing function. They made a point of rehearsing the narrative and pausing over the details. They focused on the appearance of John the Baptist. He wore a camel's skin and a leather belt, had wild hair and a wild look in his eye. They focused on the wilderness and on the banks of the river Jordan, and on John's diet of locusts and wild honey. The focused on John's message, 'Prepare the way of the Lord!'

The sensing types turned their attention to the crowd and followed the crowd as they came to hear John's message, came to John to be baptized and went away to tell others about their encounter with John.

The sensing types listened to John's message about Jesus, as being so great that John was not worthy even to untie his shoes. John said that while he baptized with water, Jesus would baptize with the Holy Spirit.

When they tried to approach the passage using their less preferred intuitive function, the questions the sensing types wanted to raise were these: Had John ever met Jesus before this? Where had John got the idea of baptizing from, and how did it fit into his Jewish background? Why was John quoting Isaiah? How had the word got around to draw so many people out to see John in the wilderness?

The sensing types never went beyond the passage that they had been asked to study.

Intuition The group of intuitive types began by using their preferred intuitive function, linking the reading from Mark's Gospel with the Church's season of Advent. They wanted from the start to explore the links between the message of John the Baptist and the Church's call to readiness. The following themes emerged.

John called people to confess their sins. The intuitive types wondered how many of us today are really ready to do that.

John went outside to call people to be ready for Christ. The intuitive types wondered how many of us go out to do this today; or do we just proclaim inside the church?

John was the voice of one crying in the wilderness. The intuitive types wondered where the voice of one crying in the wilderness was today.

John accepted everyone who came to him for baptism. The intuitive types wondered whether the church should be as open today in its baptism policy.

John said that he was not worthy to meet Jesus. The intuitive types wondered whether we have that sense of utter unworthiness in Jesus' presence?

The intuitive types then went beyond the passage they had been asked to study. They discovered how Jesus had been baptized by John and they wondered why Jesus needed to be baptized. What sins did Jesus confess? What did John feel like when he saw that he was baptizing Jesus?

Finally, the intuitive types got hold of the vision from Isaiah that a straight path would be forged through the wilderness. Was this really a good idea? Does not the long straight road break the heart of the long distance traveller, who literally sees no end to the journey?

The intuitive types never seriously tried to approach the passage using their less preferred sensing function.

Judging Process

Following a brief presentation on the characteristics of the feeling function and of the thinking function, the participants were invited to organize themselves into a horseshoe, with the most extreme feeling person at one end and the most extreme thinking person at the other end. After an appropriate period of negotiation (while individuals tested their position in relation to others), a division emerged between the three thinking types and the five feeling types. At this stage the Lucan account of John the Baptist was read (Lk 3:2b–20). The two separate groups (thinking types and feeling types), meeting in different rooms, were asked to discuss the issues raised by the passage drawing on both their feeling and thinking functions.

Feeling The feeling types recognized that this was a hard and difficult passage. They read it slowly through and then began to make sense of it by doing two things. They tried to get inside the experience of the key characters in the narrative, and also to draw on their own experiences of people and on their experiences of life.

First, the feeling types tried to get inside Herod. They began by saying that Herod came across as a very nasty man, but then they began to see a lot of good in him. One member of the group told a story about someone he knew who had been falsely accused and falsely reproached. Herod was not all bad. Herod did not want to kill John. Herod, too, was being bullied and was under pressure, frightened of his political masters. Herod was frightened that John would stir up trouble. Herod was not really a free man.

Second, the feeling types tried to get inside John the Baptist. They began by saying that John the Baptist came across as a very thinking type of person, proclaiming a God of Justice and accusing people of failure. His message is that the axe is ready to strike, but then they begin to see a lot of good in him. One member of the group told a story about how his manager at work had brought the hard message of redundancy to many of the workforce because of the need to restructure a failing company. Inside the tough management approach there was a very caring human heart, and he was torn apart by the message he had to deliver. Inside John was a very caring person. John did not rebuke the tax collectors or the soldiers for doing the work they did. Rather, John affirmed them and exhorted them to do their jobs better.

Third, the feeling types tried to get inside the crowd. Here were people who were currently looking for something but they were never quite sure what they were looking for. They were not sure that John was the right person. One member of the group told a story about some young people who had come to their church looking for baptism for their baby. They did not know what they were looking for. Inside the crowd was a deep spiritual quest that we must respect.

Drawing on their less preferred thinking function, the feeling types concluded that they would not have liked to meet John the Baptist. For them John was a real turn off.

Thinking The thinking types recognized that this was a challenging passage that gave a clear and hard message. John speaks a judgement that challenges the prejudices of his time and the political and religious leaders of the day. John issues a formal warning to the people around him because he wants them to change their ways.

Thinking types identify and analyse the major issues that are at stake in the passage. The passage is about judgement: people are judged by what they do. The passage is about responsibility: people are judged by who they are, not by their family roots. The passage is about forgiveness, but people have to repent before they can be forgiven.

The thinking types identify and analyse how John acts. John acts with honesty: people ask him questions and he tells it how it is. John acts fairly: he treats all people alike. John accepts his own exclusion because he speaks out uncomfortable truths. John upsets the expectations of his day: the 'in-crowd' are excluded and the 'outsiders' are included.

Drawing on their less preferred feeling function, the thinking types tried to identify with the human values in the story. What they ended up doing was a second exercise in logical analysis that abstracted the major value-based themes from the passage, but failed to engage with the human stories. For the thinking types the passage spoke of the values of sharing, being kind and providing others with the basics of existence to which all have a fundamental right.

Conclusion

This study set out to explore the connection between Astley's notion of ordinary theology and the SIFT hermeneutical approach. Two main conclusions can be drawn from this analysis: one concerning ordinary theology and one concerning the SIFT hermeneutical approach.

The study draws attention to the profound insights and theological reflection of ordinary theologians shaped within the liturgical life of their local church. Given the confidence to ask serious questions of sacred text and to trust their dialogue with that text, ordinary theologians can unlock significant insights through their reflective God-talk, and generate significant connections between the biblical narrative and their own experience of God active in God's church and in God's world.

In respect of the SIFT hermeneutical approach, this study confirms the key psychological insight on which the approach is based, namely that individual differences in psychological type preferences predict ways in which sacred text is interpreted. At the same time this study illustrates how ordinary theologians can be aided in their reading and interpretation of sacred text, by implementing the insights proffered by the SIFT approach. The first insight suggests distinguishing between passages of scripture rich in perceiving and other passages rich in evaluating, and then addressing to these passages appropriate tasks relevant to the perceiving functions (sensing and intuition) or to the evaluating functions (thinking and feeling). The second insight suggests that interpretation of sacred text is richer and goes deeper when several ordinary theologians holding the same psychological preferences work together. The added benefit comes in two stages. Stage one occurs when the groups are in process, and people who share the same type profile affirm one another's insights and generate confidence from these insights to go further. Stage two occurs when the groups exchange their insights and allow individuals to be enriched by fresh perspectives that they had not seen for themselves.

References

Francis, L.J. (2005), *Faith and Psychology: Personality, Religion and the Individual*, London: Darton, Longman and Todd.

Francis, L.J. (2010), 'Five Loaves and Two Fishes: An Empirical Study in Psychological Type and Biblical Hermeneutics among Anglican Preachers', *HTS Theological Studies*, 66, 1, article #811: 5 pages.

Francis, L.J. (forthcoming), 'What Happened to the Fig Tree? An Empirical Study in Psychological Type and Biblical Hermeneutics', *Mental Health, Religion and Culture*.

Francis, L.J. and P. Atkins (2000), *Exploring Luke's Gospel: A Guide to the Gospel Readings in the Revised Common Lectionary*, London: Mowbray.

Francis, L.J. and P. Atkins (2001), *Exploring Matthew's Gospel: A Guide to the Gospel Readings in the Revised Common Lectionary*, London: Mowbray.

Francis, L.J. and P. Atkins (2002), *Exploring Mark's Gospel: An Aid for Readers and Preachers using Year B of the Revised Common Lectionary*, London: Continuum.

Francis, L.J. and S.H. Jones (2011), 'Reading and Proclaiming the Resurrection: An Empirical Study in Psychological Type Theory among Trainee and Experienced Preachers Employing Mark 16 and Matthew 28', *Journal of Empirical Theology*, 24: 1–18.

Francis, L.J., and G. Smith (forthcoming), 'Reading and Proclaiming the Birth Narratives from Luke and Matthew: A Study in Empirical Theology among Curates and their Training Incumbents Employing the SIFT Method'.

Francis, L.J., M. Robbins and J. Astley (eds) (2009), *Empirical Theology in Texts and Tables: Qualitative, Quantitative and Comparative Perspectives*, Leiden: Brill.

Francis, L.J., M. Robbins and A. Village (2009), 'Psychological Type and the Pulpit: An Empirical Enquiry Concerning Preachers and the SIFT Method of Biblical Hermeneutics', *HTS Theological Studies*, 65, 1, article #161: 7 pages.

Francis, L.J. and A. Village (2008), *Preaching With All Our Souls*, London: Continuum.

Myers, I.B. and M.H. McCaulley (1985), *Manual: A Guide to the Development and Use of the Myers-Briggs Type Indicator*, Palo Alto, Calif.: Consulting Psychologists Press.

Rollins, W.G. and D.A. Kille (eds) (2007), *Psychological Insights into the Bible: Texts and Readings*, Grand Rapids, Mich.: Eerdmans.

van der Ven, J.A. (1998), *Education for Reflective Ministry*, Louvain: Peeters.

Village, A. (2010), 'Psychological Type and Biblical Interpretation among Anglican Clergy in the UK', *Journal of Empirical Theology*, 23, 2: 179–200.

Village, A. and L.J. Francis (2005), 'The Relationship of Psychological Type Preferences to Biblical Interpretation', *Journal of Empirical Theology*, 18, 1: 74–89.

Chapter 10
Extraordinary Eschatology: Insights from Ordinary Theologians

Michael Armstrong

Data reporting accounts of the final destiny of humankind and the physical creation by those not formally educated in theology ('ordinary eschatology') were collected from in-depth interviews with 26 Congregationalists (Armstrong, 2011).[1] I argued in Chapter 7 that there are two essential criteria for deciding if ordinary *theology* is being done. It was clear that for the vast majority of the subjects in this study, both the affective-volitional (subjective) and cognitive (objective) requirements were met. The majority of those interviewed had clearly given significant prior thought to the issues; and nearly all exhibited surprising focus and critical reflection within the interview itself. The vast majority of subjects also gave clear and moving testimony to the difference that their *belief in* life after death (hereafter referred to as LAD) made to them. It was rarely simply a case of their *belief that* there will be a LAD.

In several key areas these data show a quite extraordinary ordinary eschatology in comparison with orthodox eschatology, but such a reference to an established theological view of eschatology is problematic here in two respects.

First, the Congregational tradition does not require subscription to creeds and is suspicious of anything that might undermine local authority. Liturgical resources are not compulsory within Congregational churches. However, we are a federation of churches who recognize the need to understand both our own faith tradition and those of our fellow Christians. The website of the Congregational Federation states that 'Congregational churches have a broadly orthodox faith commitment'. The role of tradition is substantial, if not explicit, for most Congregationalists. Doctrine is not an alien concept and the traditional creeds are known by many. Shortly after the formation of the Congregational Union in 1831, it adopted (in May 1833) a 'Declaration of the Faith, Church Order, and Discipline' of the church, which stems from the Savoy Declaration of 1658. However, ordinary Congregationalists are far more likely today to have some awareness of the creeds as used in the Church of England, or of Catholic teaching, than of these doctrinal documents.

---

1 Twenty-four members of my own Congregational church, one member of a URC church where I was formerly minister and one who attends a local Methodist church.

Second, there is the problem of defining the normative tradition. There is a noticeable lack of clarity with regard to Protestant eschatological doctrine in general in the UK. Even the Church of England's Doctrine Commission report, *The Mystery of Salvation*, is described by its then chair, Bishop Stephen Sykes, (along with its other recent reports) as 'documents with a pastoral concern' that 'stand close to the Church's public teaching of the faith', but 'not [as] an Anglican systematic theology' (Church of England Doctrine Commission, 2005: xv–xvi).

It was useful, however, to have some clear source of views against which to compare the ordinary eschatology uncovered in this project. For this purpose I chose the recent work of another Anglican bishop, Tom Wright, who is remarkable in providing an unequivocally clear statement of what we should believe concerning 'life *after* LAD',[2] and why we should believe it. As a New Testament scholar, Wright approaches the issue of LAD from a biblical perspective. In defending the bodily resurrection of Jesus as the best explanation of the historical data recorded by early Christianity, he also clearly articulates the New Testament view of what happens to a Christian when she dies. Wright believes that a significant 'correction' is required in the way that Anglican (and other) clergy and church members understand and communicate this view, so as to counteract a liberal drifting away from biblical truths. He disparages popular ('ordinary'?) views of LAD, especially the often-expressed notion of Christian hope as 'going to heaven when we die'. 'The point seems to be that there is something called "eternity", which is regularly spoken of as though it has only the loosest of connections with space and time, and one day we are going to step into this eternal existence, whether in the form of heaven or of hell, which has almost nothing to do with this earth and this present history.' According to Wright, this is not a biblical view and is seriously misleading, if not damaging to Christian faith. By contrast, 'what we find in the New Testament, and what I commend, is the Christian hope for a new, or renewed, heaven and a new, or renewed earth, with these two integrated together' (Wright, 1999: 5).

Wright is concerned that ordinary Anglicans are apparently mistaken about the nature, timing and location of heaven; the existence of purgatory and hell; the relationship of body and soul; and the definition of soul. These are the significant and worrying results of wrong thinking, to the extent that 'the sure and certain hope of the resurrection to life has been replaced, for many Anglicans at least, by the vague and fuzzy possibility of a long winding journey to somewhere or other' (Wright, 2003: 36).

For Wright, however, the nature and timing of post-mortem life is clear from the New Testament. After death we enter immediately a disembodied state of

[2] This phrase denotes Wright's central contention that LAD is only the first, temporary stage of our post-mortem Christian destiny. The biblical view, and that of the early Christian church, is that resurrection does not mean LAD but, rather, 'was a way of talking about a new bodily life *after* whatever state of existence one might enter immediately upon death. It was, in other words, life *after* "life after death"' (Wright, 2007: 163).

paradise (or heaven), a state of 'restful happiness' where we peacefully await the future general bodily resurrection. We are conscious while in this intermediate state: by 'sleep' Paul 'means that the body is "asleep" in the sense of "dead", while the real person – however we want to describe him or her – continues' (Wright, 2007: 183–4).

But what exactly is the real person without a body? Wright denigrates what he sees as the entirely incorrect and non-Christian (Platonic) idea of an immortal soul leaving the mortal body at death; yet he is entirely convinced of an *interim* state of non-physical existence. In fact, he permits the use of the word 'soul', as long as what is meant by that is 'a whole human being living in the presence of God' (Wright, 1999: 25). But what we are in this intermediate state is not entirely clear. Wright adopts the hardware-software analogy of John Polkinghorne to illustrate how difficult and vague it is to talk of a disembodied soul, but this adds little by way of clarification. Resurrection is about a renewed world, not continuing individual existence; and it lies in the future. When Jesus says to the brigand, 'Today you will be with me in Paradise' (Lk 23:43), he means the temporary place of rest before rising from the dead. 1 Corinthians 15:51–6 speaks of the second of a two-stage process, a future point of general resurrection, when all will be raised. 'Departing and being with Christ' or 'living to God' are New Testament ways of expressing a *temporary* stage ahead of the time when God restores all things.

The ordinary eschatology of the subjects of my research, however, is notably different to this view in several key respects.

1. The final afterlife state is immediate and non-physical: there is no 'second stage'. Neither is there any 'soul-sleep' or an unconscious state. My interviewees thought that experiences of the continuing lives of the known dead confirm this; and they do not find any sense in the idea of an unconscious interim period. We continue to exist spiritually after death, so why should we not always be conscious of this? As Gregory put it, 'I don't think there's any point in having a gap of nothingness. If you've got a spirit it's there, it can't sort of suddenly go into oblivion or come back into existence a fortnight later, sort of thing. So it's immediate, no gap.' Gregory sees the spirit (soul) as something that cannot die, unlike the body.
2. One of the clearest findings from these data is that, in the view of ordinary theologians, human beings are dual in nature: there is a substantial soul (or 'spirit'), and this is what survives death and leaves the 'shell' of the body. This dualist view is based largely on the self-evident experience of the 'inner self', and a strong belief in continuing personal identity post-mortem as a feature of a substantial non-physical 'me'. Gregory is typical in thinking that 'the spirit or the soul lives on'. Joselyn thinks that 'when you're dead your body is just a shell … your soul or your spirit has been removed from it.' For Charles this was powerfully illustrated by his own near-death experience which clarified that the spirit 'leaves the body and goes'. The spirit is an 'inner being', because he could see the 'outer

being' (the body) down on the hospital bed while *he* was somewhere else. A dualist view is also seen in the way that loved ones can be considered already 'lost' to dementia, although still living. It was also pointed out that as God himself is non-physical, we too can live in a 'spiritual' form.

3. The afterlife is obviously non-physical. Bodies of dead people are clearly experienced as 'empty' and their physical remains are unimportant, just 'something that is left'. At a funeral 'we bury something, not someone.' For many interviewees, physicality is actually seen as a key *problem* for human life, presenting temptation (greed, lust, etc.) and usually ending with significant physical suffering and decline. The afterlife must be quite different, which means it must be non-physical. The subjects of this study do not want to escape the physical because they are Platonists but because they are human, because they have already lived a physical life and know what that entails. Wright fails to appreciate the strength of this popular view. Furthermore, the idea of a physical afterlife is seen as ridiculous because of various perceived practical and logical problems: space and resources, organization and regulation, meeting recognizable others, environmental and climatic issues. The point is that it is hard to see what a 'new earth' would actually be like. In fact, it is as difficult to envisage a renewed physical environment which would be 'heavenly' for all, as it is to imagine a more spiritual concept of the afterlife. Nevertheless, many subjects also believed that the non-physical afterlife will have *some* elements of physical-like experience: for example, the ability to 'hear' and 'see' others, and to have things 'to do'. Such views were held without contradiction, illustrating the non-systematic and fragmentary nature of ordinary theology.
4. So complete is this notion of a non-physical afterlife that resurrection is sometimes confused with reincarnation. The idea of 'becoming physical again' has moved so far from traditional Christian ideas in the minds of some ordinary theologians that it has become associated with this non-Christian belief. Of particular note is the way in which the resurrection of Jesus was seen. In this instance, the majority view was that Jesus was physically resurrected. Only a minority believed that it was Jesus' spirit that came back and was somehow perceived by the disciples. However, the remarkable thing about *both* positions is that those who held them thought that Jesus came back for a brief period simply to prove that what he had said was true, and to demonstrate that death was not the end of human life. His physical resurrection had nothing to do with the nature of the afterlife that *we* shall experience. After this short period of physical resurrection, Jesus returned to a *spiritual heaven*, where we will also go as *souls* or *spirits* after death for an eternal existence. Duncan provides a typical view: 'The resurrection had to be proved to the people that were there … that death had been conquered. … So Jesus had to exist physically after death.' A continuing spiritual presence would not have been enough for this; Jesus

had to be *seen*. When asked if we would also be resurrected physically, Duncan replied, 'No, it had never crossed my mind to be honest. No, I had always accepted that [Jesus' resurrection] was a one-off.'

5. An anthropocentric view of the afterlife dominates. LAD will be social: but this does not necessarily mean that we will meet everyone, or that earthly relationships will continue in the same way. God will *probably* be present in the afterlife; but, remarkably, many thought it unlikely that we would 'meet him personally'. Most felt that there would be no form of objective judgement, but perhaps some form of self-judgement. Some expected that the afterlife will be active, while others hoped for exactly the opposite.
6. There is deep scepticism concerning any claim by either academy or church to a definitive interpretation of what the Bible says concerning LAD. The most common explanation of the impossibility of a single biblical view is that it is ultimately all just a matter of opinion. In other words, no one opinion can or should prevail: the opinion of an ordinary theologian is as significant as that of a theologian or bishop. There is a Congregational influence at work here, I suspect, as well as the mutually reinforcing factors of the influence of relativism and individualism in contemporary British culture, and the failure of church and academy meaningfully to convey the results of biblical and theological scholarship. There is a bewildering (to the ordinary theologian) array of competing 'expert' interpretations of key LAD texts. The academic process itself exacerbates this situation: academic debate usually takes the form of corrections being offered to existing positions. One subject commented that 'there are so many different interpretations that … *any* [his emphasis] interpretation is covered that you can make.' This is an interesting observation by a man whose career had been in engineering. The sheer variety of academic views is a matter of significance for him, and is probably quite different from his experience of scientific disciplines where (usually) there would be, at any given time, one definitive and accepted opinion or position to learn and understand.
7. A very high level of experience of the supernatural was reported by these ordinary theologians, which reinforced their general belief in LAD. The most prevalent was experience of the known dead. Typical of this is an incident related by Janet which happened shortly after her grandfather's death.

> I'd gone to bed one night and I woke up, and I swear I'm not mad, I will swear to anybody, my granddad was sitting by my bedside, and I opened my eyes and he had his hand on me. … And I closed my eyes and opened them again and he'd gone. And I think that was his way of saying goodbye to me and just kind of saying, 'I'm OK now.'

8. Many reported a strong sense of being guided by deceased loved ones, or helped in difficult times. More than one subject clearly expected and looked

forward to undertaking this role after their death. The frequency of such experiences suggests a continuing need on the part of modern Protestant Christians for contact with the dead. For some, the Spiritualist Church had been significant in times of bereavement in confirming the ongoing life of loved ones; although others illustrated scepticism over such claims. There were also several stories of experiences of ghosts and other contact with the unknown dead, which were usually disturbing or at least uncomfortable compared with experiences of the known dead.

What These Views Tell Us

Despite the lack of Protestant doctrinal norms, the ordinary eschatology revealed in this research may seem so unorthodox that it could simply be dismissed as the ramblings of some strange, untutored Christians. However, this would be greatly to undervalue the relevance and importance of the 'ordinary voice'.

The volume of this particular ordinary voice may be relatively low: this sample of ordinary theologians is numerically small and perhaps unrepresentative. But, it is still clearly audible. Their views are remarkably consistent and nearly all find support, at least to some extent, on one 'side' of current academic theological debates. In other words, their views are not entirely unique. In fact, some aspects of ordinary eschatology may be considered to be a return to a more traditional view.

This may be argued with regard to their views of the soul. Rejection of the substantial soul is a recent phenomenon within Protestant theology (Cullmann, 1958; Stendahl, 1984) and is by no means universally accepted (cf. Barr, 1992; Swinburne, 1997). Ordinary eschatology considers the substantial soul to be the obvious explanation of both how this life is experienced, and how I can still be 'me' in the next. It is also the way that personal integrity and continuity can be understood when mind-robbing diseases such as dementia strike.

Wright would undoubtedly claim that ordinary eschatology is non-biblical. However, there really is no consensus regarding the interpretation of key LAD texts such as 1 Corinthians 15 (cf. Borg and Wright, 1999). Furthermore, even if it were accepted that Paul clearly meant a bodily 'spiritual' resurrection, and that he envisaged the recreation of the physical earth and heavens, this can be challenged in light of our total change in worldviews (Badham, 1976; Badham and Badham, 1982). What may have been a reasonable conclusion for Paul, with his understanding of a small (worldly) and young physical creation, may be less reasonable for us – who now know of an almost infinite, complex physical cosmos, which has existed for an almost unimaginably long period of time.

Competing and contradictory opinions abound, some of which would lend support to this ordinary eschatology. An 'ordinary' reading of key LAD texts, based on the idea that it has to *work* in the actual practice of human life and faith, may provide a relevant commentary on current academic debates concerning the interpretation of those texts. The results of this research suggest a number of such instances. We cannot simply dismiss the apparently naïve approach to biblical texts of ordinary theologians.

The non-physicality of the afterlife in ordinary eschatology is the key point of difference from the 'norm'. There is no future final physical resurrection, or new earth and heavens. The final afterlife state is an immediate, conscious, social, soul-spirit existence. The soul is substantial, providing the mechanism for the continuation of personal identity: this view of human beings is therefore dualist. So clear is this conviction of a non-physical afterlife, that a radical interpretation of Jesus' resurrection follows. Ordinary eschatology generally accepts that this was a physical (bodily) resurrection, but considers it solely as a necessary proof to convince the disciples and others that Jesus was the Son of God, rather than an indication of what our own afterlife will be like.

When stated in summary form like this, ordinary eschatology can seem surprising. However, the contrast between the physical ('orthodox') and the non-physical ('ordinary') appears much less stark when it is noted that ordinary eschatology expects elements of earthly physical experience to be (somehow) available in the non-physical afterlife. Rather than two extreme poles, the physical and non-physical views are better conceived as positions on a continuum. The real issue is the extent of transformation, of difference, between this world and the next.

Wright is keen to emphasize continuity with this world to comply with what he regards as biblical teaching, and to ensure that Christians in this life do not have an over-heavenly outlook that distances them from the joys and responsibilities of the present kingdom of God. These ordinary theologians are, by contrast, keen to emphasize discontinuity, although not completely because they see an obvious need for physical-like characteristics in the next life. This 'ordinary' emphasis is not based on their longing to escape this life, however, but on their clear understanding of the drawbacks of this physical life – especially the common human experience of ageing with its attendant decline and ill health. It is also clear that ordinary theologians recognize that an emphasis on the physical leads to significant logical and practical problems, the solutions to which can seem as fantastic as any non-physical afterlife.

I am not arguing that this ordinary eschatology should simply be adopted in its entirety. I wish to claim only that there are good reasons to take it seriously. If ordinary theologians have been 'Spirit signal processing' at all, and I have suggested the means to assess whether this is the case (Chapter 7), then the church and academy need to hear their results.

The strength of this 'ordinary voice' depends on several things. There is the simple matter of 'volume': the voice of 26 ordinary theologians is clearly not as loud, in one obvious sense, as the voice of 26,000. However, consistency is also important: 26 voices saying the same thing has a much greater impact than the same number of people saying several different things. The strength of the ordinary voice also relates to the extent to which it differs from the theological 'norm', and the extent to which it finds support in current theological debates. If the results of ordinary theology were *entirely* different from the theological norm and found *no* support in current debates, then it is still possible (but less likely) that it could be the result of Spiritual discernment. In such situations the most obvious implication might be that the church and academy may well need to reconsider how it conveys orthodox theology to ordinary Christians, rather than to reconsider completely such orthodoxy.

However, where the results of ordinary theology differ from the norm in key aspects, but still find support in current theological debates, then it is more likely that the guidance of the Spirit is being reflected. In such situations, church and academy should allow these views to contribute to the discussions. These data suggest that this ordinary eschatology falls into the latter category.

It is absolutely clear to me that members of my congregation do ordinary *theology*: perhaps not consistently or systematically, but sincerely and in a critically reflective manner. I believe they have now begun to realize this themselves, which is a remarkable comment on how church and academy have hitherto valued their views. It should be obvious that those who actually live the Christian faith test out the beliefs and practices of that faith. It is surely reasonable to expect that the guidance of the Holy Spirit will, at least sometimes, be discerned by such people, albeit always imperfectly.

It is surely also reasonable that church and academy should therefore seek to hear and take seriously this ordinary theological voice. If ordinary views are ignored, then potentially damaging disjunctions can appear between ordinary Christians and ecclesial and academic authority. McDannell and Lang argue that the 'modern' view of heaven is still popular, with many Christians hoping for reunion with their loved ones. However, 'while most Christian clergy would not deny that wish, contemporary theologians are not interested in articulating the motif of meeting again in theological terms' (McDannell and Lang, 2001: 312–13). This disjunction, and others, is very apparent from ordinary eschatology.

References

Armstrong, Michael (2011), 'Lay Christian Views of Life After Death: A Qualitative Study and Theological Appraisal of the "Ordinary Eschatology" of Some Congregational Christians', DThM thesis, University of Durham.

Badham, Paul (1976), *Christian Beliefs about Life after Death*, London: Macmillan.

Badham, Paul and Linda Badham (1982), *Immortality or Extinction?* Basingstoke: Palgrave Macmillan.

Barr, James (1992), *The Garden of Eden and the Hope of Immortality*, London: SCM Press.

Borg, Marcus J. and N.T. Wright (1999), *The Meaning of Jesus: Two Visions*, London: SPCK.

Church of England Doctrine Commission (2005), *Contemporary Doctrine Classics: The Combined Reports by the Doctrine Commission of the General Synod of the Church of England*, London: Church House Publishing.

Cullmann, Oscar (1958), *Immortality of the Soul or Resurrection of the Dead? The Witness of the New Testament*, London: Epworth.

McDannell, Colleen and Bernhard Lang (2001), *Heaven: A History*, New Haven, Conn.: Yale Nota Bene.

Stendahl, Krister (1984), 'Immortality is Too Much and Too Little', in K. Stendahl, *Meanings: The Bible as Document and as Guide*, Philadelphia: Fortress, pp. 193–202.

Swinburne, Richard (1997), *The Evolution of the Soul*, Oxford: Clarendon Press.

Wright, N.T. (1999), *New Heavens, New Earth: The Biblical Picture of the Christian Hope*, Cambridge: Grove Books.

Wright, N.T. (2003), *For All The Saints? Remembering the Christian Departed*, London: SPCK.

Wright, N.T. (2007), *Surprised by Hope*, London: SPCK.

Chapter 11
Ordinary Theology and the British Assemblies of God Doctrinal Tradition: A Qualitative Study

Mark J. Cartledge

Introduction

This chapter aims to offer an analysis of qualitative data gathered from a congregational study of a church in the British Assemblies of God tradition. It is based on fieldwork conducted in 2007–2008 and completed in 2010 with the publication of the book *Testimony in the Spirit*. Material not included in that book is analysed in detail here for the first time. Detailed methodological issues of this study have been discussed elsewhere, so they are not repeated here (see Cartledge, 2010: 13–28). This study focuses on a discussion of the nature of Pentecostal theological tradition and, in particular, the way the British doctrinal tradition has been expressed in the Assemblies of God. Key findings from focus group transcripts are outlined before their significance is discussed in relation to the nature of doctrinal traditions and their transmission at a congregational level.

Doctrinal Tradition and British Classical Pentecostalism

The Assemblies of God of Great Britain is one of the main classical Pentecostal denominations in the UK. The inaugural meeting of the Assemblies of God was held at Aston, Birmingham in February 1924, followed by a conference in May of the same year (Kay, 2000: 27–31). At this conference the new denomination agreed to a statement of fundamental truths. This statement was not regarded as a creed but as a basis for unity for a full gospel ministry. The reasons for the emergence of the denomination were because of the need to preserve a distinctly Pentecostal identity, especially the post-conversion experience of baptism in the Spirit as evidenced by speaking with other tongues (or glossolalia); coordination of fellowship and witness, especially in the context of social hostility to Pentecostalism; and protection against error and indiscipline, notably inappropriate use of the *charismata* (Massey, 1987: 213–98; 1992: 57–77).

Pentecostals are avid readers of the Bible as their sacred text. It comes as no surprise, therefore, that at one level they get the idea that beliefs and practices are held in memory and passed on (*traditio* – something handed over, handed down or handed on; cf. Deut 32:7). Unfortunately, their collective memory is not only short but also selective. This is partly connected to a suspicion of 'tradition', which they share to some extent with all Protestant denominations as a consequence of its use within the Roman Catholic Church in particular. As inheritors of the Reformation, they often see 'tradition' as something corrupt as well as fundamentally opposed to the authority of the Bible for life and witness (Williams, 1999: 18). Classical Pentecostals are inheritors of the Reformers' legacy in the sense that they display some wariness towards doctrinal claims from any sector of the church that cannot be attested by scripture. There is a feeling that 'tradition' *per se* has not really helped the church and what Pentecostals receive comes from the Bible directly, that is, from their own reading of it and from their contemporary experience of the Holy Spirit (Robeck, 2004: 214).

Although they published 'The Statement of Fundamental Truths' in 1924, these early Pentecostals did not wish to get bogged down in a discussion of the early Christian creeds. Nevertheless, they needed to define their identity theologically and their boundary lines sociologically. Therefore they borrowed the style of the Methodists and the Evangelicals of the period and added their own distinctive beliefs concerning the work of the Spirit, *charismata* and eschatology (Kay, 2009: 225). The denomination did not reformulate its 'Statement of Faith' formally until 2004 (Cartledge, 2010: 5–6, 193–4).

The Focus Groups

This chapter will concentrate on the main source for the ordinary theological narratives, namely focus group material.

The focus groups contained 31 men (38%) and 51 women (62%). The age range for men was 16% in 18–29 years, 19% in 30–39 years, 26% in 40–49 years, 3% in 50–59 years, 16% in 60–69 years, 13% over 70 years; 7% did not give their ages. The age range for women was 10% in 18–29 years, 16% in 30–39 years, 18% in 40–49 years, 23% in 50–59 years, 14% in 60–69 years, 15% over 70 years; 4% did not give their ages. The church is a very international and multicultural church with worshippers from many different countries, although some have now become British citizens. The men originated from Africa: Nigeria (10%), Togo (3%), Uganda (10%) and Zambia (3%); Asia: India (7%); Europe: Ireland (3%), Macedonia (3%), the UK (Black 7%, Mixed Heritage 3%, White 32%); and the Caribbean: Barbados (3%), Jamaica (10%), Montserrat (3%) and St Kitts (3%). The women originated from Africa: Ghana (2%), Nigeria (10%), Uganda (4%) and Zimbabwe (2%); Europe: Ireland (6%), Germany (2%) and the UK (Black 2%, Mixed Heritage 2%, White 33%); and the Caribbean: Barbados (6%), Dominica (2%), Jamaica (21%), Montserrat (6%) and the Turks and Caicos Islands (2%). Not everyone specified their occupation, especially if retired. The men gave the following occupations: hospital porter, cleaner, caretaker, crane worker, heavy goods driver; as well as accountant, legal practitioner, college tutor, local government manager, business adviser, teacher, engineer, IT consultant and student. The women gave the following occupations: homemaker, care assistant, cook, hospital domestic, housekeeper, cleaner, factory worker, support worker, administrative assistant, teaching assistant, administrator, traffic enumerator, sales representative, nurse, PA executive, student, evangelist and unemployed.

Each focus group member was given a copy of the 2004 Statement of Faith and asked to what extent they were familiar with the text, whether they felt able to affirm or dissent from the statements, and what issues these statements raised for them as Christians.

Research Questions

Three research questions guide this enquiry: (1) How does the Statement of Faith function at a local congregational level? (2) Do all the members affirm this statement without reservation? (3) What kinds of theological tension exist between official and ordinary theology?

Findings

A number of key findings emerged from the focus group data.

Identity Marker and Boundary Keeper

It is clear from the focus group discussions that one of the pastors of the church conducts membership classes for interested churchgoers. During these classes he discusses the contents of the Statement of Faith and explains its meaning according to the Assemblies of God denomination. If participants in the classes wish to become members of the church, they need to sign the Statement of Faith to affirm their commitment to its content and officially join this local church. Anyone can participate in Sunday worship but to be fully involved in the church a commitment is required. Two people explained:

> *Jane*: All of these things, what [it] means to be member of the Hockley Pentecostal Church, the Assemblies of God you know, the mission statement and what we believe in the essential truths and the non-essential truths and all that. Everything is gone through and then when we've done that course. And it's really open because it's a forum where one can ask questions, things are explained and there's no hurry as such. And it's really clear at the end of the day when we sign this. 'Cos I had to do that as well and apply for membership.

> *Rodney*: I mean everybody's welcome whoever you are, whatever background to attend our meeting. But if you really want to become a member … you have gone through these, as we have just witnessed, you've signed your hand to it and in the course of that that means you would automatically submit to water baptism. So you've submitted to water baptism, you accepted these as the doctrinal point of Hockley, and you are then accepted into membership.

It is interesting to observe that a third item is now brought into the discussion, namely 'water baptism'. Pentecostals use this designation to refer to baptism by immersion, which they need to distinguish from 'Spirit baptism'. A number of converts to Pentecostalism were re-baptized because their original infant baptism was not regarded as authentic. This is because the Assemblies of God stand in the Anabaptist or believers' baptism tradition.

This Statement of Faith functions as a theological identity marker and as a social boundary line, although I am informed that not all Assemblies of God churches would expect its members to sign the Statement. Generally, the denomination expects all its pastors to sign the Statement of Faith as a means of demonstrating assent. (British Assemblies of God ministers are only required to sign this statement once at the beginning of their ministry, which differs from their American cousins who are required to sign their Statement of Faith on an annual basis.) However, in this congregation it is used as part of the socialization or 'traditioning' process of would-be members.

Summary of Biblical Truths

For some people the Statement of Faith is regarded as essentially a summary of the key doctrines contained in scripture. For example:

> *Jane*: For me personally, I signed it because I believe that these statements of faith that are recorded here are the truth as they are in the Bible, and not attacking any other religion, but there have been situations where people believe that Mary intercedes for us when the Bible tells us that Jesus Christ intercedes. … When the Bible tells me, which is here also, the only way to the Father is through Jesus, so when I signed I was aware of the fact that I was signing to the truth as stated in the Statement of Faith.

It is interesting that in this comment we have a qualification of the notion that signing this Statement of Faith is simply an act of belonging. This member is confident that the Statement records truths in propositional form as they are extracted from the Bible.

A Mission Statement

Another person suggested that the statement functions more like a mission agenda than a set of regulations or rules:

> *Peter*: What I would say is that you don't sort of see this like a set of rules. It's not like that, like this is what we are gonna do day in day out. It's almost like a way of trying to describe what we do, but it's not necessarily exactly like this that or the other, you know. And you wouldn't say that it covers everything that we necessarily [believe]. It's a guarded statement within that. As I say, like in your work situation, you almost have like a mission statement in your business.

There is recognition here that the Statement should be seen as an expression of the church's way of life, a way of focusing on key values.

Reflected in Worshipping Life

Another person, in the context of a focus group discussion of worship, connected this Statement to the broader worshipping life of the church:

> *Brian*: Look at baptism, water baptism. Now I think when you are obedient to God and you get baptized with water that is an act of worship. So I'd go for that one. When you go for being filled with the Spirit then I think the Holy Spirit helps us in worship so I think that the operation of the gifts of the Spirit, some of those are within worship. Number 9, believe in the holiness of life and conduct in obedience to the command of God. Now actually part of my worship to God is, 'cos worship means what's God worth, and demonstrating our worship is not singing songs. … Living a holy life, to me, is part of my worship to God.

Here key aspects of initiation, baptism in the Spirit and *charismata*, holiness and obedience are all seen to be integrated within the life of faith.

The Essential Biblical Evidence of Baptism in the Holy Spirit

On the whole, there was very much a sense of agreement with the Statement of Faith, which is perhaps what one might expect in the context of a focus group. However, the area where there was some debate and discussion was around Article 7, and whether speaking in tongues should be regarded as the 'essential, biblical evidence' of someone being baptized in the Spirit. The following extracts give a flavour of the comments on this topic.

> *Alan*: Now I've never been quite convinced that it is the initial gift. In a lot of Pentecostal traditions they believe that it is the initial gift, although it happened

> with me personally speaking. Looking at the scriptures I don't always see that. I believe a person can prophesy, something like that you see.
>
> *Rachel*: My personal opinion is that speaking in tongues is what God wants for all filled with the Holy Spirit. I believe all can be filled with the Holy Spirit but not all speak in tongues.
>
> *Delroy*: Some can be filled but not speak in tongues.
>
> *Harry*: It is not a universal law.
>
> *Valerie*: God gives it to whom he wants. It isn't something you can create in yourself. I believe the Holy Spirit gives you what he wants you to say when he wants you to say it.
>
> *Darlene*: That is the initial evidence of speaking in tongues when you are filled with the Holy Spirit. That's the initial evidence.
>
> *Brian*: Biblically everyone who got filled with the Holy Spirit, where it specifically says in the Bible: they got filled with the Spirit, people saw a difference. Instantly there was something that happened such that other people around said: 'What's just happened to them?' And in most of those cases it specifically says 'speaks in tongues', and in a couple of places 'speaks in tongues and prophesies'.
>
> *Hannah*: Would, I mean I know we've always from the year dot said the proof of the Spirit is the speaking in tongues. But, you know, would it not be that sometimes … God could give them any one of the other nine gifts, surely he could?

These different views represent the historic debate within Pentecostalism regarding the role of speaking in tongues as initial evidence or, as currently phrased, the 'essential, biblical evidence'.

Discussion

There are two important findings from this study that invite further discussion. First, the study was interested in how the Statement of Faith functioned at a local congregational level (first research question). From the narratives and focus group discussion it would appear that the doctrine of the denomination is in fact embedded in the conversion-initiation process, forms an explicit reading tradition and informs the worshipping practices of the congregation. One of the main pastors uses it to teach enquirers about the nature of the Christian faith in general but also about what it means to be a member of a church in the Assemblies of God tradition. Therefore it functions in a boundary-keeping manner, insofar as attendees must assent to the Statement before being allowed to be fully integrated into membership (Kay, 2000: 40). He is a guardian of the tradition and therefore a key gatekeeper in the traditioning of new members (Chan, 2000: 18). From the conversations in the focus groups, it is understood to be a summary of biblical teaching and thus functions as a way of reading the Bible. It is part of 'a dialogical and dialectical encounter between the Bible and the community' (Archer, 2004: 99). It also informs the worshipping practices of the church. The practice of 'water baptism' by immersion is one example. Following the non-conformist leaders of the emerging classical Pentecostal traditions, for example Thomas Myerscough, Anabaptist sympathies were clearly in evidence (Bicknell, 1998: 215). This is seen as the only valid expression of baptism and seems to follow conversion and baptism in the Spirit, although technically conversion would suffice. People transferring from other Christian traditions where paedobaptism is practised are required to be re-baptized because it is regarded as being invalid since it was not accompanied by the faith of the believer (Bicknell, 1998: 205; Hollenweger, 1972: 391). Clearly, the Assemblies of God continues to stand in the Anabaptist tradition and this is a fairly common stance for Pentecostals (see Clark, 2004). However, it is not universal; and Robeck and Sandidge (1990) have shown that Pentecostal baptismal practices vary enormously and include paedobaptism (also see the discussion in Hollenweger, 1997: 261–3). Importantly, from a Pentecostal perspective, all of these practices (catechesis, Bible reading and sacraments) cohere in order to 'tradition' or socialize new and existing members into the community of the congregation.

Second, it is clear that while the majority of focus group members do appear to affirm the Statement of Faith in general, there are some differences of attitude towards the nature of the Statement (second research question). The first attitude is represented by the person who understood the statement as a summary of biblical truths in propositional form. She signed the form not only to identify with the ethos of the church but in order to give written assent to each and every proposition as a 'truth'. This view could be aligned with the cognitive type of doctrine defined by Lindbeck (1984: 16). The second attitude is represented by the person who understood the statement as a 'mission statement'; it is something that is limited and gives an orientation and set of values rather than a detailed prescription for daily living. This attitude is intriguing because it takes an almost coherentist approach to truth by viewing the statements as a 'web of beliefs': they form a description, but not an exact one, rather they are partial and the statement is guarded (see Cartledge, 2003: 43–4). One might be tempted to align this attitude with Lindbeck's third type, namely the 'cultural-linguistic' or 'rule' theory (Lindbeck, 1984: 18), even if the person explicitly rejects the statement as a set of rules. This is because of Lindbeck's broader argument, which has resonance here. As Lindbeck observes: 'The chanting of the Nicene Creed … can be an immensely powerful symbolization of the totality of the faith even for those who do not understand its discursive propositional or regulative meanings' (1984: 19). However, one does not need to assume a lack of understanding to appreciate the power of the totality of a credal statement, even if it is never read or sung in a liturgical context. For this person, the statement provides a means of orientation, and signing it is simply an alignment with the worldview, or the 'web of beliefs', represented in general rather than in atomistic and precise propositional form. In other words, it is 'the medium in which one moves, a set of skills that one employs in living one's life' (Lindbeck, 1984: 35). Although these two attitudes are not necessarily mutually exclusive, and indeed the types proposed by Lindbeck could be considered as complementary (see McGrath, 1997: 32), I would suggest that the differences between them can be seen to lie behind the key issue on which the members disagree.

The particular area of disagreement focuses around the signification of glossolalia, especially as it accompanies the event of baptism in the Spirit and is the 'essential, biblical evidence' (third research question). This official view is still maintained by some, perhaps even the majority, and again an argument from the Bible is employed. Those arguing for a propositional correspondence between the Statement and the biblical texts would, no doubt, fall into this category on this particular point of doctrine. But it is openly disputed by others on the basis that there are a number of different *charismata* and these should also have the right to be seen as 'evidence' of Spirit baptism.

What does this disagreement among Pentecostals tell us regarding the nature of the doctrinal tradition as it is currently mediated? Certainly it tells us that an issue which divided Pentecostals in the earliest days still divides them today. Shuman's (1997) appropriation of Lindbeck's theory to this very issue suggests that a constellation of Pentecostal practice provides the context in which specific texts are interpreted and is, to some extent, subverted because of the broader set of ecclesial practices located within the Pentecostal constituency. Some might say that experience of the Holy Spirit is reshaping Pentecostal cultural-linguistic tradition (Stell, 1997: 693). In the context of a very diversely constituted church there is some room for latitude in interpretation, even on such an important doctrinal point as 'essential, biblical evidence'. Other charismatic signs are accepted in a secondary sense; and this suggests that an implicit compromise has been reached and there is a convergence with the Elim tradition at the ordinary level, despite merger failures at an official level, for example in 1963 (Kay, 2000: 58).

Conclusion

The findings from this qualitative research indicate that the 2004 Statement of Faith plays an important role in the conversion-initiation process of the local church and is significant for the traditioning of prospective members. Its role is enhanced by being embedded in catechesis and supported by specific sacramental practices. Closer scrutiny of attitudes among the focus group members suggests that there are some differences in how the Statement is approached, and these may lie behind the key disagreement around the doctrine of glossolalia as the 'essential, biblical evidence' of baptism in the Holy Spirit. Further research is required in order to test this finding more widely.

References

Archer, Kenneth J. (2004), *A Pentecostal Hermeneutic for the Twenty-First Century: Spirit, Scripture, Community*, London: T. & T. Clark (Journal of Pentecostal Theology Supplement Series 24).

Bicknell, Richard (1998), 'The Ordinances: The Marginalised Aspects of Pentecostalism', in Keith Warrington (ed.), *Pentecostal Perspectives*, Carlisle: Paternoster, pp. 204–22.

Cartledge, Mark J. (2003), *Practical Theology: Charismatic and Empirical Perspectives*, Carlisle: Paternoster.

Cartledge, Mark J. (2010), *Testimony in the Spirit: Rescripting Ordinary Pentecostal Theology*, Farnham: Ashgate.

Chan, Simon (2000), *Pentecostal Theology and the Christian Spiritual Tradition*, Sheffield: Sheffield Academic Press.

Clark, Matthew S. (2004), 'Pentecostalism's Anabaptist Roots: Hermeneutical Implications', in Wonsuk Ma and Robert P. Menzies (eds), *The Spirit and Spirituality: Essays in Honour of Russell P. Spittler*, Sheffield: Sheffield Academic Press, pp. 194–211.

Hollenweger, Walter J. (1972), *The Pentecostals: The Charismatic Movement in the Church*, London: SCM Press.

Hollenweger, Walter J. (1997), *Pentecostalism: Origins and Developments Worldwide*, Peabody, Mass.: Hendrickson.

Kay, William K. (2000), *Pentecostals in Britain*, Carlisle: Paternoster.

Kay, William K. (2009), *SCM Core Text: Pentecostalism*, London: SCM Press.

Lindbeck, George A. (1984), *The Nature of Doctrine: Religion and Theology in a Postliberal Age*, London: SPCK.

Massey, Richard D. (1987), '"A Sound and Scriptural Union": An Examination of the Origins of the Assemblies of God of Great Britain and Ireland during the Years 1920–1925', PhD thesis, University of Birmingham.

Massey, Richard D. (1992), *Another Springtime: The Life of Donald Gee, Pentecostal Leader and Teacher*, Guildford: Highland Books.

McGrath, Alister E. (1997), *The Genesis of Doctrine: A Study in the Foundation of Doctrinal Criticism*, Grand Rapids, Mich.: Eerdmans.

Robeck, Cecil M., Jr (2004), 'An Emerging Magisterium? The Case of the Assemblies of God', in Wonsuk Ma and Robert P. Menzies (eds), *The Spirit and Spirituality: Essays in Honour of Russell P. Spittler*, Sheffield: Sheffield Academic Press, pp. 212–52.

Robeck, Cecil M., Jr and Jerry L. Sandidge (1990), 'The Ecclesiology of Koinōnia and Baptism: A Pentecostal Perspective', *Journal of Ecumenical Studies*, 27, 3: 504–34.

Shuman, Joel (1997), 'Toward a Cultural-Linguistic Account of the Pentecostal Doctrine of the Baptism in the Spirit', *Pneuma: The Journal of the Society for Pentecostal Studies*, 19, 2: 207–23.

Stell, Stephen L. (1997), 'Hermeneutics in Theology and the Theology of Hermeneutics: Beyond Lindbeck and Tracy', *Journal of the American Academy of Religion*, 56, 4: 679–703.

Williams, D.H. (1999), *Retrieving the Tradition and Renewing Evangelicalism: A Primer for Suspicious Protestants*, Grand Rapids, Mich.: Eerdmans.

Chapter 12
Congregational Hermeneutics: Towards Virtuous Apprenticeship

Andrew Rogers

Congregational hermeneutics, in my usage, explores how people in churches say, do and learn biblical hermeneutics. Hermeneutics here is taken in the broad sense of reflection on how such Bible readers move between the text and their context.[1] In Jeff Astley's terms, then, congregational hermeneutics is nearly a subset of ordinary theology study, given that most people in congregations have received limited Bible-related theological education of 'a scholarly, academic or systematic kind' (Astley, 2002: 56). It developed out of liberation hermeneutics and its emphasis on 'ordinary' readers of scripture (cf. Chapter 13).

This volume as a whole engages with a rationale for studying ordinary theology. For congregational hermeneutics, there is growing recognition of the need for ecclesiology to be informed by the practices of actual churches (e.g., Ward, 2012). Furthermore, an increasing number of Christian thinkers are being drawn towards a theological hermeneutics that typically makes the church the primary locus for hermeneutics (e.g., Davis and Hays, 2003). The theological logic of such a position has been set out recently by Stephen Holmes, where he argues that 'the study of biblical interpretation ought to be responsible in some sense to the lived interpretative practices of ecclesial communities and attentive to their proposed or enacted principles of interpretation' (2011: 414). Attention to and reflection on lived hermeneutical practices is what congregational hermeneutics is about, and a sample of such is given here. Further motivation for this specific study arose from disquiet regarding the place of biblical hermeneutics in UK churches, especially within my own tradition of evangelicalism, and this has subsequently been borne out by other research (e.g., ComRes, 2008; Dickson, 2007).

[1] The term 'congregational hermeneutics' was coined by the Anabaptist theologian Stuart Murray as a historical characterization of Anabaptist hermeneutics with 'conversation partner' potential for contemporary hermeneutics (2000: especially chs 7 and 10). I am using the term in a related but broader sense to refer to both descriptive and prescriptive aspects of contemporary hermeneutics in congregations.

The Congregations

Two contrasting evangelical congregations were the focus of my study, namely 'Holder' and 'The Fellowship'. Holder had a Reformed tradition and belonged to an association of independent churches,[2] whereas the Fellowship was a charismatic 'new' church belonging to a regional network of similar congregations. Set within an interdisciplinary practical theology framework, I adopted 'an ethnographic perspective' (Green and Bloome, 1997) by observing hermeneutical practices in services and small groups in both churches, as well as interviewing congregants about 'how' they read the Bible. I understand the process of congregational hermeneutics to be at least a three-way conversation between the researcher, the congregation and Christian tradition(s). As with all conversation partners, the researcher brings their initial categories; in my case, these included the Gadamerian hermeneutical categories of horizon and fusion (Gadamer, 2004: 301–6). My interest was to see how these categories worked in actual churches in relation to scripture – how personal, small group and public horizons interacted to form congregational horizons, and how these horizons at the 'coal face' of their tradition were 'fused' with the horizon of the biblical text.[3]

Congregational hermeneutics were embedded within the broader life of the church through a complex 'configuration' of resonant and dissonant features. Despite this complexity, it was possible to detect hermeneutical patterns and even hermeneutical traditions within the congregations. One could distinguish in broadly Gadamerian terms between horizonal and fusion patterns, although the specifics were shaped substantially by the ethnographic experience. Congregational horizons included certain *beliefs* that were significant for hermeneutical practice (e.g., the status of scripture), as well as *goals* for Bible encounter (e.g., to hear God speak). Fusion patterns related to the specific *processes* that congregants used to make connections between text and context, such as 'text-linking' (i.e., cross-referencing and the linking of biblical texts in songs and sermons). These configurations of congregational hermeneutics were carried by *mediators* including more or less expected items such as sermons, liturgy, prayers, songs, house groups, congregants, Christian publications, church interior layout, web site design and hand-held microphones.

I have spoken of hermeneutical traditions, yet this should be prefaced by the admission that congregational hermeneutics were implicit in many aspects. Horizonal aspects, such as beliefs and goals, were sometimes made explicit, but fusion processes rarely so. Some scholars have argued that there are no

---

2 Fellowship of Independent Evangelical Churches (FIEC, 2011).

3 'Fusion' can be rather misleading, as it suggests that horizons may be assimilated; but Gadamer did not intend this, since in every horizonal encounter there is 'the experience of a tension between the text and the present'. The task of hermeneutics is not to cover up this tension 'by attempting a naïve assimilation' but to 'consciously bring it out' (2004: 305).

hermeneutical traditions within at least evangelical congregations (e.g., Malley, 2004), but I contend that this assumes a very narrow definition of hermeneutics. To say that congregational hermeneutics are implicit is not the same as saying there are no common hermeneutical beliefs, goals and processes. The nature of these hermeneutical traditions is our focus for the rest of this chapter, although space means it must be quite selective.

Both congregations were explicit in their beliefs about scripture, although these were construed in different ways. In Holder this was formally expressed as 'Bible-centeredness', whereas the Fellowship preferred the phrase 'Bible passion'. Holder exhibited Bible-centeredness through its doctrinal statement (FIEC, 2004), which included reference to the inerrancy of scripture, as well as scripture being incorporated into nearly every possible congregational setting and event. Regarding inerrancy, an elder explained, 'it is a view that we would expect [congregants] to adopt, because … it's part of our basis of faith …', adding that this view of scripture had been taught in house groups and formed part of a 'subculture of expectation'. The effectiveness of the mediation of this position was evident in interviewees' comments that largely conformed to this view.

The Fellowship's Bible passion was more activist than doctrinal, evident in a flurry of new initiatives designed to encourage the congregation to 'get into the Word'. There was, however, a formal statement of faith that referred to the Bible's 'divine inspiration' and 'supreme authority', as well as the Bible being 'fully trustworthy' (Evangelical Alliance, 2005). The pastor wanted to avoid inerrancy and infallibility positions, which he characterized as 'this must be exactly right, I'm going to hit you over the head with it'. Little effort appeared to be expended on mediating any specific doctrine of scripture, except that the Bible ought to be important – interviewees had a wide range of views on the Bible's status.

The most explicit hermeneutical goals for both congregations were to hear God speak through encounter with scripture, and its twin, that scripture should be relevant for life today. Holder's website combined these goals: 'The teaching of the Bible in a relevant and understandable way is central to our activities. It is our conviction that when God's Word is explained, God's voice is heard – and lives are changed!' These goals were repeated in most Holder interviews, so one person wanted sermons to be 'purposeful for life … not just abstractly "this is what the Bible says", but "this is how it impacts in life today"'. The Fellowship intensified these goals in coherence with their charismatic tradition, since they understood God to speak to the church and individuals directly today through a variety of means, including the Bible. The existential cast of this goal for the Fellowship was expressed by one interviewee, who declared: 'I want to hear from God, in my life. I want to hear what he's saying about what's relevant to what's happening in my life today, like *today*, not just generally in this period of my life, but today, what's going on.'

One further explicit hermeneutical goal was evident at the Fellowship and in their wider charismatic sub-tradition, which was described by the pastor as follows: 'the idea of Jesus hermeneutic, or Jesus-centred hermeneutics, so Jesus is God's answer, word to us, and so we interpret the written word in the light of who Jesus is, and we look back at the Old Testament in the light of who Jesus is. I think that's the goal.'

Such 'Jesus hermeneutics', which can also function as a process, were evident in interviewee comments. So one remembered learning on a church-based course that: 'when we read the Bible, even the Old Testament, it's important to look at it in terms of Jesus being at the centre of the Bible and, really, the whole thing is about Jesus.'

The 'saying' of Jesus hermeneutics in interviews was also found at Holder, but this goal was much less explicit. The 'doing' of the same through fusion processes in public settings and small groups was evident in both congregations, but it was a more substantial and explicit Jesus hermeneutics tradition at the Fellowship.

Explicit reflection on how congregants moved/should move between biblical texts and their context was occasional at the Fellowship and uncommon at Holder. By 'explicit' I mean some way of 'naming' their hermeneutical processes. Biblical 'context' and 'application' were the two favoured names given in both congregations, although the latter seemed to merge with the goal of relevance in many instances. The most explicit naming at Holder came from an elder who prioritized examining the text horizon in terms of 'the real essence of communication at the time', then continued: 'to then draw from that, if that was what was happening then and that was relevant at that time, how can this potentially apply to us in our situation today? So that there's a measure of consistency.'

Since this comment was the most explicit characterization of hermeneutical processes during the Holder fieldwork, it suggests that a substantial number of congregants learnt their hermeneutics intuitively, aided by the intense level of Bible exposure within the congregation. There was a little more space for reflection on processes at the Fellowship, with a few sermons referring to the big picture or story of scripture and one leader running an ambitious Bible study on 'The Exegesis and Hermeneutics of the Epistles'. Another leader characterized his process as 'What does it say?' and 'What does it say to me?', stressing the importance of the first question, since 'we can so often come to the Bible with preconceptions and we don't actually read what's there'. Explicit hermeneutics were closer to the surface of congregational discourse at the Fellowship, but there was markedly less exposure to scripture for the majority of Fellowship congregants.[4]

Given my characterization above, it follows that the majority of congregational hermeneutics encountered were implicit, albeit to varying degrees. Functioning as both belief and goal, an emphasis on the individual as the addressee of scripture was evident through the practice of personal Bible reading in both churches, although the emphasis was more striking within the Fellowship's configuration, especially in worship songs that incorporated scripture. Unsurprisingly, the theological

[4] Fifty-four per cent read the Bible at least once a day at Holder compared to 20 per cent at the Fellowship (N = 101/71). A wider survey rate for non-leaders lay in-between at 35 per cent (N = 1929) (ComRes, 2008).

traditions of the church shaped their hermeneutical processes, evident in practice through the core traditions of Bible-centeredness embedded in Calvinism at Holder and atonement within Christocentrism at the Fellowship. Most hermeneutical processes in both churches moved in one direction, from the text to congregational horizons, and, in coherence with the goal of relevance, congregants often made connections between horizons rapidly and on the basis that these horizons were quite proximate. Engagement with the text horizon in both churches was witnessed through closer readings, exemplary biblical characters, and grammatico-historical approaches (cf. Marshall, 2004), although this emphasis was more consistent at Holder. Displaying some 'Bible passion', the pastor at the Fellowship started mediating his recently started formal theological education through running Bible studies where he took groups through a grammatico-historical process, albeit without naming it in any way. The youth pastor, who subsequently replicated this process with the youth group, identified it as: 'you just go through it, bit by bit, looking at what it means, what the implication is of that. I love Bible studies where there's application, where there's learning … and maybe even going back to the original stuff … the culture content, and stuff like that.'

The most striking emic ('insider') hermeneutical process in both churches was the practice of linking Bible texts. Since it was not named I refer to it as 'text-linking', and it draws on, but is not exhausted by, the 'scripture interprets scripture' principle and the prevalence of study Bibles. Over half of the worship songs in both churches reconstructed multiple portions of scripture within their lyrics; sermons at the Fellowship regularly strung pearls of scripture together (cf. Longenecker, 1975: 115); and, given their level of Bible knowledge, small groups at Holder were able to text-link quite proficiently.

Towards Virtuous Apprenticeship

There was a strong contrast between the two congregations, in terms of how they mediated hermeneutical beliefs, goals and processes. Holder had very strong homogeneous mediatory dynamics, compared to the Fellowship's *laissez faire* approach that embraced more heterogeneous mediators. Nevertheless, hermeneutical patterns were evident in both churches, the 'saying' and 'doing' of which invited imitation from other congregants. Consequently, one might characterize the churches as operating ad hoc hermeneutical apprenticeships with mostly 'anonymous' apprentices.

The three-way conversation referred to earlier led to the development of a model of congregational hermeneutics.[5] Congregational traditions in the broadest sense were formed by a combination of their engagement with scripture, Christian

5 I have followed an analytic induction approach (Hammersley and Atkinson, 1995: 234–5) in which models are generated from 'telling' rather than 'typical' cases, which may well have resonance beyond their original contexts (Mitchell, 1984: 238–9).

tradition, reason, experience and culture, as well as other internal and external mediators – but the fieldwork also indicated there were latent hermeneutical traditions embedded within those congregational traditions. The contemporary edge of congregational tradition is the congregational horizons. Hermeneutical engagement with scripture was one means by which congregational tradition is affirmed, formed and transformed (cf. Rogers, 2007). This model is the basis for my critical theological reflection on the lived hermeneutical practices narrated.

Finding a place to engage in critical and constructive reflection upon congregational hermeneutics is not easy. It is claimed by some that no such place exists and that the academic always constructs the critique in the form of 'be more like us'. The three-way conversation includes the Christian tradition, but there sometimes needs to be an imaginative moment in order to get the theological and ethnographic partners talking. In this study, it arose from considering the purpose of the Bible in the church, alongside being alert to what appeared to enrich that purpose during the generation and reading of the ethnographic accounts. The purpose of the Bible in the church has been expressed in many ways, but one broad understanding is of scripture ideally acting to draw the congregation into the Christian story, in order that the congregation, in Christ, might faithfully improvise that story in their contemporary context. Such an understanding recognizes the eschatological nature of Christian communities as those being formed and transformed into the likeness of Christ (e.g., 2 Cor 3:12–18; Rom 8:18–30; cf. Briggs, 2007), where engagement with scripture through the agency of the Spirit is a critical feature of this congregational story. For our purposes here, therefore, one should be alert to signs of such formation and transformation within the ethnographic narrative as they relate to congregational hermeneutics, whilst recognizing the provisionality of those signs.[6]

There were many such signs in these two ordinary churches. For example, a discussion in one Holder small group, in response to a question on Malachi 1:6–14 regarding 'empty and useless religious practices', led to an exchange about tradition not necessarily being bad, although sometimes 'Reformedness gets in the way'. Similarly, at the Fellowship, the pastor told of a visiting monk who had noted their Christocentrism, and questioned whether they were even trinitarian – the pastor spoke of a 'swing back in our circles to taking a more explicitly trinitarian approach'. Another Fellowship congregant in interview spoke of a change in his understanding of the Bible: 'for a lot of years, I … read the Bible from a very me centred perspective, and how does this passage relate to me, what's God saying to me about this? And … in doing that, I think I've weakened the message of the Bible very significantly.'

These and other signs seem to point to the importance of being aware of one's hermeneutical horizons, where congregants explicitly recognize their contribution

[6] This is where theological and hermeneutical language run very close to each other, in that Gadamer speaks of 'the possible expansion of horizon, of the opening up of new horizons' (2004: 301).

to the hermeneutical task. Such examples fit with the language of being honest about one's horizons.

A second set of signs included a Bible study in another Holder small group, where the leader had suggested that the book of Jonah 'was just a story to illustrate Christ', knowing full well what the group reaction would be – 'Don't be ridiculous.' He justified this strategy for pedagogical reasons, as he wanted to 'push the barriers' and 'really challenge people to make sure they knew what their scriptures were'. Congregants at both churches offered a number of critiques of contemporary worship song lyrics, especially at the Fellowship. One congregant refused to sing a song that included the line 'You give and take away' from Job 1:21, because that was not her understanding of God's character. Of the song 'These Are The Days Of Elijah' (Kingsway Music, 2003: #1047), another congregant commented 'it's like you're … jumping from thousands of years … from then to now … there's this … odd time-shift.' These and many other instances identified the habit of some congregants to question the hermeneutical practices of their congregation. It seemed to me that such examples highlighted the courage of these congregants in challenging and possibly changing their congregational tradition.

These indicative signs of formative/transformative hermeneutics within the congregations have been described using the ethical language of honesty and courage – the language of virtue. This was mostly not an emic terminology,[7] unsurprising given their largely implicit hermeneutics, but it fits well with the different types of formative/transformative hermeneutics taking place in the congregations. Identifying the language of virtue, then, is our imaginative moment for bringing the theological and ethnographic into conversation within congregational hermeneutics. Virtue ethics makes the connection between character and behaviour, in that it 'encapsulates the idea that my ability to make good decisions is directly related to the on-going practices, behaviours, and habits that I live out' (Bretherton and Rook, 2010: xii). Stretching back to Plato and Aristotle, the virtue ethics tradition has been recast in Christian categories over the centuries, within the Bible (cf. Briggs, 2010; Wright, 2010), and in subsequent Christian history where faith, hope and love have been understood as the theological virtues received as gift through sanctification. Since the virtue tradition has always been teleological, a key feature of that recasting has been to establish a Christian *telos* for the virtues – a *telos* that fits with the eschatological nature of the church.

Recent insights see hermeneutics as intrinsically ethical (Sinn, 2008: 583). In particular, a number of biblical scholars and theologians have argued that the character of the interpreter must be significant for interpreting the scriptures. Therefore, growth in virtue should not only be the outcome of reading the Bible, but virtues should inform the reading itself – a truly virtuous circle. Congregants

[7] There were two nearly emic virtues in the congregations, given the prevalence of the terms 'faithful' at Holder and 'radical' at the Fellowship, which applied to most aspects of church life, including the Bible.

should learn the habits for handling scripture through being apprenticed within their congregation, where those habits are formed through the development of certain hermeneutical (or 'interpretative') virtues. Stephen Fowl has offered charity (1998: 86–7); to faith, hope and love, Kevin Vanhoozer adds honesty, openness, attention and obedience (1998: 377); Ellen Davis and Richard Hays name their prominent virtues as receptivity, humility, truthfulness, courage, charity, humour and imagination (2003: 4); Richard Briggs considers humility, wisdom, trust, love and receptivity (2010: 43). The rationale for selecting such virtues stems from a mixture of theological reasoning, relation to the attributes of critical scholarship and the character of the implied reader of the Bible.

Congregational hermeneutics deals with the relatively unexplored terrain of real, not implied, Bible readers (cf. Briggs, 2010: 193–4). It explores the operation of hermeneutical virtue for real readers, and so sketches the grammar or structure of lived hermeneutical virtue within a congregational story (Hauerwas and Pinches, 2010). From this research, I have also identified a number of hermeneutical virtues (developed further in Rogers, forthcoming). All the proposers agree that such virtues need to be developed together, not in isolation, as they balance one another and enable an enriched hermeneutical apprenticeship. Such a virtue account links hermeneutics to discipleship, where growth in hermeneutical virtue is for every disciple. Consequently, any potential divide between 'expert' and 'ordinary' readers is lessened, since the connection between critical scholarship and virtue is not direct, and the 'expert' reader may not be more honest or courageous (for example) than an 'ordinary' one (cf. Rowland, 1997: 131).

The congregational hermeneutics conversation can contribute towards our theological and educational formulations regarding the Bible in the church, thus underlining the value of the wider ordinary theology project this volume addresses. Readers are invited to reflect on how far this congregational hermeneutics model may relate to their own congregational context.[8]

References

Astley, Jeff (2002), *Ordinary Theology: Looking, Listening and Learning in Theology*, Aldershot: Ashgate.

Bible Society (2011), *H+ Making Good Sense of the Bible* [online], www.hplus.org.uk [accessed 26 May, 2012].

Bretherton, Luke and Russell Rook (eds) (2010), *Living Out Loud: Conversations about Virtue, Ethics, and Evangelicalism*, Milton Keynes: Paternoster.

[8] This research had an unexpected afterlife, in that I was asked to generate a course for churches structured around enriching hermeneutical virtues and skills within the congregational context (Bible Society, 2011). This was piloted in eight churches and, to date, 200 facilitators have been trained to lead the course in the UK.

Briggs, Richard S. (2007), 'The Role of the Bible in Formation and Transformation: A Hermeneutical and Theological Analysis', *Anvil*, 24, 3: 167–82.

Briggs, Richard S. (2010), *The Virtuous Reader: Old Testament Narrative and Interpretive Virtue*, Grand Rapids, Mich.: Baker Books.

ComRes (2008), *Taking the Pulse: Is the Bible Alive and Well in the Church Today? A Survey of Congregation Members and Church Leaders*, Swindon: Bible Society.

Davis, Ellen F. and Richard B. Hays (eds) (2003), *The Art of Reading Scripture*, Grand Rapids, Mich.: Eerdmans.

Dickson, Ian (2007), 'The Bible in Pastoral Ministry: The Quest for Best Practice', *The Journal of Adult Theological Education*, 4, 1: 103–21.

Evangelical Alliance (2005), *Evangelical Alliance Basis of Faith* [online], www.eauk.org/about/basis-of-faith.cfm [accessed 25 February 2006].

FIEC (2004), *Beliefs* [online], www.fiec.org.uk/about-us/beliefs [accessed 6 September 2007].

FIEC (2011), *Fellowship of Independent Evangelical Churches* [online], www.fiec.org.uk [accessed 6 September 2012].

Fowl, Stephen E. (1998), *Engaging Scripture: A Model for Theological Interpretation*, Oxford: Blackwell.

Gadamer, Hans-Georg (2004), *Truth and Method*, London: Continuum.

Green, Judith and David Bloome (1997), 'Ethnography and Ethnographers of and in Education: A Situated Perspective', in James Flood, et al. (eds), *Handbook of Research on Teaching Literacy through the Communicative and Visual Arts*, New York: Macmillan, pp. 181–202.

Hammersley, Martyn and Paul Atkinson (1995), *Ethnography: Principles in Practice*, London: Routledge.

Hauerwas, Stanley and Charles R. Pinches (2010), 'On Developing Hopeful Virtues', in Luke Bretherton and Russell Rook (eds), *Living Out Loud: Conversations about Virtue, Ethics, and Evangelicalism*, Milton Keynes: Paternoster, pp. 80–99.

Holmes, Stephen R. (2011), 'Kings, Professors, and Ploughboys: On the Accessibility of Scripture', *International Journal of Systematic Theology*, 14, 4: 403–15.

Kingsway Music (2003), *Songs of Fellowship: Combined Words Edition*, Volumes 1–3, Eastbourne: Kingsway.

Longenecker, Richard (1975), *Biblical Exegesis in the Apostolic Period*, Grand Rapids, Mich.: Eerdmans.

Malley, Brian (2004), *How the Bible Works: An Anthropological Study of Evangelical Biblicism*, Walnut Creek, Calif.: AltaMira.

Marshall, I. Howard (2004), *Beyond the Bible: Moving from Scripture to Theology*, Milton Keynes: Paternoster.

Mitchell, J. (1984), 'Typicality and the Case Study', in R.F. Ellen (ed.), *Ethnographic Research: A Guide to Conduct*, New York: New York Academic, pp. 238–41.

Murray, Stuart (2000), *Biblical Interpretation in the Anabaptist Tradition*, Kitchener, Ontario: Pandora Press.

Rogers, Andrew P. (2007), 'Reading Scripture in Congregations: Towards an Ordinary Hermeneutics', in Luke Bretherton and Andrew Walker (eds), *Remembering our Future: Explorations in Deep Church*, Milton Keynes: Paternoster, pp. 81–107.

Rogers, Andrew P. (forthcoming), *Congregational Hermeneutics: How Do We Read?* Farnham: Ashgate.

Rowland, Christopher (1997), 'Reflection: The Challenge to Theology', in Christopher Rowland and John Vincent (eds), *The Gospel from the City*, Sheffield: Urban Theology Unit, pp. 126–31.

Sinn, Simone (2008), 'Hermeneutics and Ecclesiology', in Gerard Mannion and Lewis S. Mudge (eds), *The Routledge Companion to the Christian Church*, Oxford: Routledge, pp. 576–93.

Vanhoozer, Kevin J. (1998), *Is There A Meaning In This Text? The Bible, The Reader and The Morality of Literary Knowledge*, Leicester: Apollos.

Ward, Pete (ed.) (2012), *Perspectives on Ecclesiology and Ethnography*, Grand Rapids, Mich.: Eerdmans.

Wright, Tom (2010), *Virtue Reborn*, London: SPCK.

Chapter 13
The Bible and Ordinary Readers

Andrew Village

> No people are uninteresting.
> Their fate is like the chronicle of planets.
> Nothing in them is not particular,
> and planet is dissimilar from planet.
>
> (From 'People' by Yevgeny Yevtushenko)

The poet Yevtushenko reminds us to be cautious with the term 'ordinary' lest we imagine it means simple, mundane or uninteresting. The term 'ordinary reader' has been current in the discourse of biblical studies for some years now, and it is easy for those who use it frequently to forget that it is easily misunderstood. 'Ordinary reading' has similar connotations to 'ordinary theology': it is a phrase designed to contrast the general with the particular. The particular in this case is the discourse of biblical studies and 'ordinary' refers to Bible reading by people who are not part of that discourse. Such people are by far the majority of Bible readers and what they do represents 'normal' reading. Biblical scholars represent a tiny minority who use the Bible in an extraordinary and peculiar manner.

Ordinary readers of the Bible may be *extra*ordinary in many ways. They may be highly educated and articulate, profoundly spiritual, live in the depths of poverty or rank among the most famous and powerful people on earth. They may be ordained ministers or people who rarely attend church. What makes them ordinary readers is that they interact with the Bible in ways that are not driven primarily by the concerns of the academic community. They would not call themselves 'ordinary readers', for this is a term coined by the scholarly community.

Some decades ago that community began to realize that their discipline was becoming so specialized that it was in danger of losing connection with its roots in the faith communities who use the Bible as their sacred text. For some this represented the triumph of criticality over dogma, and much contemporary biblical scholarship is driven by the same Enlightenment principles that inspired the rise of 'higher-criticism' in the eighteenth and nineteenth centuries. For others, however, 'real' readers have become an increasingly important object of study.

The shift in biblical studies from historical to literary and then to reader-centred criticism has been well documented and need not be recounted here. Biblical scholarship has gone through a protracted internal debate about hermeneutical method over the past half century or more.[1] For most scholars, interest in 'real' readers has meant interest in real *scholarly* readers. Even ideological approaches such as liberationist or feminist interpretation, which focus on what it means to read the Bible in particular 'social locations', are mainly an internal debate within the scholarly community (see, for example, Segovia and Tolbert, 1995a, 1995b; or Kitzberger, 1999). A few biblical scholars have managed to listen to real *ordinary* readers but, as with theologians, they have had to turn to the methods of other disciplines to do so.

In this chapter I will examine some of the ways in which scholars from various disciplines are trying to understand ordinary readers of the Bible. The field can roughly be divided into those who come from a biblical studies background and those who come from a social science background. In terms of approach, the majority use qualitative methods and a few, such as myself, use quantitative methods.

'Reading With' Ordinary Readers: Socially Engaged Scholars in Africa

The term 'reading with' was coined by Gerald West and Musa Dube (1996), who edited a seminal volume of the journal *Semeia* that reported the work of African biblical scholars working with ordinary readers. The expression 'reading with' points to the way that these scholars engage with poor and politically marginalized readers in South Africa and elsewhere. This follows the earlier work of people such as Carlos Mesters (1991) in South America, and is engagement that intends social transformation. There is strong awareness of the unequal distribution of power between scholarly and ordinary readers, and an explicit effort to ensure that this power is not abused. This is not disinterested engagement, and scholars offer themselves to ordinary readers on the understanding that both are shaped by the interaction.

This work has now been going on for over two decades, and while it has found a niche among the mainstream of biblical scholarship (West, 2007: 1), it remains primarily an exercise in enabling community change. The growing body of published work sheds light on the way in which the context of ordinary readers feeds into their understanding of particular biblical texts. A good example is the work of the Institute for the Study of the Bible among the women of Amawoti, a township in KwaZulu-Natal (Sibeko and Haddad, 1997). The institute facilitated a group of women who read Mark 5:21–6:1, the stories of Jarius' daughter and the woman with a haemorrhage. These women were members of an African Independent Church, where the laying on of hands for prayer and healing was a key part of their church life. However, menstruating women were taboo and could not receive this ministry. These women focused entirely on the woman

[1] Anthony Thiselton (1980, 1992, 2009) has done more than anyone else to document these changes.

in the passage, strongly identifying with her and noting the way that she broke taboo to obtain her healing. These unnamed, ordinary readers bonded with an unnamed, ordinary character in the narrative and this reading opened possibilities of challenging the status quo.

Through the Eyes of Another: Intercultural Reading of the Bible

This project began in the Netherlands through a joint initiative between the Uniting Protestant Churches and the Free University of Amsterdam in the late 1990s. It was intended as an exercise in both ecumenism and empirical hermeneutics. The aim was to get ordinary Bible readers from different contexts to read the same passage (the Samaritan woman at the well in John 4) and enter into a conversation. The project was a major undertaking, involving 120 reading groups from over 25 countries. Groups first read the story and discussed it in their particular context. Texts of these discussions were then exchanged across cultures, and groups then read the passage in the light of the other group's comments. Finally, groups responded to this interaction. Around half the groups completed the entire process.

Like the South African studies, this was also a bringing together of scholars and ordinary readers in an attempt to promote change: in this case, specifically, a greater intercultural understanding. However, the main report on the project suggests a slightly more detached approach that included room for research on 'empirical hermeneutics' (Wit, 2004: 41). The method is qualitative, with the 3000 or more pages of text resulting from the exercise being transcribed and then analysed using hundreds of different codes. The researchers drew on 'grounded theory' (Bryant and Charmaz, 2007; Glaser and Strauss, 1967), a method whereby analysis and interpretation of data go hand-in-hand so that key constructs emerge from the data, rather than being imposed upon it *a priori*.

The project has created a global network of readers from many nations (under the auspices of the Intercultural Bible Network) and rich narrative descriptions of how different readers engage with a particular passage. Using a single text has limitations, but it does allow very different groups to be compared. To date the analyses have tended to show what might have been guessed: cultures varied in how they understood the story, and western readers found it harder to apply the passage than those from the southern hemisphere. However, this ongoing study represents a major attempt to understand ordinary Bible readers across the globe, and doubtless more nuanced findings will continue to emerge.

Observing Ordinary Readers: Ethnographic Studies in North America

A number of researchers from the United States have studied ordinary readers of the Bible from the perspective of cultural, social or political locations. An abiding interest has been conservative Protestant churches, for whom the Bible is both the central source of authority and the shibboleth that gives them identity as 'Bible believing' Christians (Ammerman, 1987; Bielo, 2009; Boone, 1989; Malley, 2004; Watt, 2002). These studies use the methods of anthropology, ethnography or social science to observe and analyse congregations or Bible study groups. A common aim is to understand the role of the Bible as cultural icon, and how it is related to attitudes, beliefs and behaviours that are more widely linked to political conservatism. There is less interest in how the Bible is interpreted, and certainly less sense of intervening to change readers. The methods to date have mainly been qualitative, using interviews and observation (detached or participant).

Brian Malley's (2004) study of 'Creekside Baptist Church' makes the Bible the central interest as he seeks to understand how it operates within this particular congregation. He uses his observations to propose a model of 'American evangelical Biblicism', claiming that for these readers hermeneutical activity is mainly about aligning the biblical text with the central beliefs of the tradition: 'The maintenance of transitivity between the Bible and a set of beliefs is the core of the interpretative tradition' (ibid.: 145–6). Evangelicals, he argues, are constantly seeking the relevance of the text, but this often requires a certain amount of hermeneutical freedom, which threatens the integrity of the tradition. Literalism is thus the 'norm' which restricts freedom, but it may be modified as necessary in the service of relevance.[2] The way in which ordinary readers strive to connect what they read with how they live their lives has been noted in other ethnographic studies (e.g., Bielo, 2009), and is perhaps a key feature that distinguishes 'ordinary' from 'scholarly' readings.

The Bible and Lay People: Quantitative Studies of Ordinary Readers

My work on ordinary Bible readers has been within the British tradition of empirical theology, which has tended to use the quantitative methods of the social and psychological sciences. The intention is to try and understand ordinary reading, rather than to engage with and change ordinary readers. This more detached approach has its detractors, not least from socially engaged theologians (Malan, 2010), but in common with ordinary theology it recognizes that it is all too easy for scholars to rush in and 'help' ordinary readers, and more difficult to observe and learn from them. The use of quantitative rather than qualitative methods is unusual (if not unique) and stems partly from my particular background in the natural sciences, and partly from the belief that quantitative methods offer a useful means of analysing, rather than simply describing, ordinary reading.

The Bible and Lay People project (Village, 2007) was a study of 404 Anglicans from 11 churches in England from 1999 to 2001. They completed a questionnaire that included a test passage (the exorcism of a boy in Mk 9:14–29) and a number of instruments designed to measure beliefs about the Bible, biblical literalism,

2 James Barr (1981) made much the same point some years ago.

horizon separation, horizon preference, and interpretative styles. In addition, the questionnaire gathered information about participants such as their social background and psychological profile. The congregations sampled came from Anglo-Catholic, broad church and evangelical traditions within the Church of England, and it soon became clear that even within this one denomination there was considerable variation in how individuals understood and interpreted the Bible. The rest of this chapter examines three key aspects of the study.

Biblical scholars have developed a multitude of interests in the Bible, with increasing specialization in the content and method of study. The text has been worked and reworked to reveal its sources, forms, redaction, literary structures, implicit ideologies and theological messages. To some extent, what counts as 'interesting' or a 'valid' method of reading depends on what the text is understood to be. Is it multi-sourced Ancient Near East writing, the product of a sophisticated writer, the embodiment of a patriarchy or a window into the nature of God? Ordinary readers may share some of these interests, but mostly they do not. When Gerald West looked for an 'ordinary reader' to act as a respondent to a collection of scholarly engagements with ordinary readers, he could not find one: they were not that interested in what scholars do (West, 2007). The Bible and Lay People project worked mainly from the perspective of ordinary readers to investigate those things that seemed important to them. Some of these, such as biblical literalism, were things that scholars had long left behind, and which they consider to be uninteresting if not rather vulgar. However, for many of the lay people I spoke to at the start of the project, literalism was a key issue and one that preoccupied them. The project also included concepts that scholars are familiar with, such as interpretative 'horizons' (Thiselton, 1980, 1992), but which may be less familiar to ordinary readers. The following represent some key parameters that shape ordinary reading.

Bible Beliefs: Liberalism and Conservatism

A key predictor of how ordinary readers engage with the Bible is what they believe *about* the Bible. For many the Bible is not simply a source of theology, it is a theological object in its own right. It is the *Holy* Bible and may shape attitudes, beliefs and behaviours, even if it is rarely read and often misunderstood. Indeed, many ordinary 'readers' are in fact ordinary 'hearers', who know the Bible exclusively through hearing it read as part of collective worship.[3] The Bible and

[3] Several surveys of national populations have indicated that while Bible ownership may be common, the number of people who read the Bible frequently is much lower (for example, see Phillips, 2011). Among churchgoers, Bible reading is more frequent, especially among Protestant congregations, but in some countries less than a third of churchgoers read the Bible by themselves (see, for example, the surveys reported by the Catholic Biblical Federation website at http://www.c-b-f.org/start.php?CONTID=09_06_00&LANG=en [accessed 6 September 2012]).

Lay People questionnaire included a 12-item scale designed to assess liberal versus conservative beliefs about the Bible (Village, 2005a, 2007). Conservative belief holds the Bible to be the word of God: authoritative in all matters of faith and conduct, uniquely inspired, infallible or inerrant, and offering exclusive insight into the divine nature and will. Liberal belief holds the Bible to be important, but not necessarily authoritative in all matters, containing a mixture of literal and symbolic truth, some human errors, and offering truth about God that stands alongside that offered by other religions. Ordinary readers in the Church of England hold these views to a greater or lesser extent, and the scale allowed individuals to be scored on a single dimension of liberal versus conservative belief.

Biblical conservatism was, as expected, more prevalent among evangelicals than among Anglo-Catholics, with people from broad churches lying somewhere between the two. There were no correlations with sex or age, but a slight decline in conservatism with increasing levels of education. The more detailed analysis made possible by quantification showed that among evangelicals greater conservatism was associated with more frequent attendance at church and more frequent Bible reading, whereas among Anglo-Catholics this was not so. This highlights that the encounter of ordinary readers with the Bible can vary even within a single denomination: some Anglo-Catholics may read scripture regularly as part of their daily office, but this does not necessarily mean that they hold conservative beliefs about it. Other traditions encounter scripture through hearing it read on Sunday, in Bible study groups and during personal 'quiet times'. Among these traditions, more frequent reading is associated with more conservative beliefs about the Bible (Village, 2007: 46), implying that belief and practice go hand-in-hand.

Biblical Literalism

Literalism is strongly linked to biblical conservatism, but represents a distinct interpretative approach to scripture. I have used a 10-item scale to assess literalism, rather than the more general statements frequently used in surveys in the United States (Village, 2005b, 2007, 2012). This asks if events are fictional stories or if they actually happened, and examples ranged from Jonah to the raising of Lazarus. Some people object that the distinction is too crude, but experience suggests that for many ordinary readers this is not a strange or inappropriate question, even if it is difficult to answer. Judgements about literalism are not straightforward for all readers. A surprisingly high number agreed that most of the ten events had happened, but endorsement was highest for events carrying doctrinal weight (such as the virgin birth, which 81% agreed actually happened), and lowest for Old Testament 'mythic' accounts (such as Adam and Eve in the garden of Eden, which 47% agreed actually happened). Evangelicals were much more likely to think that events definitely happened, but this was not unthinking literalism. Alongside the literalism scale were items that referred to the parables of Jesus: evangelicals were much more likely than others to be firm about parables being stories, rather than actual events (Village, 2007: 66).

Literalism among Church of England ordinary readers seemed to be shaped mainly by two independent forces: education and tradition. For evangelicals, literalism was high, and was not related to levels of education. Even those with degrees in science maintained the historical nature of seemingly impossible events. For evangelicals, literalism is not about ignorance, it is a very explicit choice made because of particular views about the status of the Bible and the nature of God's interaction with the world. For other traditions, literalism declined with increasing levels of education, and education may encourage readers to find others ways of interpreting such accounts. The quantification of literalism in this way enables us to see more clearly than before the important role it has for many ordinary readers.

Biblical Horizons: Author, Text and Reader

The notion of interpretive horizons was made famous by the philosopher Hans-Georg Gadamer (1960) and for biblical studies by Anthony Thiselton (1980, 1992). The metaphor reminds us of the gap that exists between our world and that which gave rise to the biblical texts. Gadamer pointed out that once a text is produced it may be interpreted by different people at different times, each with their own understanding which is limited by their particular cultural horizon. A similar, but slightly different, notion is that of Paul Ricoeur (1981) who referred to textual 'worlds' associated with different horizons: the historical world of the author ('behind' the text), the imaginary world created by the text ('in' the text), and the world of the contemporary reader ('in front of' the text).

These different horizons are familiar to scholars, but what about ordinary readers? I was interested to know if (a) they noticed the gap, and (b) whether they preferred particular horizons, and why. Measuring this is not easy. I used the test passage, and created a 'horizon separation' scale that measured how strange or alien the story seemed to readers. They were then offered interpretations of 'what the passage tells us', with options located in the worlds of the author, the text or the contemporary reader (Village, 2007: ch. 5; forthcoming).

In general, readers in the study tended to 'fuse' rather than 'separate' horizons: that is, the exorcism story seemed familiar, recalling people who are 'just like us' and things going on that 'I could imagine happening today'. This is rather striking, given that exorcisms are not a regular feature of worship in most Church of England congregations. Most people had read the story before, but those who had not done so scored higher on separation, suggesting that familiarity with a passage may inure ordinary readers to the 'strangeness' of the biblical world. Not surprisingly, people who accepted the possibility of supernatural healing, who took the Bible literally or were part of a church healing team were all more likely to find this story 'familiar'. For ordinary readers, beliefs, experience and practice make the world of the Bible part of their world.

Horizon preferences were shaped by a range of factors, but, as might be expected, the world of the author (the traditional horizon of biblical scholarship) was not as popular as the worlds 'in' or 'in front of' the text. Evangelicals were particularly uninterested in the world of the author but, in all traditions, those with more education were slightly more likely to recognize that the passage might tell us something about that world. The striking difference was the way that those with little education were much more likely than those with higher degrees to prefer interpretations that related to what disciples should do today. The reluctance for the more educated to apply this sort of New Testament story to their lives links to the findings of the Intercultural Bible Network mentioned earlier, which found that western readers struggled to apply John 4 to their lives. Education in the West clearly has a profound influence on ordinary readers and ordinary theology. This influence is not uniform across Bible readers, but is related to other factors, notably church tradition. Follow-up work on horizon with Anglican clergy has also shown that psychological profile can shape horizon preferences (Village, forthcoming).

Conclusions

The study of ordinary readers is in its infancy, and is developing along a number of quite distinct lines. Some scholars engage with the explicit purpose of promoting change, while others take a more detached stance. These are different approaches with different aims and should not be confused, as some have (Malan, 2010). The tools used to understand ordinary readers also vary, and include constructs linked to liberation theology, anthropology, ethnography, social science and psychology. Most scholars employ qualitative studies, but these are enhanced by some of the quantitative methods reported briefly here. The field looks set to develop rapidly in the coming years.

References

Ammerman, Nancy T. (1987), *Bible Believers*, New Brunswick, NJ: Rutgers University Press.

Barr, James (1981), *Fundamentalism*, London: SCM Press.

Bielo, James S. (2009), *Words Upon the Word: An Ethnography of Evangelical Group Bible Study*, New York: New York University Press.

Boone, Kathleen C. (1989), *The Bible Tells Them So: The Discourse of Protestant Fundamentalism*, Albany, NY: State University of New York Press.

Bryant, Antony and Kathy Charmaz (2007), *The SAGE Handbook of Grounded Theory*, Los Angeles and London: SAGE.

Gadamer, Hans-Georg (1960), *Truth and Method* (English translation, 1979), London: Sheed and Ward.

Glaser, Barney G. and Anselm L. Strauss (1967), *The Discovery of Grounded Theory: Strategies for Qualitative Research*, Hawthorne, NY: Aldine de Gruyter.

Kitzberger, Ingrid Rosa (ed.) (1999), *The Personal Voice in Biblical Interpretation*, London and New York: Routledge.

Malan, Gert J. (2010), 'Can the Chasms be Bridged? Different Approaches to Bible Reading', *HTS Teologiese Studies/Theological Studies*, 66, 1: article #404, 10 pages.

Malley, Brian (2004), *How the Bible Works: An Anthropological Study of Evangelical Biblicism*, Walnut Creek, Calif.: AltaMira.

Mesters, Carlos (1991), '"Listening to What the Spirit is Saying to the Churches": Popular Interpretation of the Bible in Brazil', in W. Beuken, S. Freyne and A. Weiler (eds), *The Bible and its Readers*, London: SCM Press, pp. 100–111.

Phillips, Peter (2011), 'The CODEC Research Project', *Epworth Review*, 38, 2: 60–71.

Ricoeur, Paul (1981), *Hermeneutics and the Human Sciences: Essays on Language, Action and Interpretation*, Cambridge: Cambridge University Press.

Segovia, Fernando F. and Mary Ann Tolbert (eds) (1995a), *Reading from this Place, Volume 1: Social Location and Biblical Interpretation in the United States*, Minneapolis, Minn.: Fortress.

Segovia, Fernando F. and Mary Ann Tolbert (eds) (1995b), *Reading from this Place, Volume 2: Social Location and Biblical Interpretation in Global Perspective*, Minneapolis, Minn.: Fortress.

Sibeko, Malika and Beverley Haddad (1997), 'Reading the Bible "With" Women in Poor and Marginalized Communities in South Africa', *Semeia*, 78, 1: 83–92.

Thiselton, Anthony C. (1980), *The Two Horizons*. Exeter: Paternoster.

Thiselton, Anthony C. (1992), *New Horizons in Hermeneutics*, London: HarperCollins.

Thiselton, Anthony C. (2009), *Hermeneutics: An Introduction*, Grand Rapids, Mich.: Eerdmans.

Village, Andrew (2005a), 'Assessing Belief about the Bible: A Study among Anglican Laity', *Review of Religious Research*, 46, 3: 243–254.

Village, Andrew (2005b), 'Factors Shaping Biblical Literalism: A Study Among Anglican Laity', *Journal of Beliefs and Values*, 26, 1: 29–38.

Village, Andrew (2007), *The Bible and Lay People: An Empirical Approach to Ordinary Hermeneutics*, Aldershot and Burlington, Vt.: Ashgate.

Village, Andrew (2012), 'Biblical Literalism: A Test of the Compensatory Schema Hypothesis Among Anglicans in England', *Review of Religious Research*, 54, 2: 175–196.

Village, Andrew (forthcoming), 'Biblical Interpretative Horizons and Anglican Readers: An Empirical Enquiry', in C. Amos (ed.), *Anglican Approaches to the Bible*, Norwich: Canterbury Press.

Watt, David Harrington (2002), *Bible-Carrying Christians: Conservative Protestants and Social Power*, Oxford: Oxford University Press.

West, Gerald O. (2007), 'Reading Other-Wise: Socially Engaged Biblical Scholars Reading with their Local Communities: An Introduction', in G.O. West (ed.),

Reading Other-Wise: Socially Engaged Biblical Scholars Reading with their Local Communities, Atlanta, Ga.: Society of Biblical Literature, pp. 1–5.

West, Gerald O. and Musa W. Dube (eds) (1996), *"Reading With": An Exploration of the Interface between Critical and Ordinary Readings of The Bible. African Overtures* (*Semeia*, Vol. 73), Atlanta, Ga.: Scholars Press.

Wit, Hans de (2004), *Through the Eyes of Another: Intercultural Reading of the Bible*, Elkhart, Ind.: Institute of Mennonite Studies.

Chapter 14
How Far is it to Bethlehem? Exploring the Ordinary Theology of Occasional Churchgoers

David Walker

Introduction

Occasional Churchgoing

Behind the surface statistics showing that the number of people attending Church of England services each Sunday has been in decline over many decades, there lies a complex story. As lifestyles change, the pattern of a settled parish worshipping community, found in its local church on almost every Sunday of the year, is less the norm. Among this heterogeneous population some still have a habit of reasonably frequent churchgoing, but less than weekly. Others focus their experience of public worship on a monthly Family Service or All Age Worship, or make a commitment to a fresh expression of church as identified and promoted in the influential book *Mission-Shaped Church* (Archbishops' Council, 2004). That book takes as a central theme that there is a major shift in current British society, in which people experience belonging less through communities of geographical propinquity and more by their membership of communities of interest: more succinctly, a shift from neighbourhoods to networks. While this reconceptualization of church belonging still looks primarily at those who are engaged frequently and habitually with church activity, it raises the question as to what other ways are possible of imagining church belonging and whether other forms of it are more capable of capturing the experience and engagement of occasional churchgoers. In seeking to address this question, the prior issue arises as to how occasional constitutes occasional? While a variety of answers are possible, the consensus within the field of congregational studies is to identify this as comprising those who report their attendance as less than six times a year.

Belonging Through Events

In a study of 1,450 individuals who attended rural harvest festival services, Walker (2006) set out a fourfold model of belonging: activities, events, people and places. This model takes as its starting point the understanding of belonging as self-defined religious affiliation, following the definition of Francis and Robbins (2004), rather than collapsing it into either doctrinal affirmation or participation in specified activities. Each of these modes of belonging is given a brief theological grounding and a characterization in terms of how different individuals may adopt this mode for their engagement with the church. For the purposes of this present study, it is the dimension of belonging through an event (the cathedral carol service) that provides the lens through which the engagement of occasional churchgoers is to be studied. Walker writes:

> The notion of expressing religious belonging through events is evident in the various covenant makings of ancient Israel as well as in the rites for circumcision, purification of women, and cleansing of lepers. Baptism lies to the fore as the main event based expression of religious affiliation in the early church. The notion of affirming religious identity at a variety of rites of passage builds on this over successive centuries. (Walker 2006: 91)

The key distinction between a church activity and an event is that the former carries some explicit or implicit expectation on the part of the individual attendees, others present or the church leadership, that attendance on one occasion creates a commitment or obligation for future occasions. By contrast, an event stands alone; while the individual may attend a similar event, no wider contract is imputed or implied. Part of what avoids the creation of such obligations may be that, even if an event is held regularly, it is held only very infrequently. Although at one level it is arbitrary, the conceptualization of occasional churchgoing as being less than six times a year fits well here, as it is plausible that this is a frequency at which it becomes less likely that a sense of obligation will arise (see, for example, Francis and Richter, 2007). The Christmas carol service occurs too infrequently for such expectations to arise and hence falls into the category of event, where it might be anticipated that a significant number of those who attend church only occasionally would be present.

Cathedral Studies

Recent Church of England statistics indicate an average growth in attendance at the 43 English cathedrals of 37% over a 10-year period (Archbishops' Council, 2011). This context of substantial growth makes it plausible that cathedrals may be attracting significant numbers of individuals who are not regular churchgoers. As well as shedding light on occasional churchgoers in general, studying them in a cathedral setting is therefore likely to provide insights to support the cathedral in the ministry and mission it has among them.

The Cathedral Carol Service

The cathedral carol services studied in this essay took place on two evenings in Worcester in December 2009, and on one afternoon and one evening in Lichfield in December 2010. The worship followed the pattern established since the first half of the twentieth century: congregational participation was limited to singing a small number of hymns, while the remainder of the service comprised the reading of traditional biblical passages and the performance of a range of carols, dating from the medieval to the present day, by a semi-professional cathedral choir.

The carol service is far from the only example of an 'event', on Walker's classification, to be held in the cathedral. For the purposes of study, however, it offers a number of advantages:

- It provides an opportunity to explore the ordinary theology of those present in relation to the Christmas story and their attitudes, beliefs and practices with respect to Christmas within a wider enquiry;
- It is an open and widely advertised event, to which large numbers turn up, offering a potentially more varied and representative sample than would be the case with an event focused on a school, university or commercial organization, a diocesan occasion such as an ordination service, or a personal event like a wedding or funeral;
- The popularity of the service and the absence of ticketing means that the majority of those attending are seated about 30 minutes before the service begins, affording a good opportunity to gather a significant body of data.

A general discussion of the whole sample can be found in Walker (2012).

Research Question

Against this background, the research question addressed by this study was to describe the ordinary theology of occasional churchgoers attending the cathedral carol services: their understanding and beliefs about Christmas and the Christmas story, their motivations for being present at the service, their wider attitudes towards significant or contemporary issues of Christian doctrine, their moral stance and their attitudes towards the place of the Christian religion in public life.

Method

Procedure

Some 1,151 participants completed a questionnaire distributed at the point of arrival at the *Service of Nine Lessons and Carols* in Worcester or Lichfield

Cathedrals. Pencils were provided and completed questionnaires collected after the service was over. The survey forms were anonymous and confidential. From this sample, the responses of the 460 individuals who were categorized as occasional churchgoers were extracted for analysis.

Measures

Respondents were asked about gender and age (measured largely in decades, but starting at 15 and with a final category for '80 and over'). Frequency of church attendance was assessed by a choice of six responses: once a week or more, nearly every week, at least once a month, at least six times a year, at least once a year, never. The remainder of the survey invited participants to respond using a five-point Likert scale: agree strongly, agree, not certain, disagree, disagree strongly. For each statement the percentages of those agreeing and those agreeing strongly were added to produce a single percentage for agreement. Those who chose not to answer a particular question were excluded from the calculation. The response rates for individual questions were almost all above 90%.

Participants

The sample contained 44% men and 56% women. There was a good level of familiarity with the concept of a carol service, with 70% claiming to attend one somewhere most years and almost half (46%) claiming to do so in that cathedral.

By comparison with most surveys of churchgoers, the present sample includes a much higher proportion of younger people; some 30% were below the age of 40, 41% between 40 and 59, and just 29% were aged 60 and above. The figures in the same age categories for a sample of 322 adults from two rural cathedral Sunday morning congregations, reported by Francis and Williams (2010), were 12%, 27% and 61% respectively.

Notwithstanding the low levels of churchgoing, this was a population with a significant Christian background: four out of every five (81%) had been baptized, over half of whom (42% of the sample) had also been confirmed – most of them (as implied from their ages) in an era when confirmation for cultural reasons, or as an expected rite of passage, had died out. Very few (only 8%) were currently on a Church of England Electoral Roll, a good measure of an individual's ongoing commitment. Three fifths (59%) agreed with the statement, 'I go to church less often nowadays.' These are people who would often be categorized and studied as 'church leavers' (see, for example, Francis and Richter, 2007). A few were potentially on a return path, with 8% agreeing with the statement that they go to church more often nowadays.

For a significant minority, relationships would appear to be an important dimension of faith, with some 30% agreeing that most of their friends were Christians, over a quarter (26%) having a friend with whom they could talk about faith, and the same proportion claiming to pray at least once a week. By contrast, virtually none of them (1%) said that they read the Bible at least once a week.

Despite the low levels of churchgoing, a little over half (52%) defined themselves as Church of England and a further 12% as a member of another Christian denomination, almost two thirds in total. Nearly one in five (19%) claimed to belong to the cathedral congregation itself.

Results and Discussion

The responses to the questions asked in the survey fell into six sections. In the first section respondents were invited to reflect on their motivations for attending the service, in order to understand whether they saw it in purely cultural and aesthetic terms, or were bringing significant religious and spiritual expectations with them. The nature of these expectations was then explored through a second set of questions which tested the way in which the respondents sought to engage with the service.

Moving the focus from the service itself, the third section turned to the Christmas story as a means of beginning an investigation into the ordinary theology of the participants as regards the Bible and Christian doctrine. This exploration was widened in the following section, where more general questions of Christian belief were asked. This twofold approach allowed a focus on the event at which the survey took place, anticipating that participants would find it easier to offer views in this context than they would in response to more general questions.

The remaining two sections took this study in ordinary theology into the wider fields of moral behaviour and the public face of religion. In each case a number of questions were used exploring issues that are or have recently been matters of public debate in Britain. This allowed some investigation of the ways in which the participants' faith affected their attitudes. The same questions offered insight into the extent to which they expect society to hold a place for faith, and faith institutions to be subject to the consensus of public morality.

Reflecting on Attending the Carol Service

Cathedral carol services are noted for the very high level of choral performance; hence it was not surprising that some 94% cited the music as one of their reasons for attending. As the service was designated 'lessons and carols', it is not surprising that three quarters (75%) were present to be reminded of the Christmas story. This should confirm to those planning such occasions that what is being offered fits with the wishes of those attending. Three other statements explored more overtly religious aspirations for attendance; in each case over half expressed agreement: 'I have come to feel close to God' (55%), 'to worship God' (55%), 'to find the true meaning of Christmas' (52%). It was a slightly more general question with an implicit spiritual element, however, that gained the highest level of support, with

94% of the occasional churchgoers present agreeing that the service should be uplifting. Taken together, the responses to these questions suggest that the finding of meaning, the possibility of encounter and the significance of public worship are important concepts within the ordinary theology of many of these occasional churchgoers; and that this theology is worth more detailed analysis.

Reflecting on the Carol Service Experience

Responses to four statements about elements of the carol service were then invited. The two statements where agreement indicated a preference for a traditional view, 'I prefer traditional hymns to modern ones' and 'I prefer carol services to be candlelit', gained significantly higher levels of assent (76% and 78% respectively) than did two that suggested support for a modern idiom, where less than half (45%) expressed a preference for the use of modern English in carol services and very few indeed (11%) agreed that they preferred modern carols to traditional ones. It is possible that these responses might be conveying nostalgia for a time when these occasional churchgoers had been more involved in church life, as we have seen to be the case for many of them. This was tested by offering the statement, 'carol services are not as good as they used to be'; that only 8% expressed agreement with this opinion statement is a good indicator that nostalgia is not a significant factor for many.

The remaining statements in this section explored ways in which the service might engage the attendees, producing what at first may appear to be conflicting answers. Three quarters (75%) agreed that 'I like carol services that get the congregation involved', while little more than a third (36%) affirmed that 'I like carol services that make me ask questions of myself.' Taken together with the statements investigated in the previous section, however, these suggest that the occasional churchgoers are not seeking to be passive recipients of entertainment but to be engaged in the occasion, and to be engaged at a level that is better described as 'opening up to being affected by the experience', rather than being challenged over theological or other beliefs.

Reflecting on the Christmas Story

Several statements sought to gauge responses to individual elements of the Christmas story. Levels of support were highly consistent, with belief in the stable (58%), shepherds (57%) and wise men (55%) being all a little over the halfway mark. Given the sample's lack of engagement with scripture, it is not surprising that there was no significant difference between belief in these elements and the entirely non-biblical donkey (52%). However, a second set of belief statements that more obviously required respondents to consider the possible theological import of their answers received levels of agreement well below the halfway point: such as the virgin birth (42%), the Bible's prediction of Jesus' birth (43%) and the existence of angels (34%). Invited to consider the statement that the biblical account is not literally true, almost half (47%) agreed and over three fifths (62%) agreed that the Christmas mystery is more important than the historical facts.

These responses build up a consistent picture of a group of people who want to enter into the story, rather than to assent to any particular theological import. As the previous sections suggest, this is not a refusal to engage with the story as a matter of significance in their lives; rather it expresses a clear preference for mystery over history.

Reflecting on Christian Belief

The light-touch stance taken by the sample with regard to Christian doctrine came across clearly in their responses to statements about Christian beliefs: the more specific a belief, the less likely was it that the sample agreed with it. So while two thirds (67%) agreed that 'I consider myself a Christian', this dropped to a little over half (55%) who agreed that 'I believe in God'. The level of agreement fell to two fifths (40%) for the belief that Jesus was 'fully human', less than a third (31%) for the statement that he was 'fully God', while fewer than a quarter (23%) agreed that he was 'fully God and fully human'. The numbers make clear that some didn't agree with any of these last three statements. Consistent with the negligible level of Bible reading reported, the lowest figures for Christian belief came in the responses to statements focused on the literal truth of scripture: only 22% agreed that Jesus turned water into wine, one in seven (14%) that God made the world in six days and rested on the seventh, one in twenty (5%) that the Bible is without error.

With this attitude to doctrine, it is not surprising that very few (13%) believed Christianity to be the only true religion and a majority (53%) believed that Christians should not try to convert people, while almost half (48%) agreed that 'all world faiths lead to God'. The ordinary theology of these occasional churchgoers places pluralism above dogma.

Reflecting on Moral Issues and Concerns

Respondents were offered one fairly general statement of attitude and one of personal practice, followed by two that focused on currently contentious issues. With regard to the first, when offered the statement that 'what you believe matters less than how you live your life', a clear majority (58%) agreed. Almost three quarters of the sample (71%) claimed to give to charity most Christmases. Compared with the relative low significance placed on doctrine, the answers to these two questions suggest that the respondents recognized an important ethical dimension to faith.

The remaining questions focused on homosexuality, in particular the two areas where this is contentious in Church of England circles. Invited to agree that it should be possible for a gay man to be made a bishop and that homosexual couples should be allowed to marry, there was support around or above the halfway mark in both cases (55% and 50% respectively). This suggests that the official negative stance of the church to both issues holds less sway in the theology of occasional churchgoers than does the wider moral climate. If anything, the slightly higher figure of support for a gay man as a bishop than for same-sex marriages indicates that the participants do not see the church as exempt from the normal ethical standards of society (for more detail see Walker, forthcoming).

Reflecting on Public Religion

The final area of study explored the attitudes of the sample to the visibility and public face of religion. This, too, has been contested in Britain in recent years, with challenges from secularist organizations and atheists on topics ranging from church schools, through prayers at council meetings, to the very use of the word 'Christmas' to describe a public holiday.

Notwithstanding the strongly pluralist view taken by participants, when asked directly whether 'Christianity should have a special place in this country' almost two thirds (63%) agreed. Nearly three fifths agreed with the principle of church schools (58%), while only a third (35%) thought that 'Christianity and politics don't mix.' Faith clearly has a place in the public realm for most of these individuals. Once attention was turned to Christmas itself the responses became overwhelming; only 1% thought that Christmas should not be a public holiday and just 6% believed that all shops should be allowed to open on Christmas Day.

Conclusions

This survey has made it possible to construct a picture of what the Christian faith looks like among a population cut adrift from the ties and influences of regular churchgoing. In particular, it has put the spotlight on those who attend church at Christmas at a type of service that is still extremely well attended, from village church to cathedral. Rather than faith collapsing into a combination of sentiment, culture and aesthetics, it retains for many a significant religious content from which can be constructed a picture of the ordinary theology of the participants.

Within this theology a high expectation is placed on the possibility of encounter with God through participation in the style of worship offered at a carol service; the high return rate to the service suggests that their past experience supports that expectation. The attraction and positive experience of carol service worship may owe much to the fact that the Christmas story is heard there as a narrative gateway to the mystery of God, rather than as coded doctrine; and it would seem that there is a real intention on the part of the occasional churchgoers present to enter through that gateway, rather than passively to observe what is going on beyond it.

The faith engendered and supported by this encounter has been shown to be centred on doing rather than dogma. However, this is not a theology of a privatized religion; indeed, levels of private piety were quite low and Bible reading almost non-existent. Moreover, the consequence of a strong belief in pluralism is not the ejection of religion from the public realm, but a clear view that faith is a public phenomenon with a right to its place in public life, and that society needs to acknowledge it in the ordering of business, politics and education. At the same time, the values of wider society are clearly visible in the attitudes of the majority of the sample when reflecting on matters of church order. The arrow of influence in their understanding of public religion goes both ways.

Allowing the voices of this group of occasional churchgoers to be heard through their responses to the present survey permits a picture of their ordinary theology to be painted. Attention to this theology should enable those planning church worship, including carol services, to consider the needs and expectations of the occasional churchgoers who attend them, and to determine to what extent their hopes and aspirations are to be met – or challenged. Furthermore, this description of ordinary theology supports the notion that an important dimension of Christian belonging is mediated and expressed through attendance at one-off events rather than habitual and frequent Sunday worship, and suggests that further study of this type of belonging would be profitable.

References

Archbishops' Council (2004), *Mission-Shaped Church*, London: Church House Publishing.

Archbishops' Council (2011), *Church of England Cathedrals: Headline Mission Statistics 2010*, http://www.churchofengland.org/media/1243690/cathedralattendances2000to2010.pdf [accessed 23 April 2012].

Francis, L.J. and P. Richter (2007), *Gone for Good? Church-Leaving and Returning in the 21st Century*, Peterborough: Epworth.

Francis, L.J. and M. Robbins (2004), 'Belonging without Believing: A Study in the Social Significance of Anglican Identity and Implicit Religion among 13–15-Year-Old Males', *Implicit Religion*, 7: 37–54.

Francis, L.J. and E. Williams (2010), 'Not all Cathedral Congregations Look Alike: Two Case Studies in Rural England', *Rural Theology*, 8, 1: 37–50.

Walker, D.S. (2006), 'Belonging to Rural Church and Society: Theological and Religious Perspectives', *Rural Theology*, 4, 2: 85–97.

Walker, D.S. (2012), 'Attending the Service of Nine Lessons and Carols at a Rural Cathedral: An Empirical Study in Religious Orientation and Motivational Style', *Rural Theology*, 10, 1: 56–69.

Walker, D.S. (forthcoming), 'The Association between Homonegativity and Religious Orientation: An Empirical Enquiry Among Those Attending an Anglican Cathedral Carol Service'.

Chapter 15
Ordinary Prayer and the Activity of God: Reading a Cathedral Prayer Board

Tania ap Siôn

Introduction

A number of empirical studies have examined the beliefs of ordinary theologians in relation to central Christian doctrines, through interviews with churchgoers. A complementary tradition of empirical studies has also sought to gain insight into the beliefs of ordinary theologians, both churched and unchurched, through content analyses of personal intercessory prayer requests left in church or chapel-related settings in England (Brown and Burton, 2007; Burton, 2009, 2010; ap Siôn, 2007, 2008, 2009, 2010, 2011, 2012; ap Siôn and Edwards, 2012a, 2012b; Hancocks and Lardner, 2007), the USA (Cadge and Daglian, 2008; Grossoehme, 1996; Grossoehme et al., 2011; Grossoehme et al., 2010) and Germany (Lee, 2009; Schmied, 2002). Qualitative data of this type has enabled relatively large, broadly based groups to be surveyed within the contexts of church, hospital, shrine and website, where both churchgoers and non-churchgoers used open-access intercessory prayer facilities.

Unlike other empirical methodologies that may be employed to examine beliefs of ordinary theologians, analyses of prayer requests are distinctive insofar as the prayer authors generate data from within natural contexts without intervention on the part of the researcher. This means that when prayer authors engage in personal prayer (understood as communication between the individual and God, rather than as a corporate activity) they provide glimpses into a range of theological assumptions that underpin and shape their prayer requests, without externally prompted reflection on these belief processes.

However, whichever methodology is employed in the study of ordinary theology, there is often a common concern that the research is relevant for 'those who are engaged in Christian communication, pastoral care and worship [who] need to know about the beliefs of those in their care, and their patterns and modes of thinking and believing' (Christie and Astley, 2009: 178) and that this should influence their practice.

The aim of the present study is to focus on one specific theological theme and examine how ordinary theologians perceive God's activity in the world through an analysis of over 1,000 personal intercessory prayer requests left in a cathedral in Wales, using an analytical framework devised and tested for this purpose (ap Siôn, 2011).

Method

Sample

Bangor Cathedral is situated in a central location on the High Street of the City of Bangor, in the northern part of this Anglican diocese. Within the Cathedral's Lady Chapel visitors were offered the opportunity to pause, reflect and pray. Explicit prayer aids included a statue of the Virgin Mary with a single prayer desk, a candle and flowers, suggestions in English for introductory prayer stems or content (such as 'Lord, I am troubled …' and 'Give me wisdom …'), and the text of the 'Hail Mary' prayer in Latin, Welsh and English. To one side of the statue, a prayer board was positioned on which 'pray-ers' (i.e., the prayer authors) were able to attach their written prayers. For this purpose, blank paper was provided of varying sizes. The present study is based on a random selection of 1,000 prayer cards which were left on the prayer board between 2005 and 2009.

Analysis

Of the 1,000 prayer cards analysed, 915 cards were concerned either wholly or in part with intercessory and supplicatory prayer forms (92%), and were written in either the English or Welsh language. Prayer cards excluded from the study were 20 other-language prayer cards, 51 prayer cards for thanksgiving alone, five prayer cards for confession or repentance alone, three prayer cards for adoration alone, one prayer card for confession and adoration, and five unintelligible prayer cards. Within these 915 prayer cards, there were 1,143 individual requests, which were analysed using a conceptual framework for intercessory and supplicatory prayer devised by ap Siôn (2011) to explore pray-ers' perceptions of the activity of God. It is these 1,143 individual requests that form the basis of the following study.

The conceptual framework used in the analysis distinguished between three elements defined as prayer intention, prayer reference and prayer objective (ap Siôn, 2011). *Prayer intention* distinguished between nine views of God drawn from God's perceived activity in the world, and are styled as: gift-bestower, confidant/e, intervener, protector, intermediary, revealer, strength-giver, helper (general) and comforter. *Prayer reference* distinguished between four key foci with which the individual authors were concerned: themselves, people known personally to the author, animals known personally to the author, and a world or global context. *Prayer objective* distinguished between two effects that the individual authors envisaged as a consequence of their prayers: primary control and secondary control. In primary control, prayer authors explicitly suggest the desired consequences of their prayers. In secondary control, prayer authors place prayers and their consequences entirely in the hands of another. Alongside this conceptual framework, each prayer request was also placed into one of eleven subject categories, derived from previous analyses of prayer requests by ap Siôn (2007, 2009), which are styled as health and illness, death, affective or spiritual growth, relationships, conflict or disaster, work, travel, housing, sport, open intention and miscellaneous. This enabled the various activities of God categories and the eleven prayer subject categories to be cross-tabulated in order to provide a fuller picture of how God's activity in the world was presented by prayer authors.

Results

Within the 1,143 individual prayer requests, there were 1,234 examples of prayer request content that fell in the nine intention categories describing God's activity in terms of gift-bestower, confidant/e, intervener, protector, intermediary, revealer, strength-giver, helper (general) and comforter.[1] The frequency of prayer requests appearing in these intention categories and their relationships with prayer reference and prayer objective are displayed in Table 15.1 below.

The relationship between the various activities of God and the 11 prayer subject categories is described in the exemplification. The exemplification focuses on aspects of prayer content most relevant to the question of how ordinary theologians understand the nature and activity of God.

Set within the context of ordinary theology, prayer authors showed various degrees of familiarity with Christian beliefs and forms of expression, ranging from those who employed explicitly religious language in prayer with confidence to those who included no explicitly religious elements at all in their prayer requests. Where the addressees of prayer requests were identified, 'God' or 'Lord' featured most frequently; but groups of prayers were also addressed to Mary, Jesus or 'Father', and individual prayers were addressed to 'Master', 'Divine Spirit', 'Great Spirit', Light, St Anthony and St Luke, among others. A number of prayers were addressed to those in the Cathedral offering intercessory prayers on their behalf.

Gift-bestower

God was recognized as 'gift-bestower' in 219 requests (18%). Although a quarter of requests in this category made only general reference to 'gifts', the majority was associated with specific contexts, which included concern for those who had died, spiritual and affective growth, health and illness, conflict and disaster, relationships, work, travel and housing. The most common request in both general and specific contexts was for 'blessing', most often for family or friends but also

[1] The last three categories (representing 8%, 10% and 1% of the requests, respectively) are not discussed here.

Table 15.1 Content of intercessory and supplicatory prayer by prayer intention, reference and objective

	Prayer reference and prayer objective										
	Other people		**Global**		**Self**		**Animals**		***Total***		**TOTAL**
	pc	sc	pc	sc	pc	sc	pc	sc	*pc*	*sc*	
Prayer intention											
Gift-bestower	150	0	40	0	29	0	0	0	*219*	*0*	**219**
Protector	163	0	17	0	13	0	6	0	*199*	*0*	**199**
Confidant/e	96	42	5	1	32	6	1	1	*134*	*50*	**184**
Revealer	82	1	36	4	38	2	1	0	*157*	*7*	**164**
Intermediary	78	18	15	0	28	2	5	1	*126*	*21*	**147**
Helper (general)	85	0	9	0	22	0	3	0	*119*	*0*	**119**
Intervener	64	0	25	0	12	0	1	0	*102*	*0*	**102**
Strength-giver	62	0	5	0	25	0	1	0	*93*	*0*	**93**
Comforter	5	0	1	0	1	0	0	0	*7*	*0*	**7**
Total	785	61	153	5	200	10	18	2	*1156*	*78*	**1234**
TOTAL	**846**		**158**		**210**		**20**		***1234***		**1234**

Note: pc = primary control; sc = secondary control.

for world settings, for the prayer authors themselves, and for those offering the intercessory prayer in the cathedral on their behalf. The importance of having or receiving such blessings and 'gifts' was particularly significant in prayer requests for 'world' concerns, where a quarter of all the prayer requests included this element.

Where specific types of gift were included in the prayers, authors cited 'peace', 'serenity', 'love', 'happiness', 'contentment', 'gift of cooperation', 'gift of mercy' and 'hope'. Occasionally, the source and nature of the gifts were explicitly linked to God, which is illustrated by the request for 'your [God's] love and peace'. Included in this category was a small group of prayers that requested the religious gifts of God's presence, the Holy Spirit and 'Grace'.

The prayer authors presented the blessings or specific gifts in three ways. First, most often the gifts were perceived as required but currently lacking, appropriate to request, and – if God were willing – able to be granted (for example, 'grant us peace' and 'please give me hope'). In some requests, the certainty that God was able to bestow these gifts was shown by language that asked God to 'allow' or to 'let' their bestowal (for example, 'let' a person be 'happy' or have 'peace'). In other requests, the image of 'sending' blessings or specified gifts such as 'happiness' was used (for example, 'Send a blessing …' and 'Send your love …'). Second, some prayer authors recognized the gifts as a present reality in people's lives, and asked either for the gifts to remain with them or for the presence of the gifts to be recognized (for example, in relation to the former, the wedding anniversary request for 'our continued blessings' and the request for God 'to remain with me'; while in relation to the latter, the prayer for individuals to 'know your blessing at this time' and the prayer to 'help them to recognize your presence in all things'). Third, some prayer authors suggested that people play an active role in acquiring gifts by praying that they or others 'find' peace, happiness or contentment (for example, 'pray for me to find peace').

Protector

God was recognized as 'protector' in 199 prayer requests (16%). Over a third of requests in this category made only general reference to 'protection', while others were associated with specific contexts of health and illness, the death of loved ones, affective and spiritual growth, relationships, conflict or disaster, work, travel and housing. 'Protection' was the activity of God most frequently requested for family and friends and animals, and it was considerably less significant in prayers for the prayer authors themselves and for world situations.

Expressions used to describe this activity of God included 'protect', 'look after', 'keep safe', 'take care of', 'watch over', 'keep' and 'guard'; the images used included being lifted up on God's shoulders, being safe in God's arms or hands, and God laying the hand of protection on someone. Some prayers did not specify the reason why protection was required, although many cited a concrete situation (for example, an ill person, soldier/s in war zones, the safe birth of a baby or safe travel), and others expressed the need for protection in less tangible terms, some of which were explicitly religious (for example, from evil, the devil, danger or themselves; and for protection from anything perceived to threaten the current situation of happiness, safety and security). Prayers falling into this category presented God's role as protector in terms of 'warding off' the undesirable and also 'sustaining' those for whom prayer was offered. Usually the prayers focused only on the need for protection, but some prayers understood protection as part of a broader picture of the activity of God and human beings (for example, 'Please keep my son safe as he drives around in his first car. Please give him wisdom and care for other road users').

Confidant/e

God was recognized as 'confidant/e' in 184 prayer requests (15%). Nearly two-thirds of the requests in this category were situated in contexts related to illness, death of loved ones and relationships, while the remaining requests were either not contextualized or related to affective and spiritual growth, work, housing, conflict or disaster, and travel. 'Confidant/e' (alongside 'revealer') was the most frequently accessed activity of God in requests made for the prayer authors themselves, as well as an important feature in prayers for family and friends, while it was considerably less significant in prayers for world contexts and animals. God acting as 'confidant/e' was found in the discursive affective content of prayers, and was present in three forms: an articulation of emotions in relation to the recipient of prayer, reflection on the person or situation for which the prayer was offered, and a personal statement of the prayer author's own wishes or hopes in relation to the request (rather than a direct request). This aspect of prayer requests may illustrate belief in a God who takes a personal interest in the thoughts and feelings of people, and that these in some sense matter to God and may influence the outcome of the prayer (either in relation to God directly, or to the intercessors and how they present the prayer).

Revealer

God was recognized as 'revealer' in 164 prayer requests (13%). Over two-thirds of requests in this category were concerned with affective or spiritual growth, while the other requests, if they were placed in a context, were related to illness, relationships, work, death of loved ones, conflict or disaster, travel and housing. 'Revelation' was the most frequently requested activity of God in prayers for the prayer authors themselves (alongside confidant/e) and for world contexts (alongside gift-bestower), while it was considerably less significant in prayer requests for animals and family and friends.

God's activity as 'revealer' was present in three forms. First, a number of prayer requests referred to religious truths or qualities: for example, requests for knowledge of God and God's will, faith or growth in faith; revelation of God's love, wisdom and peace; and 'release from the bond of self' so that 'thy will be done' (a form of salvific revelation). In addition, there were a number of global requests for the return of Christ to the world and for a 'fresh anointing of your Holy Spirit and a revival again to come to Wales'. There were questions that related to theodicy, such as why do some people suffer more than others and how will God 'save' on Judgement Day. Frequent requests were made for God's presence to be felt (usually expressed with the general term to 'be with'), and for God to guide through providing a 'sign'. 'Light' was a particularly frequent image used both to address God and as an attribute to be requested (for example, requests to 'keep lighting the path we walk', for help in seeing the 'light' and an expressed desire to be touched by God's 'light'). This 'light' was variously described as 'eternal' and 'perfect', and related to 'God', 'Spirit' and 'Christ'. In a few examples, revelations took the form of proclamations, where the prayer author proclaimed a religious, spiritual or moral 'truth'.

Second, a number of prayer requests referred to spiritual, moral or emotional guidance or support: for example, guidance when embarking on a new path or direction in life, help in understanding 'loss', help in being 'a better person' or in learning how to 'forgive' or to say 'sorry', and help in being 'kind … and looking after others'.

Third, a number of prayer requests referred to guidance in concrete situations: for example, help in guiding a missing cat home, guidance through illness, difficult times and in purchasing a house, and recognition of the 'truth' so that families and friends could be reconciled.

These prayer requests illustrate belief in a God who reveals Godself in a number of ways to groups of people as well as to individuals. This revealing often relates to religious, spiritual and moral guidance, but it is also concerned with practical, everyday issues. In many cases the revealing is understood in terms of God's presence.

Intermediary

God was recognized as 'intermediary' in 147 prayer requests (12%). Nearly four-fifths of requests in this category were concerned with relationships and the death of loved ones; while the other requests, when placed in context, were related to disaster, illness, work, affective or spiritual growth, and housing. 'Intermediary' was a frequently requested activity of God in prayers for the prayer authors themselves, family and friends, animals and world contexts.

These requests are concerned with the activity of God in human relationships (and occasionally pets). They included requests that sought to establish, re-establish or maintain relationships in various contexts; to invoke God (or another) to 'pass on' or 'tell' information to others (such as feelings or messages, for example); or to address and communicate with others directly. The prayers encompassed relationships among the living, relationships among the living and the dead, and relationships among the dead.

These requests illustrated belief in a God who is concerned about and actively involved in human relationships, which includes both the living and the dead. Many of the prayers attested to belief in an afterlife, often depicted as 'heaven' and 'being with God'; and God's role was perceived as significant in ensuring that loved ones were kept 'safe' and 'watched over', and had 'peace'. Occasionally, reference was made to alternative beliefs concerning life after death: for example, the request for the spirit of a child to move with the family from their old home into their new home.

In a number of cases, the intercessory prayer request was used as a medium to convey messages directly to others, without any religious references included.

Intervener

God was explicitly recognized as 'intervener' in only 102 prayer requests (8%). Over two-thirds of requests in this category were concerned with illness; while the other requests, if they were placed in a context, were related to conflict or disaster, relationships, sport, death, affective or spiritual growth, work and housing. 'Intervener' was the most frequently requested activity of God in prayers for world situations, although it was also present in prayers for the prayer authors themselves, friends and family, and animals.

These prayers requested miraculous activity on the part of God, Jesus or a saint. In a few requests the significance and efficacy of those praying on their behalf was noted. The requests were expressed in three ways. First, there was a direct request for intervention, such as 'Make him walk again', 'Pray that it rains', 'Let Stoke win the league next season', 'Find me a job that I enjoy', 'Free the slaves.' Sometimes, these requests were accompanied by expressions of faith in God's ability to intervene, such as 'for you nothing is impossible' and 'the hospital cannot do anymore for him, but we know Father can.' Second, in some examples reference was made to God's successful interventions in the past and God was invoked to continue to act in the present: for example, after giving thanks for healing one request asked 'Father' to 'continue please to make her fully fit and well', and another asked for the continuation of prayers on behalf of named people in hospital after reporting miraculous activity resulting from earlier petitions. Third, in some examples the requests for physical intervention were placed within a broader divine plan. For example, some requests referred to the need for prayers to be considered in light of 'God's will' and that ultimately 'God's will be done'; one request asked for doctors to resolve treatment issues but 'with your [God's] overruling'; and one request asked for miraculous healings as a sign so that the affected will 'recognize your [God's] presence in all things'.

Common images used in these types of prayer were references to laying 'your healing hands' on a person or on their affected part, and for God to 'touch' them.

Conclusion

From this analysis five conclusions may be drawn.

First, the analysis illustrates belief in a God who is perceived to be actively involved in human concerns (both at an individual level and at a wider group or global level), and who is able to respond positively to the largely affective needs of the prayer authors as illustrated by the focus on requests for non-material gifts, protection, revelation, strength, comfort and communication. Many of the contexts in which the requests for God's action were set related to crises and situations over which the authors could exercise little personal control (for example, illness, death, global conflict or disaster) as well as everyday concerns (for example, relationships, housing, travel and work). However, there were substantial differences among prayer authors concerning the way in which they presented God's action, ranging from requests presented without any explicitly sacred terminology to the very 'religious' presentation of requests that employed Christian concepts and language with confidence, at times located within a broader appreciation of God's will or plan. Differences were again evident in the portrayal of the relationship between God and human beings in relation to how God acts in the world. For example, the language used in many prayer requests focused on the agency of God alone in responding to the request, although a substantial minority appeared to suggest that both God and humans had complementary roles to play, while other prayer authors were prepared to act on receipt of a 'sign' or other such prompt from God, which would make God's will known.

Second, compared with requests for affective help, surprisingly few prayer requests (8%) asked God to intervene directly in the material world (that is, miraculously); although it is recognized that some of the unspecified requests for 'help' (10%) may also fall into this category. Differences emerged in the prayer requests as to how this intervention was conceived by the prayer authors. For example, most of the prayer authors requested God to intervene miraculously in response to individual cases of need, but a minority of prayer authors understood intervention as necessary for bringing about a new order of some kind and, for some, a miracle would act as God's 'sign' to the world. Occasionally, being a witness to miracles provided the basis for new requests for miracles. As with requests for affective help, the language used by the prayer authors ranged from being without any explicitly religious terminology to very 'religious'.

Third, differences were observed among the prayer authors in relation to the prayers' addressees, which included God, Jesus, the Holy Spirit, Great Spirit, Light, a saint (often Mary), the Cathedral community, or an individual who may be living or dead, among others. This reflects the presence of different theological positions in relation to how or through whom prayer may be offered (e.g., one prayer author cited scripture to explain that he or she could not pray to Mary, as Jesus was the only mediator). It was often unclear whether references to the Great Spirit or Light were Christian in any conventional sense.

Fourth, many prayer authors understood God's activity as not being limited to this world or this life, but used language which suggested belief in a continuum of God's sustaining care which extended from this life into an afterlife, often described as heaven or 'being with God'. This was an area of real concern for the prayer authors. A particularly striking use of intercessory prayer was to ensure that relationships and communications with loved ones were continued both in this life and in an afterlife.

Fifth, the analysis highlights the challenge for the church to respond to the different needs of the ordinary theologians who make use of its personal intercessory prayer facilities, and these include both the churched and the unchurched. Informing a response to this challenge, the present study has identified the main concerns of the prayer authors and the wide variety of ways in which the authors understand the nature of God's activity in the world, and God's relationship with human beings and the physical world.

References

ap Siôn, Tania (2007), 'Listening to Prayers: An Analysis of Prayers Left in a Country Church in Rural England', *Archiv für Religionspsychologie*, 29: 199–226.

ap Siôn, Tania (2008), 'Distinguishing between Intention, Reference, and Objective in an Analysis of Prayer Requests for Health and Well-being: Eavesdropping from the Rural Vestry', *Mental Health, Religion and Culture*, 11: 53–65.

ap Siôn, Tania (2009), 'Ordinary Prayer and the Rural Church: An Empirical Study of Prayer Cards', *Rural Theology*, 7: 17–31.

ap Siôn, Tania (2010), 'Implicit Religion and Ordinary Prayer', *Implicit Religion*, 13: 275–94.

ap Siôn, Tania (2011), 'Interpreting God's Activity in the Public Square: Accessing the Ordinary Theology of Personal Prayer', in Leslie J. Francis and Hans-Georg Ziebertz (eds), *The Public Significance of Religion*, Leiden: Brill, pp. 315–42.

ap Siôn, Tania (2012), 'Coping through Prayer: An Empirical Study in Implicit Religion concerning Prayers for Children in Hospital', *Mental Health, Religion and Culture* (forthcoming).

ap Siôn, Tania and Owen Edwards (2012a), 'Praying "Online": The Ordinary Theology of Prayer Intentions Posted on the Internet', *Journal of Beliefs and Values*, 33: 95–109.

ap Siôn, Tania and Owen Edwards (2012b), 'Say One for Me: The Implicit Religion of Prayers from the Street', *Mental Health, Religion and Culture* (forthcoming).

Brown, Alec and Lewis Burton (2007), 'Learning from Prayer Requests in a Rural Church: An Exercise in Ordinary Theology', *Rural Theology*, 5: 45–52.

Burton, Lewis (2009), 'The Dear Departed: Prayers for the Dead on a Prayer Tree in a Rural English Parish Church', *Rural Theology*, 7: 83–97.

Burton, Lewis (2010), 'Prayers on a Prayer Tree: Ordinary Theology from a Tourist Village', *Rural Theology*, 8: 62–77.

Cadge, Wendy and Melanie Daglian (2008), 'Blessings, Strength, and Guidance: Prayer Frames in a Hospital Prayer Book', *Poetics*, 36: 358–73.

Christie, Ann and Jeff Astley (2009), 'Ordinary Soteriology: A Qualitative Study', in Leslie J. Francis, Mandy Robbins and Jeff Astley (eds), *Empirical Theology in Texts and Tables: Qualitative, Quantitative and Comparative Perspectives*, Leiden: Brill, pp. 177–96.

Grossoehme, Daniel H. (1996), 'Prayer Reveals Belief: Images of God from Hospital Prayers', *Journal of Pastoral Care*, 50: 33–9.

Grossoehme, Daniel H., Jeffrey Jacobson, Sian Cotton, Judith R. Ragsdale, Rhonda VanDyke and Michael Seid (2011), 'Written Prayers and Religious Coping in a Paediatric Hospital Setting', *Mental Health, Religion and Culture*, 14: 423–32.

Grossoehme, Daniel H., Rhonda VanDyke, Jeffery Jacobson, Sian Cotton, Judith R. Ragsdale and Michael Seid (2010), 'Written Prayers in a Pediatric Hospital: Linguistic Analysis', *Psychology of Religion and Spirituality*, 2, 4: 227–33.

Hancocks, Graeme and Mary Lardner (2007), 'I Say a Little Prayer for You: What Do Hospital Prayers Reveal about People's Perceptions of God?', *Journal of Health Care Chaplaincy*, 8: 29–42.

Lee, Daniel B. (2009), 'Maria of the Oak: Society and the Problem of Divine Intervention', *Sociology of Religion*, 70: 213–31.

Schmied, Gerhard (2002), 'God Images in Prayer Intention Books', *Implicit Religion*, 5: 121–6.

Chapter 16
A Tune Beyond Us, Yet Ourselves: Ordinary Worship and Ordinary Theology

Bridget Nichols

Introduction

In 1937, the American poet, Wallace Stevens, published a long poem called 'The Man with the Blue Guitar'. The poem is thought to be a response to one of Picasso's blue paintings, depicting a lone hunched guitarist. It is also a powerful meditation in its own right on creativity, aspiration, the longing to inhabit the known and the value of human existence itself in the long view of history. Here is its opening section:

> The man bent over his guitar,
> A shearsman of sorts. The day was green.
>
> They said, 'You have a blue guitar,
> You do not play things as they are.'
>
> The man replied, 'Things as they are
> Are changed upon the blue guitar.'
>
> And they said then, 'But play, you must,
> A tune beyond us, yet ourselves,
>
> A tune upon the blue guitar
> Of things exactly as they are.'
>
> (Stevens, 1990: 165)

As the dialogue changes from factual observation to demand and prescription, a conflict becomes apparent. On the side of the audience, there is the wish for a tune that is out of the ordinary, yet still comfortably in a recognizable idiom, something in which they can see and hear themselves. On the side of the guitarist, there is the knowledge that music once made is out of the musician's control. Between them is the blue guitar, the folk instrument trusted to produce familiar tunes yet somehow bringing a new and strange reality.

This configuration of musician, instrument and people is a suggestive image for another common experience of gathering for an activity that is believed to have transformational consequences, amid complex feelings of hope, longing and fear – ordinary Christian worship. By that broad term I understand the habitual rhythms and practices of those who in some way share an ecclesiastical identity and gather regularly to pray together. The level of formality might vary considerably, but there will be a shape to the gathering, and an element of repetition. Part of its attraction is its power to evoke something beyond the worshippers, while providing a familiar environment. This is what makes it what it is. It does not confine what it does.

Worship has much to do with learning languages, both verbal and non-verbal. The languages – or perhaps dialects – of worship are culturally learned. Anglicans have learned to classify church styles by listening to the way people pray. Evangelical Christians will frequently begin, 'Lord, we just want to praise/thank you for …', whereas their more restrained co-religionists normally adopt a more formal tone: 'Heavenly Father, we pray that/give you thanks for …'. Knowing what language to use is very important – this is how you show that you are at home, comfortable with the conventions. Worshippers have to become functionally literate in the church worlds they inhabit. Once they own the language, interesting things can happen as they become not only users, but interpreters and even creators. They may become articulate about how prayer makes them feel. They may appropriate, or even misappropriate, shared words in a personal way, since statements of orthodoxy will not be natural starting points. They will watch the ritual presentation of worship and take from it a meaning where no explicit explanation is offered.

This chapter contends that many illuminating challenges to the familiar might come from within ordinary worship, as participants interpret for themselves what seems to be happening.

An anecdotal approach has seemed the most truthful one to adopt and the examples that follow draw on fact, fiction and poetry. They testify to the extraordinariness of the ordinary and lead to preliminary conclusions about the nature of ordinary worship itself.

Changing Things as They Are? Three Creative Misreadings

Vera and her husband were faithful churchgoers of long standing in a suburban parish. He served on the church council. She was a pillar of one of the women's organizations. When the parish commissioned a local artist to redecorate the Lady Chapel, its sober, monochrome style was transformed by the addition of a dark blue starry ceiling and the installation of an icon of Mary holding the Christ Child. Vera found the new arrangements very conducive to prayer and reported to another parishioner that she felt 'sanctuous' when she had prayed in the Chapel. This intriguing coinage meant something wholly positive for Vera. She was sanctified, virtuous, a better person for having been in what felt to her like an unusually holy place. Others were ambivalent. They heard the traces of 'unctuous' and suspected an element of smug self-righteousness. Yet this was word-making by a woman without much education, in response to an intense experience of place and prayer. Suddenly, a place had freed her to communicate with God. We are accustomed to acclaiming God as holy, but seem to cope less easily with the idea that worshipping might have, as one of its purposes, making us holy.

Another kind of meaning-making occurred at the closing eucharist of an international conference of liturgists. The preacher quoted Gerard Manley Hopkin's sonnet, 'God's Grandeur', which celebrates a world infused with divine glory. No matter how much human beings have damaged and neglected this beauty, it is irrepressibly there:

> And for all this, nature is never spent;
> There lives the dearest freshness deep down things.
>
> (Gardner, 1981: 27)

It is clear to anyone reading the text that 'deep down things' describes a location in the profoundest and most essential part of the natural order. The preacher, however, had perhaps only ever heard the poem read aloud, because she developed a sermon on the theme of 'deep-down things' – those concerns with an enduring and universal integrity and importance that distinguished them from the superficial and trivial. Yet there is something arresting about the idea of 'deep-down things'. It may be a misquotation, but it is richly meaningful in its own right.

Again, it might be the liturgical text itself that allows itself to be creatively subverted. Few pre-teenage girls read L.M. Montgomery's *Anne of Green Gables* series any more. There will, however, be a middle-aged to elderly constituency with fond memories of the red-headed orphan adopted by an austere brother and sister on Prince Edward Island. When Anne grew up, her adoptive parents took on orphaned twins called Davey and Dora. Dora was biddable; Davy had a great propensity for error. One evening, he helped himself illicitly to the plum jam that was reserved for visitors. Fortunately for him, it was Anne who was there to deal with the offence, which she did with firm but gentle reasonableness, prompting Davy to promise never to repeat it. The following exchange then took place:

> 'Anyhow, there'll be plenty of jam in heaven, that's one comfort,' he said complacently.
>
> Anne nipped a smile in the bud.
>
> 'Perhaps there will … if we want it,' she said, 'but what makes you think so?'
>
> 'Why, it's in the catechism,' said Davy.
>
> 'Oh no, there is nothing like *that* in the catechism, Davy.'

> 'But I tell you there is,' persisted Davy. 'It was in that question Marilla taught me last Sunday. "Why should we love God?" It says, "Because He makes preserves, and redeems us." Preserves is just a holy way of saying jam.'
>
> 'I must get a drink of water,' said Anne hastily. When she came back it cost her some time and trouble to explain to Davy that a certain comma in the said catechism question made a great deal of difference to the meaning. (Montgomery, 1969: 106–7)

Seeing a better world through misunderstanding is theologically irregular, but the evidence of lively engagement with formulae that for many have long since ceased to be anything other than weary rote-learning suggests the potential that might be harnessed by good teaching, receptiveness to questions and not laughing at mistakes. In fact, what may be important in these circumstances is the very act of allowing people to get things wrong, because in the process they may discover something that is curiously right. Over-anxious correction often betrays an institutional insecurity, a need to keep people 'on message' not so much for the proper formation of their opinions and beliefs, as to protect holders of the 'correct' view from any form of challenge or exposure.

Beyond Us Yet Ourselves

Ordinary worship has a penumbra beyond the church, in the largely private devotional lives of individuals. This spectrum stretches from disciplined rigour to apparently unambitious forms of prayer. For some, that will be enough, however much the churches might wish to nurture people into more rigorous and sophisticated forms of prayer. U.A. Fanthorpe's self-ironizing poem about Patience Strong illustrates this exactly.[1] The first part describes the sentimental content and likely provenance of Strong's verse in calendars and women's magazines in condescending and disparaging terms. The second part describes a particular episode. The speaker (perhaps the poet herself) recalls assisting in an outpatients' department of a hospital as a volunteer, and taking a cup of tea to an epileptic man. His condition, he explained, had prevented him from having the career he coveted in the Ambulance Brigade. Having drunk some tea, he extracted from an inside pocket

[1] Patience Strong, a pseudonym for Winifred Emma May (1907–1990), regularly contributed sentimental poems to *The Daily Mirror* from 1935 to 1946, when her column moved to *The Sunday Mirror*. She continued to write for the paper for many years, and also published in *Woman's Own* and *This England*. Her success as a writer of popular songs is less well known.

A booklet muffled up in cellophane,
Unwrapped it gently, opened at a page –
Characteristic cottage garden, seen
Through chintzy casement windows. Underneath
Some cosy musing in the usual vein,
And See, he said, *this is what keeps me going.*

(Fanthorpe, 2010: 34–5)

Liturgical language and practice are often subject to judgements of taste. There are occasions when this is necessary because what is being offered is careless or ill-prepared or irreverent, and consequently not good enough for God. There is still room, though, to have regard and respect for the profit others find in what we might find facile or unworthy of attention. Sentimental poetry, trite worship songs or saccharine hymns come under attack often enough. The value of what is made out of these things is of a different order. Should we despair over the failure to seek more enriching wells of inspiration, or should we salute those who manage to make much of little, to live richly within their means? Is the chintz-curtained world of Patience Strong one in which people have grown and found a form of prayer in the hope of adversity, on a scale they can manage? Some may even have grown beyond this to something better, but they could not have done so without this starting point.

There is another side to the substitution of sugary and vapid forms of devotion for more rigorous approaches to prayer. Sometimes, we may recoil from a strong doctrinal claim abhorrent to the way our own faith, practice of worship and understanding of God has been formed. Hymns and songs are as likely a source of such claims as any for ordinary worshippers and deserve much more attention than I can offer here. Stuart Townend's enormously popular composition 'In Christ Alone' must stand as a single example. When this is sung at gatherings of people who do not normally worship together, it is easy to see that as the lines, 'And on that cross where Jesus died/the wrath of God was satisfied' approach, the lips of those opposed to penal substitution as an account of the atonement are not moving. Yet imposing our prejudices is nearly always premature. The hymn's theology of the cross is what keeps a great number of people going.

Ordinary worship involves forms of shared activity which do not require a foundation in perfect agreement. This is not because the divisions and disagreements do not matter, but because it is often easier to approach them when other bonds of trust and cooperation and mutual regard have been established. If you have sat beside someone in church, received communion together, helped at fundraising events and worked together in a children's work group, the exploration of belief and theological outlook will be in the context of a much denser sense of the person and certain shared commitments.

Not Ourselves? Worship and Difference

In 1985, the Church of England published a report called *Faith in the City*. It was the work of a Commission set up to establish a framework for a proper response to the situation of inner city populations in what were termed Urban Priority Areas (UPAs). The Commission's primary task was to report on the church in these areas and its response to unprecedented social changes. But the church's setting in the world was essential to the enquiry, and investigations revealed stark poverty, unemployment, poor housing and despair in cities which had once been prosperous industrial centres. The report divided its material between the challenge to the church and the challenge to the nation posed by conditions in UPAs. Worship was addressed in a sub-section called 'Developing the People of God', drawing on evidence collected by diocesan liturgical committees.

It was, however, a project of its time, and it is now impossible to imagine how some of the findings and recommendations could ever have sounded other than patronizing and out of touch.

The assertion that 'the roots of liturgy must be found in the ground of society' is not contentious. It is harder to swallow uncritically the notion that the church in its worshipping life in UPAs must be prepared 'to communicate through feeling rather than the mind, through non-verbal communication rather than verbal', though this claims to report findings in one urban diocese. The Commission recommended that worship in UPAs should 'reflect the concern of local UPA people for things to be more concrete and tangible, rather than abstract and theoretical', an aim which could be met by introducing banners and crucifixes. Worship and study, they proposed, should 'lay more emphasis on the history, the story, the narrative. Local UPA people often love to tell the stories of their lives, how God changed them, of problems overcome, and of great events and disasters.' People were to be 'encouraged to come and go' in a way unusual for those churches whose spirituality made 'prayer and worship available only to those who turn[ed] up in the right place at the right time and [went] through the correct motions corporately from start to finish'. The Commission felt that worship should embody 'good dreams' when real life was so hard for those who attended. 'UPA Christians want a beautiful service, but they may have to go home to domestic violence or a leaking roof' (Archbishop of Canterbury's Commission on Urban Priority Areas, 1985: 135–6).

There is something folkloric about all this, as though the quaint practices of a remote and recently discovered population were being self-consciously preserved by the more sophisticated and powerful group which had found them. But the powerful group appears not to have understood that what it perceived as marked cultural and sociological differences could never be so clearly separated. Why should working class status and lack of educational opportunity make inner city Christians less sensitive to language, or less able to sustain the orderly unfolding of a formal or 'traditional' act of worship? Ordinary worship for many, right across the social spectrum, has dispensed entirely with prayer books (except as collections of resources), and where words are provided they are as likely to be projected onto a screen as distributed in printed form. Worship may rely heavily on projected images. Banners are more likely to distinguish Evangelical from Catholic styles of church adornment in Church of England circles, than poor from rich. Some city churches with largely Afro-Caribbean congregations may even have acquired *more* formal habits, repatriated with the immigrants who first learned them in churches abroad (Lampard, 2009).

Why should domestic violence and leaking roofs be features only of these populations? Easy as it is to romanticize the dauntless efforts of nineteenth-century slum priests in the poorest areas of English cities like London and Portsmouth to offer elaborate worship, train choirs and run Sunday Schools and organizations for young people and adults, their efforts never condescended to the people they served (Haynes, 2011).

Things Exactly As They Are: Seeing and Believing

After you have been worshipping with a community over a period of time, you begin to realize that a great deal of what the worshippers would claim to believe, and of their understanding of their ritual practice, is derived as much from what they see as from what they say and hear. Those who lead worship should not underestimate the power of the observer to ascribe meaning to the visual, and even to actions that are in fact pragmatic and not really ritual at all. Members of a single congregation will offer different reasons for the priest's kissing the altar before commencing the eucharist. These might include reverence for the sacrament, or a way of reverently acknowledging the presence of God. It is unlikely that there will be any mention of relics, yet it is from the practice of reverencing the relics of the saints interred in altars in the earliest basilicas that this initial kiss stems.

The visual teaching promulgated by the 'establishment' may not always be consistent. Take Sunday baptisms in one English cathedral. These are conducted in front of the nave altar, and a portable font is used. The candidates are invariably infants or very small children; and parents and godparents, together with any other children in the congregation, gather on the platform with the priest performing the baptism. It has become the norm for officiants to interpolate a good deal of commentary which is explanatory in its intention, and deliberately informal and slightly jocular in style.

A great deal is made of the anointing with chrism (oil blessed by the bishop and used for baptism and confirmation in Anglican and Roman Catholic practice) after the child has been baptized. Here, two distinct models have evolved. One regular officiant invites the parents and godparents to anoint the child following his example. Another officiant makes it clear that he alone will anoint the child. In the first model, the act of baptism with water is trumped by the elaborate anointing. This produces a very different theological rationale from the second model. For the regular congregation, questions must surely arise. Why is anointing a shared action when Canon X baptizes, but a distinctive priestly act when Canon Y baptizes? Does it matter, and is there a right answer? Is baptism valid if the wrong method is applied?

It is also possible to use ritual to conceal practical transactions which might indirectly facilitate the liturgy, but have no part in it. The Rector of one parish suffered from a dry throat and kept a supply of throat lozenges in his pocket. He would suck one during the offertory procession while the congregation was singing a hymn, and be in good voice to begin the eucharistic prayer. There were times when he felt in his pocket and discovered that he had not replenished the stock. On those mornings, he would signal to a member of the choir, who had a preference for the same brand of lozenges. As the collection plate passed the choir stalls, she would drop two lozenges into it. There would be a slight silence, noticeable only to those who were aware that consumption had been delayed, before the normal pattern resumed. Such resourcefulness is not irreverent. In fact, a great deal of solemn liturgical behaviour – processing, bowing, vergers directing people into particular seats – is formalized to give ordinary necessities like moving from one place to another a certain dignity. This must be carefully judged. Elaborate ritual is in proportion in a cathedral, but in a small church or a school hall, it can look pompous and absurd. Worship needs to be set in the scale of its surroundings. That in itself is a kind of ordinariness, in the sense of being 'ordinary for us'.

Changed Upon the Blue Guitar

Kenneth Stevenson wrote at the time of the great period of revision in Church of England liturgy of the 'soft points' in the eucharist. By this, he meant those moments which are particularly susceptible to inflation and elaboration in a way that sometimes obscures the clear progress of a rite, dominates simpler celebrations, and generally gives excessive emphasis to elements of worship which are not as important as the performance might suggest. He points to three instances of actions which hardly require words at all – the entrance into the church, the preparation of the gifts, the fraction, distribution of communion and dismissal – but which have steadily acquired accompanying words through the course of history (Stevenson, 1991: 29).

There is room to recapture that term, but with a different meaning. Might 'soft points' not also be those opportunities within a rite or any structured form of worship for a kind of escape, for the fabric to become translucent or a crack to open up in the structure, allowing worshippers just for a short time to escape beyond it? This might not be completely predictable. For some, the effect of hearing a passage of scripture read in the context of worship will be a sudden personal summons, or a new way of seeing the world. For others, the words of a prayer, or a particular hymn sung at a strategic point will open a window onto a theological meaning which has never opened before.

Some might argue that the whole principle of 'common prayer' which has informed the practice of the Protestant churches in the development of their service books might seem rather against transcendence. There is a way of praying that makes us recognizable to each other, and which forms us because it is consistent in shape and outline and in the regular repetition of a number of greetings, prayers and statements of belief. We talk of the 'ordinary' of the mass or the eucharist – the elements repeated at every celebration: the *sursum corda*, *sanctus*, *benedictus* and *agnus dei*.

Yet, unsystematic though it must necessarily be, the evidence is that there are points where ordinary worship becomes transcendent. Ordinary worship is about engagement in a process, about the abandonment of self, yet also about a level of intellectual and emotional reflection in which the selves we receive back may be changed. It does not part company with theological models and paradigms which have been helpfully applied to the interpretation of worship (the heavenly banquet and the wedding feast of the Lamb in the case of the eucharist, the hallowing of time in the case of the daily offices). But instead of beginning with an externally imposed model, 'a tune beyond us', we might profitably begin where we are and move towards these interpretations of our practice, gathering language, vision and confidence sufficient for this en route.

A 'blue guitar' kind of worship, therefore, begins with worshipping people, and not with models of what worship means. It attends to their questions, uncertainties, hopes and longings, and it offers them a tune in which they can recognize themselves yet also encounter something infinitely greater. It lets them misunderstand, on the wager that sometimes a more glorious understanding will result. What it does not do, is return them to themselves unchanged. Things as they are/Are changed upon the blue guitar.

References

Archbishop of Canterbury's Commission on Urban Priority Areas (1985), *Faith in the City*, London: Church House Publishing.

Fanthorpe, U.A. (2010), *New and Collected Poems*, London: Enitharmon Press.

Gardner, W.H. (ed.) (1981), *Gerard Manley Hopkins: Poems and Prose*, Harmondsworth: Penguin.

Haynes, Catherine (2011), 'Liturgy and Mission Among Children in Late Victorian Anglican Ritualism', *Anaphor*a, 5, 2: 1–19.

Lampard, John (2009), 'The Empire Strikes Back: The Impact of Ghanaian Methodism on Methodist Worship in London', *Anaphora*, 3, 2: 23–38.

Montgomery, L.M. (1969), *Anne of Avonlea*, London: George Harrap & Co.

Stevens, Wallace (1990), *The Collected Poems*, New York: Vintage.

Stevenson, Kenneth (1991), 'Soft Points in the Eucharist', in Michael Perham (ed.), *Liturgy for a New Century*, London: SPCK, pp. 29–43.

Chapter 17

A Study in Ordinary Theological Ethics: Thinking about Eating

Matthew Barton and Rachel Muers

The study of ethics is often assumed to be the study of what ought to be done – and the study of Christian ethics to be the study of what 'Christianity' says ought to be done. Despite a concerted effort by Christian theologians and ethicists in recent years to critique dilemma-focused approaches to ethical reasoning (Cunningham, 2008; Hauerwas and Wells, 2004), it is probably still fair to say that (for example) students beginning courses on ethics expect to learn about contrasting and conflicting responses to the question of what ought to be done in specific 'problem' situations.[1] If they are studying religious ethics, they expect to investigate and critique accounts, derived from sources recognized as authoritative within specific religious traditions, of what ought to be done.

As Linda Woodhead and others have noted (Woodhead, 2001; see the discussion in Muers, 2007), this model of theological ethics assumes and reinforces an authoritarian – and patriarchal – pattern of communication that is theologically as well as ethically problematic; the voice of the ethicist tends to become the commanding voice from above, passing on instruction to the uninformed hearers. This model also tends to misrepresent, or to ignore, the everyday practical reasoning undertaken by ordinary Christians, and the complex ways in which Christianity is interpreted and reinterpreted in their lives. The rise, noted above, of accounts of Christian ethics based on the core community-forming practices of Christianity, and on virtues learned through membership of Christian communities, goes some way to redress these problems. However, there is still in this work a tendency to idealize Christian practical reasoning, and in particular to assume that the church community gathered in worship forms the primary context for nurturing and challenging Christians as practical reasoners.[2] We would argue that in order to do justice to the 'extensity' of Christian life (Hardy, 2001: 109–12) – the fact that the church is gathered from people who live out their Christian lives in numerous other communities – more attention needs to be paid to the particularity and diversity of ordinary Christians' practical reasoning. It may be especially

[1] Mathewes (2010) is one recent textbook that makes a very good attempt at bridging the gap.

[2] Note, for example, the way in which the influential collection edited by Hauerwas and Wells (2004) is structured around eucharistic liturgy.

illuminating, for the critique and extension of existing theological ethics, to focus on those areas where numerous ordinary Christians find themselves, on the basis of what they understand to be Christian reasoning and practice, at odds with the assumed positions and settled practices of their church communities – and find themselves, also, unable to engage in sustained dialogue with these communities.

In this chapter we present and summarize some of the results of a small-scale study of the ordinary ethical reasoning, and relationships to church communities, of Christians who are vegetarians. The study points to three conclusions that are of importance for future work in ordinary theological ethics. First, Christian vegetarians without explicit training in theology and ethics engage in complex scripturally and traditionally informed ethical reasoning about their practice, producing a significant although largely undocumented body of reflection. Secondly, Christian vegetarians' action and reflection often places them in an uneasy relationship with the church communities in which they worship, and in which we might, on standard models of Christian ethics, expect them to find their primary sources of norms and patterns of action. Thirdly, Christian vegetarians do often find Christian 'communities of character' (Hauerwas, 1981) within which they can explore and develop their ordinary theological ethics, but these communities are not part of recognized church structures and do not conform to the paradigm of the local congregation.

Ordinary Christian Vegetarians

The initial reason for talking, and listening, to ordinary Christian vegetarians was to consider how ordinary vegetarian theology related to, and differed from, its academic counterpart. The interviews conducted did not disappoint on this account, but they did surprise: a surprise that stemmed at least partly from the interviewer's presumption that ordinary theological reasoning would be substantially different from that conducted in the academy. Explicitly contextual (Astley, 2002: 60) and relatively unsophisticated (47) it may be, but conscious and complex engagement with scripture and tradition was evidenced by all 12 interviewees;[3] and often the

[3] Because the population to be studied is so small, a self-selection approach was used to obtain the sample. Christian vegetarians were approached who had already identified themselves as such, through membership of organizations such as Christian Vegetarian Association UK (CVAUK), the Anglican Society for the Welfare of Animals (ASWA) and Catholic Concern for Animals (CCA). In addition, an open call was put out on online Christian message boards such as the Student Christian Movement (SCM) forum and Ship of Fools, and on online vegetarian message boards such as *veggieboards*. Potential respondents provided a statement of their faith and dietary practices before entering into conversation. The interviews were semi-structured, focusing on faith, theology, diet, ethics and relationships within Christian communities, and lasted roughly one hour.

end product was closer to academic formulations than critics of doing ordinary theology might suspect.

That communities of belief and practice, in the process of forming the character of their members, engage in serious and complex moral reasoning is not a fresh revelation within academic theology and philosophy. Alasdair MacIntyre described casuistry, the process of communal ethical reflection, as a 'kind of tradition-constituted, craft-constituted enquiry' (MacIntyre, 1990: 81); and Stanley Hauerwas makes frequent reference to the vital place of scripturally based casuistry in the life of the church as a 'community of character' (Hauerwas, 2003: 116–34). In theory, then, it has long been known that ordinary theologians engage in complex ethical reasoning, informed by scripture and tradition, with significant and important output. In practice, however, this is not always so readily admitted: that scholars wishing to engage with ordinary theological ethics feel the need to defend their methodology (e.g. Astley, 2002: 125–45; Scharen and Vigen, 2011: 47–74) is evidence of this. Studies such as these conversations with ordinary Christian vegetarians serve to support the argument for the strength of ordinary theological ethics.

Kevin, a middle-aged Anglican and member of ASWA, was representative of the ordinary Christian vegetarians spoken with, in that he expounded a personal theology drawing on scripture and tradition, and demonstrated serious ethical reasoning.

> *Matthew*: What would you say is central to your vegetarianism?
>
> *Kevin*: I would say a love of God, and the world he has made, and the sort of creatures he has brought into being, um, through love of God love and respect for them …
>
> *Kevin's written statement*: My basic feeling and belief is that all life is 'good' and has value in the eyes of God, and the 'dominion' we have been given as human beings implies a duty of care. Lordship and authority, in the light of Jesus the Servant-King, is seen to be characterised by service rather than exploitation. My guiding principles, therefore, are that I should play my part in caring for Creation, only take life where it is necessary for health or survival, and work to minimise suffering.

Kevin's testimony concerning his connection between faith and diet displays both the learning context within which his Christian character was formed, and how the process of embracing his faith involved understanding and internalizing it in a way which was meaningful – and therefore salvific – for him (cf. Astley, 2002: chs 1 and 2). For Kevin, this meant that the learned concepts of the love of God, the goodness of creation and the significance of Jesus-as-servant could not be limited in their theological and ethical significance only to the human element of creation. His dietary practice, directly impacting upon creation and individual creatures, is informed by his tradition-constituted enquiry.

Helena, an Anglican in her twenties, demonstrated a similar process of transmission from learned faith to theological praxis in her placement of stewardship – defined as compassionate care for creation – at the centre of her ethical reasoning. 'Animals are a part of God's creation and we're stewards of that creation and so we need to care about all of it, not just a little bit. I think that's part – you know, I think that's part and parcel of being a Christian is being compassionate on all creation.' Drawing on Genesis 1, and depicting stewardship in a manner analogous to some academic proponents of Christian vegetarianism (Linzey, 1994; Northcott, 1996; Bauckham, 2010),[4] it is difficult to contest that Helena employs scripture, tradition and reason in working through the ethical problems that she recognizes in the ways humans relate to non-human animals. George, a middle-aged Catholic and member of CCA, showed parallel scripture-rooted ordinary theological reasoning when he described vegetarianism as an eschatological practice: 'a choice for the kingdom rather than worldly ways'.

Alison, a Baptist with Mennonite heritage,[5] did not solely draw on her learning context when reflecting on dietary matters; she consciously criticized her tradition, and in dialectical fashion spoke of her intent to move from this criticism to a praxis that better embodied what she had been taught.

> I've always admired the Mennonites I was raised amongst, many of my relatives are of a more conservative sect who are very obviously removed from mainstream life, and the strong commitment to pacifism. I have been confused, however, about the pacifist disconnect when it comes to animals and food. I really appreciated your emphasis on this point and the encouragement it gives me to rebrand my background into something that fits me better today.

Note that Alison was thankful for the chance to discuss her ordinary theology in more detail, and was encouraged by it to 'rebrand' her theological inheritance. Upon perceiving a 'disconnect' between Mennonite theology and Mennonite dietary practice, Alison wants to engage with the problem casuistically, moving towards a more holistic living out of her pacifist beliefs.

In the conversations with Kevin, Helena, George and Alison we hear the product of scripturally and traditionally informed ethical reasoning. These ordinary theologians recognize their learning context and engage casuistically with it, striving for an embodied praxis with regards to diet, and in so doing embracing

[4] Gen 1:26 (NRSV): 'Then God said, "Let us make humankind in our image, according to our likeness; and let them have dominion over the fish of the sea, and over the birds of the air, and over the cattle, and over all the wild animals of the earth, and over every creeping thing that creeps upon the earth."'

[5] In her thirties, Alison hails from the American south, but currently lives and works in London.

the faith they have been taught. Some, like Alison, recognize what they see as disconnects between faith as they have been taught it – the ecclesial theology they inherited – and the lived practice of their faith community, and want to work in their ordinary theological reasoning to bridge the gaps. In living, practising and reasoning differently from their community at large, however, do ordinary Christian vegetarians run the risk of marginalizing themselves at a local level? And if they do, what does this say about community-centred accounts of Christian ethics, which privilege the role of communal casuistry as theologically important?

Ordinary Heretics?

As mentioned in the introduction to this chapter, community-centred approaches to Christian ethical reasoning, currently academically popular, are seen by some as a corrective to the 'top-down' dilemma-based understanding of ethics still commonly taught to students in further and higher education. In setting out this approach, Hauerwas stresses the role of the church as the formation of truthful Christian characters (Hauerwas, 1981: 115), and argues that situational responses cannot be adequately formulated in advance (Hauerwas, 2003: 123–5). Embodied ethical reasoning is, therefore, key to the Hauerwasian framework (Hauerwas, 2003: 119–21). Concerns remain, however, that the idealization of the church as casuistical community of character may further marginalize and silence those members of church communities whose theological and ethical reasoning sets them at odds with those who first taught them faith. Alison, reflecting on how to 'rebrand' her Mennonite heritage, is one such example. The series of interviews sheds light on the tensions and conflicts faced by other 'ordinary heretics'.

Ingrid, an older Baptist woman who shares Hauerwas' emphasis on casuistry in community, recently stopped attending her local church as a result of feeling that neither holistic casuistry nor respect for one's fellows were being practised.

> [The church is] incredibly important, because as we know what happens to a piece of coal that is left on its own rather than together with the other pieces of coal, and forsaking the assembling of ourselves together in the manner of some is, it's very important …
>
> You know I never made an issue in Christian circles 'cause I know where those guys are coming from, so you know never sort of bonding together with others, seeing if we could change something. I once suggested that we could have for Sunday lunch spaghetti bolognese made with soya. Oh my goodness! That was my only venture into … how can you have this as a Sunday meal? You know, and then you would need to have different food for different people, um, now how can you – you need to have roast on Sunday, of course! But nut roast was not considered as an alternative either, you know …

The rejection of soya bolognese as an option for the communal lunch may seem, at an academic level, a minor issue. Such a presumption, however, would only emphasize the need for a more nuanced understanding of community-centred ethical reasoning: in the everyday life of real churches, such issues can have significant and potentially destructive impact.

Communities which do not seriously engage in ethical discussion with members who have well-developed ordinary theological accounts of their vegetarianism are more likely to engender dissatisfaction, even resentment, in those they push to the margins. Daisy, a charismatic evangelical in her fifties, spoke of being seen as 'extreme, or a bit wacky', as well as being accused of misinterpreting scripture: something that, having engaged in serious personal casuistry, she felt strongly about. 'It's turned me against some of my Christian peers, and I shouldn't let it do that, but I can see how it could.' Fiona, a middle-aged Anglican who is also on the committee of ASWA, offered a similar story.

> The church? I think they think we're all barking … I do get quite irritated I have to say. I get, um, slightly resentful …
>
> I know there's quite often you know sort of slightly sarcastic comments made about me because I am the one who's always cracking on about animals, and they know that given half the chance I will always bring it up, and if ever I'm asked to do prayers I will always slot animals into it somewhere. I mean I'm tolerated and people aren't unpleasant but I do think they think I'm a bit of a crackpot, and I get very, very little support for anything I do, so you know nobody ever comes to my services, you know, if I'm speaking at a service no one will ever come and listen, so that is quite depressing, that's quite a depressing side of it really …

The rejection of vegetarianism as a Christian practice, involving the rejection of the ordinary theology of the community's own vegetarians, is clearly a negative experience for those Christians for whom non-human animals and diet are important in their ethical reasoning. Even more troubling are those instances where dietary casuistry appears to have been rejected out of hand, leaving the ordinary Christian vegetarian with no engagement in his or her community and without any tangible justification for their isolation. In speaking about differences in interpretation of scripture, Daisy suggested that her church community was, at minimum, prepared to enter into conversation on ethical matters pertaining to diet. Fiona and other ordinary Christian vegetarians interviewed, however, felt marginalized, without having entered into any genuine ethical discussion. At odds with the majority position and practice in their communities, such individuals are left without the opportunity for sustained dialogue: their learning context, which provided much of the material for the reasoning through which they reached a vegetarian conclusion, in this way implicitly rejects their personal embracing of faith. When attendances at the services in which Fiona is involved are noticeably lower than normal, such rejection is no longer implicit but has become explicit.

In the concerns of Ingrid, Daisy and Fiona we find our own concerns validated about the communitarian-ethical idealization of the church community as it is. In an effort to counter the authoritarian presumptions inherent in a dilemma- or quandary-based understanding of ethics, the community of ordinary casuists is put forward as the alternative. We agree that the sustained and complex ethical reasoning of ordinary Christians, informed by scripture and tradition, should be given more attention within the academy. But an idealized picture, which neglects to attend to the prejudices, personalities and pitfalls involved in community-based casuistry, can only contribute to the marginalization of those voices which deviate from the majority. Hauerwas himself appears to anticipate such a problem, writing that: 'There are certainly differences in the church which may even cause separation, but that is why the church should learn to value her heretics. We never know what it is we should believe or be until we are reminded by another' (Hauerwas, 2003: 107).

Implicit in the call to casuistry is the call to value the heretic: to honestly enter into conversation with those whose ordinary theology differs from one's own. An emphasis on casuistry in community without a parallel emphasis on the reality that churches are constituted by different people with different perspectives – and that some Christians will then logically find themselves in a distinct minority on some issues – can and does lead to some heretics being marginalized. Where standard models of Christian ethics might have expected Ingrid, Daisy and Fiona to find their norms and patterns of action within their church community, the reality of their experiences of marginalization suggests that community-centred ethical models require further nuance if they are to be relevant for real churches and real ordinary theologians.

Alternative Communities of Character

Ordinary Christians who, as described above, find themselves marginalized in their local communities do often find communities within which to explore and further develop their ethical reasoning. A fact that further suggests the need for a more nuanced account of community-centred ethics is that these communities are not part of recognized church structures and do not conform to the paradigm of the local congregation. In particular, the conversations with ordinary Christian vegetarians highlighted how shared concerns with extra-ecclesial organisations such as CVAUK, ASWA and CCA can lead to marginalized individuals increasingly identifying with, and being formed by and into, the communities these organizations constitute.

Fiona, who felt she was either ignored or treated as 'barmy' and 'a crackpot', offered one example of this:

> It is really quite depressing really, if I think about it too much. I mean thank God I've got people, you know sort of like my fellow committee members, so I do know that there are other Christians who do care about animals, because I think if I didn't have them it would actually be quite a lonely old journey actually.

The learning context of Fiona's community, which shaped her character such that in embracing the faith she moved to reflect on dietary ethics, proved to her to be exclusive of dietary ethics itself. Feeling isolated and marginalized, Fiona spoke of her relief at having fellow Christian vegetarians. Whether the 'lonely old journey' to which she referred would be continuing as a vegetarian, continuing as a member of her local community, or both is unclear – and so could have been explored further in the interview – but what is clear is the nourishment and community she finds in ASWA, but which is absent from her local church. Carol, a middle-aged Christian who attends both Baptist and United Reformed churches, and Alison offer similar testimony with regard to CVAUK and its American equivalent.

> *Carol*: I went to a conference last year with the CVAUK … And I must admit that I felt so, so good there because I was with people that were like-minded and I've never come across people that have been, you know, with that kind of attitude before, so.

> *Alison*: The CVA group was really encouraging … Not to feel such the weirdo.

Particularly in the Internet age, ordinary Christian vegetarians like Fiona, Carol and Alison can find in organizations like ASWA and CVAUK the fundamental ingredients of the church as community of character. Without the physical proximity of typical congregations, it might seem that the opportunity for such alternative communities of character to be deeply involved in Christian formation is limited. The learning context of CVAUK, for example, can play an important role in developing the character and ordinary theological ethics of its members; but unless a new member is the offspring of one or more CVAUK parents, it is unlikely that anyone will begin their education into faith there. This does not reduce the significance of what CVAUK does do as a community: character is developed and shaped, and casuistry engaged in. A learning context is provided, rooted in scripture and with reference to tradition, which is open and actively sympathetic to ordinary Christian vegetarians' personal ethical reasoning, and encouraging of their dietary practice. In short, alternative communities of character can become the vital 'network of giving and receiving' (MacIntyre, 1999: 142) for ordinary Christians who feel marginalized in their local church community.

There is the danger that, in being communities oriented to a specific manifestation of theological praxis, organizations such as ASWA and CVAUK may invert theological ethics, making vegetarianism the end and Christianity the means, in a move memorably portrayed by C.S. Lewis's Screwtape as 'Christianity

And' (Lewis, 2002: 135). This is indeed a danger facing any Christian community that makes its mission so specific; but the other side of the problem lies in church communities that marginalize those members who, through scripture-and tradition-rooted ethical reasoning, reach an ordinary theology that calls them to abstain from eating animal flesh. If we are to note where alternative communities of character fall short of the paradigmatic church community, we must remember that real church communities fall short too – something of which conversation with ordinary theological ethicists is bound to remind us.

References

Astley, Jeff (2002), *Ordinary Theology: Looking, Listening and Learning in Theology*, Aldershot: Ashgate.

Bauckham, Richard (2010), *The Bible and Ecology: Rediscovering the Community of Creation*, Waco, Tex.: Baylor University Press.

Cunningham, David (2008), *Christian Ethics: The End of the Law*, London: Routledge.

Hardy, Daniel W. (2001), *Finding the Church*, London: SCM Press.

Hauerwas, Stanley (1981), *A Community of Character: Toward a Constructive Christian Social Ethic*, Notre Dame, Ind.: University of Notre Dame Press.

Hauerwas, Stanley (2003), *The Peaceable Kingdom: A Primer in Christian Ethics*, London: SCM Press.

Hauerwas, Stanley and Samuel Wells (eds) (2004), *The Blackwell Companion to Christian Ethics*, Oxford: Blackwell.

Lewis, C.S. (2002), *The Screwtape Letters*, London: HarperCollins.

Linzey, Andrew (1994), *Animal Theology*, London: SCM Press.

MacIntyre, Alasdair (1990), *Three Rival Versions of Moral Enquiry: Encyclopaedia, Genealogy, and Tradition*, Notre Dame, Ind.: University of Notre Dame Press.

MacIntyre, Alasdair (1999), *Dependent Rational Animals: Why Human Beings Need the Virtues*, London: Duckworth.

Mathewes, Charles (2010), *Understanding Religious Ethics*, Oxford: Wiley-Blackwell.

Muers, Rachel (2007), 'Feminist Theology as Practice of the Future', *Feminist Theology*, 16: 110–27.

Northcott, Michael S. (1996), *The Environment and Christian Ethics*, Cambridge: Cambridge University Press.

Scharen, Christian and Aana Marie Vigen (eds) (2011), *Ethnography as Christian Theology and Ethics*, London: Continuum.

Woodhead, Linda (2001), 'The Implicit God of Christian Ethics', unpublished paper presented at the Society for the Study of Theology.

Chapter 18
Ordinary Discipleship

Roger L. Walton

There are a number of many-layered problems connected with accessing ordinary believers' views of discipleship. First, there is the issue of words. Discipleship is not always part of the vocabulary of how people see the practice of Christian faith. A number of Christians evidently do not see themselves as disciples. They associate the term with the first followers and, in line with a good deal of the New Testament (Dunn, 2009: 8), do not adopt it as a self-understanding of their faith vocation. This reluctance is in part to do with the feeling that the first disciples, later 'apostles', were special and their calling different in kind from the faith to which contemporary Christians are called.

Moreover, for some, discipleship carries associations of particular churchmanship. The words 'discipleship', 'disciple' and 'discipling' have been a major focus of the new Network churches and evangelical churches inside and outside the mainline denominations. To adopt the language would be to identify with certain areas of Christianity where some feel neither comfortable nor convinced. Despite discipleship becoming a major discourse among broad denominations in recent years – through, for example, the Church of England's 'Education for Discipleship' emphasis (Ministry Division, 2006) and the Methodist Church's vision of itself as a 'discipleship movement shaped for mission' (Atkins, 2011) – it remains true that for many this is not their preferred description of their Christian faith commitment.

Then there is the issue of the relationship between belief and practice. The all-inclusive nature of discipleship means that the whole of life is to be encompassed. Astley's taxonomy of Christian learning identifies eight Christian attributes or aspects of learning that make up the range of Christian living and growth (Astley, 1994: 112–13). Even for those who have no knowledge of these dimensions, there is an intuitive idea that being a Christian is all-pervasive. It involves not only what we believe, but what we do, feel and think: at home, at work, in the shops and at the theatre, the football match and the pub. Everything is discipleship, and it is thus difficult to describe being a Christian as a separate, discrete belief.

Add to this some epistemological concerns – how do people know what they know? – and the investigation becomes still more complex. Unlike some areas of ordinary theology, discipleship is largely a lived form of theology where we may wonder whether it is possible to identify what people believe separate from their actions. Some theories of learning, such as situated learning theory (Lave and Wenger, 1991), would question whether knowledge and belief can be separated from participation or practice. In this perspective, the doing is the knowing and the practice is the belief.

One way to overcome these difficulties is to come at the investigation within another research project where the primary aims are focused elsewhere, but within which notions of Christian discipleship can be explored. My own research on church-related small groups allowed such an entry point into the world of ordinary discipleship. By engaging those who involve themselves in small groups, and seeking data on the details of the working of the small groups and their effects on the participants, it was possible to embed some questions about discipleship. In particular, I asked about how people saw being a mature Christian. This approach had three distinct advantages. First, it had the benefit of being couched in more neutral, less partisan language. Second, because the enquiry came late in questionnaires and interviews that were primarily about small groups, it was indirect and did not make people self-conscious about the topic, allowing more spontaneous and revealing responses. Finally, the particular question was teleological or aspirational in orientation, and asked people to describe what they were aiming at, rather than what they believed about the subject of discipleship or what they did by way of discipleship. Thus it sidestepped the question of the relation of belief to practice, and teased out the direction of travel and the goals of the discipleship of those participating.

The research involved interviews with over 40 local church leaders, 691 questionnaires received from members of church-related small groups and three case studies (see Walton, 2012). Here we analyse and compare the views about mature discipleship of those in leadership and 'ordinary disciples'.

Leaders

Four themes recurred in the interviews when leaders were asked what a mature disciple looked like.

Personal Qualities

It is unsurprising that Christian maturity should be seen in terms of personal qualities. The New Testament gives several lists of qualities and characteristics that mark out Christ-likeness (Gal 5:22–6; Col 3:12–17; Rom 12:9–21; 1 Cor 13; Phil 2:1–11; 2 Pet 1:5–8; and perhaps also Mt 5:1–12; Eph 6:10–17). One might expect that these qualities, perhaps especially love, would be identified as signs of following Jesus. Many church leaders did in fact identify the love of God, love of other Christians and love of people in general as signifying maturity. Occasionally they quoted short sections of scripture to describe aspects of maturity, such as 'speaking the truth in love'. In the main, however, the vocabulary was more contemporary.

Married Salvation Army officers at a small but growing corps spoke about the nurture of empathy as a sign of a maturing Christian:

> trying to encourage people to maybe think about their lives differently. So there would have been somebody – who I have in mind [from] back in Bangor – who would, on a sort of a regular basis, talk to young and old with a sense of, sort of, I suppose … empathy. (CL16)

This empathy, one said, was evident in personal relationships and the ability to listen, but was not confined to the local. Rather, it would gradually extend a sense of sympathy and identification with those in need across the world, especially if affected by natural disaster or war.

A number of church leaders gave me the name of someone they knew who embodied maturity and in each case they referred to qualities which characterized their lives. So Charlie was 'passionate about people', which seemed to indicate his sensitivity and responsiveness to individuals. Mary was 'gracious and kind'; and, because of her 'openness', Angela was skilled at 'seeing need and creating opportunities' and 'sharing faith' with others.

However, the most frequently mentioned and admired quality in a mature Christian was stability. 'Not blown here and there, by what the scripture calls "every wind of doctrine"' (CL20). Another church leader said:

> firstly someone who is stable and convinced in what they believe, to have a firm foundation of understanding of the gospel and therefore a conviction in the light of that in every area; so seeking to transform every area of their life to be more like Christ. (CL3)

This sense of steadiness and solidity was, as in this last quote, often linked to a certain kind of secure knowledge which provides the basis for Christian living. Others used the idea of confidence in God and one's faith to convey the same kind of bedrock of maturity. 'For us mature discipleship is someone who is growing in confidence in who they are and who God has called them to be, and is able to somehow translate that into everyday life, everyday living, everyday following of Jesus' (CL28). This deep-rooted stability or confidence also provides the ability to remain faithful in the face of adversity and difficulty. 'Another aspect in mature Christianity, though, I think for us would be about the capacity to live with difficulty and not pull out' (CL24); 'to face whatever life throws at you and know the peace and presence of God within it' (CL5).

It would seem that most thought that a mature Christian would have grown or be growing in particular virtues, though some church leaders were keen to stress that maturity would not always take the same form, nor be expressed in the same qualities. Yet the notion of stability with accompanying confidence and resilience was widely held to be a hallmark of maturity.

Practices

Another way mature discipleship was envisaged was via the medium of disciplined living. Mature Christians could be identified through their regular engagement with the means of grace and through practices that marked out their distinctive orientation to Christ. One person called this the 'biblical disciplines'. So one would expect mature Christians to be 'daily reading their Bibles and praying' (CL16), and to be regularly in worship (CL20); those of a sacramental tradition expected frequent participation in the eucharist, whilst those from charismatic and Pentecostal traditions emphasized the regular practice of spiritual gifts.

On deeper inspection, however, the practice of the means of grace is seen as instrumental to maturity rather than the final sign of its achievement. It is a pattern of nurture which enables Christians to be reflective in the world:

> What is mature Christian discipleship? It's about … people who are learning under a discipline, some sort of rule of life that works, that enables them to sustain their spiritual life under God; it will be a combination of prayer, scripture and public worship and sacramental worship. The other side of it, I think, will be the capacity to listen to the voices [in the life of the world] and interpret and to make sense of and to articulate perhaps what God may be saying to us through all these voices. The … third thing would be maturity in relationships; … the capacity to go the extra mile not only with the [people] outside but also the inside [church].

In this view, the practice of the means of grace enables the discernment of God and a strengthening of the ability to love beyond expected boundaries. As with qualities, practices integrate and deepen a lived relationship with God and God's world. This relationship is fed by and manifest in practices. Grace is encountered in the life of the faith community and its spiritual rituals, but also met and manifest in pragmatic, value-filled actions. As one person put it, Christian maturity is known in ethics:

> you expect [mature Christians] to be honest, you expect them to be kind to people, you expect them to think about other people. You wouldn't expect them to be out there profiteering at the expense of other people – it would be something to do with values and attitudes, and behaviour. (CL12)

The notion of practices or disciplined living also indicates another widely valued feature of mature discipleship, taking responsibility for one's own spiritual growth: 'someone who takes the initiative in their own relationship with God' (CL25), 'a concern for their own godliness' (CL30), 'the expectation of a continuing spiritual growth' (CL17).

Some wanted to include the notion of taking responsibility for the spiritual lives and growth of others, and a few saw 'discipling others' as a defining feature of mature discipleship. One leader of a fresh expression of church built on cell groups wanted to make the five values of Cell UK the benchmarks of growing maturity (Potter, 2001). In all, the sense of personal responsibility for discipleship and a self-conscious intention to go on growing and developing one's faith life was indicative of maturity.

Gifts Used in Service

For many church leaders, a key sign of the moment of transition from infant to adult Christian faith is the desire to want to use one's gifts self-consciously for Christ in the service of others.

> What's the mark of a [mature] disciple? Certainly a learner, and certainly someone who's looking for opportunity to serve, or they're knocking on my door saying, 'David, I've really been studying, reading, I've been in the group, I really want to serve the Lord, where do you think my gifting lies?' I think that's an indicator. (CL15)

This idea of serving being a sign of maturity was echoed by others:

> I think serving, maturity in serving, is making sure you're being effective in what you're doing. You get beyond, 'I'm doing the church a favour', you get beyond, 'Well I'm faithful in what I do because I'm committed'; but you're looking to be more effective and develop that gift. (CL18)

The same leader goes on to argue that this stage of wanting to be effective and to develop the gift is the movement into mission. It is accompanied by a growing sense that God is calling and opening up possibilities for the person to be active individually and with others, and is accompanied by an emerging consciousness of divine providence in action: in formal theological terms, taking one's place in the *mission Dei*.

Others make the same point through their remarks about Christian faith relating to paid employment and other forms of work. While most Church leaders felt that they did not equip people well enough through preaching, study or small groups, nevertheless Christian maturity is seen in 'how am I being more Christ-like in the workplace?' (CL18).

It is in this theme that I think we can best locate and understand the emphasis by some church leaders on 'discipling others', 'mentoring and taking responsibility for others' and 'helping others find faith'. It is clear that for some church leaders this is the acid test for maturity. For the majority, it would not be the defining feature, but if seen as one manifestation of the broader call to witness to Christian faith and to use gifts in God's service, it would be owned by almost all of those interviewed. There was a strong sense that not to make the transition into using gifts in ministry and mission, in at least one of church, home, community or civic society, would be to fall short of Christian maturity.

Perception of One's Life as Part of a Larger Divine Plan

A final strand to the understanding of mature discipleship is caught in the next extract.

> if I needed to sum it up, it would be about a couple of things. One is honouring God in the place he's put you. It's about being a witness to Christ wherever you are. ... And I think the second is having a very strong consciousness that this life of discipleship is being worked out in the context of the purpose of God – I suppose, if one wanted to use missiological language, in terms of the mission of God ... and the way we're living our lives, is not about us, it's about what God is about, ... I think we would understand that in very strong eschatological terms, there is a culminating purpose of God in human history and in the cosmos ... So producing, if you like, hopeful Christians, hope-filled Christians, where the Christian hope is part of their vision, where the cross and the resurrection, and what God's final intention is, is part of who they are. (CL1)

The idea here seems to be an extension of the point about stability that came through strongly in the section on qualities. What leaders desire for disciples, including themselves, is a deep-rootedness in God which leads to resilience of faith in all life's various circumstances. Mature disciples here find a quality of faith that can withstand the radical ups and downs of life, with a continued willingness to look for God in all things. The extension is in the place of the person in the plan of God. Whereas deeply-rooted and confident faith can continue to stress a human centredness (e.g., 'I have a strong faith in God and am confident that it can see me through all things'), the emphasis that occasionally came out among church leaders was that fully mature faith will take a small place in a big plan. Thus the emphasis shifts to a God-centred understanding of things in which one is happy to play a part, small or large, in the divine drama. With this comes a willingness to embrace paradox and doubt as unthreatening to faith. 'I think a mature disciple is someone who acknowledges the doubts and difficulties of following Jesus Christ, but still desires to do so' (CL8); 'they can live with doubts, they can live with some sense of mystery and paradox' (CL21).

The overall picture of the mature disciple that emerges from these conversations is of a person who is deeply rooted in their faith, stable, confident and resilient; who lives a disciplined life, taking responsibility for their own spiritual growth and drawing on the means of grace for the transformation of their daily living; who sees the need and takes up the challenge of using their gifts in the service of others; and who locates themselves within the divine plan, able to live faithfully with doubt and complexity.

'Ordinary Christians'

The data for the views of ordinary believers comes in the main not from interviews but from the questionnaire. In relation to discipleship, the questionnaire asked what participants thought being a mature Christian meant. This was not an open question, as in the interview, but listed various aspects, attributes or practices and invited people to agree or disagree using a five-point Likert scale. All the items on the list were taken from the content of interviews with church leaders but, as the questionnaires were sent out prior to the detailed analysis above, the four themes were not explicitly represented or tested. However, it is possible to comment on at least three of the themes.

Ordinary Christians agreed that particular qualities were a sign of mature Christian faith. Sixty-four per cent strongly agreed that 'showing qualities such as kindness and forgiveness' would characterize a mature Christian, with a further 30% agreeing, combining to 94% agreeing or strongly agreeing, making this the highest ranked of all the attributes. Confidence, in terms of 'having a grasp of Christian belief', was also ranked highly, with some 92% seeing this as a feature of mature faith. There was some support, too, for the particular quality of empathy, as 34% agreed and 45% strongly agreed that being a mature Christian would involve 'sharing in the suffering of others'. Whether or not these features could be said to represent the practice of ordinary Christians, it is fair to say that virtuous qualities and stable, confident faith are the goals to which these Christians aspire.

With regard to living a disciplined life, those answering the questionnaire were highly committed to worship and to small group attendance. Ninety-six per cent attended worship at least once per week. In relation to their small groups, 46% said they attend every meeting and 51% most meetings. In this frame, attendance at small groups would be a signal of living a disciplined life, as all the participants belong to churches which place a high value on small groups. Seventy-six per cent said that belonging to the small group was vital or very important to their Christian faith. In terms of benefits, 72% said belonging to a small group had made them more accepting and forgiving of others; 79% said it had strengthened their prayer life; 87% said that belonging to the small group has brought them closer to God, and a similar number said that it had helped them mature as a Christian. Thus, the practice of participating in the life of their small group is an important Christian discipline, an expression of their commitment to the way of Christ and an effective way of pursuing discipleship. What is more, participation in small groups had, they said, a significant outward effect. In addition to the positive effects cited above, 68% said it had given them more confidence in speaking about their faith to others, and about half (51%) said that belonging to the group had made them more likely to help their neighbours. When asked about the facets of mature Christian faith, 83% said that the ability to shape workplace and home life in a Christian way would be seen in a mature Christian, and 82% that 'witnessing to your faith to your non-Christian friends' was to be associated with maturity in faith.

Service of others can be seen in attributes such as 'supporting other Christians', 'tackling local issues such as crime and poverty' and 'being involved in campaigns for justice and peace', which were all listed as possible signs of mature faith. Here we see less conviction among the ordinary Christians when compared with church leaders. While 93% thought that 'supporting other Christians' was a characteristic of mature Christian faith, rather less (62%) were convinced that getting involved in neighbourhood concerns signalled maturity, and less than half (43%) considered involvement in justice issues to be a hallmark.

So there is some degree of correlation between the views of church leaders and the thoughts of ordinary Christians. Apart from the theme of 'one's life as part of a larger divine plan', which was untested, there are points of correspondence between the notions of church leaders and the aspirations and self-understanding of certain actions of these ordinary Christians.

However, the overall rankings appear to convey another significant message about discipleship: not so much the features that ordinary Christians identify but the way in which those features are related to each other.

Table 18.1 Features of mature Christians

Being a mature Christian means …	**Strongly agree**	**Agree**	**Total**
showing qualities such as kindness and forgiveness	64.4%	29.2%	93.6%
supporting other Christians	40.4%	52.5%	92.9%
having a better grasp of Christian belief	50.8%	40.8%	91.6%
trying to shape my workplace and home life in a Christian way	41.2%	42.1%	83.3%
witnessing to your faith to your non-Christian friends	36.3%	45.4%	81.7%
sharing in the suffering of others	34.0%	44.9%	78.9%
inviting others to become Christian	32.9%	44.4%	77.3%
tackling local issues, e.g. crime, poverty and loneliness	18.1%	43.8%	61.9%
being involved in campaigns for justice and peace	11.9%	31.5%	43.4%

The three scores in the 90s probably tell us most about the core concept carried by ordinary group members. In this view, a mature disciple is one who lives out the virtuous qualities, who loves and supports other Christians, and has a firm understanding of her beliefs. Issues of practice, witness, caring for the world's needy and tackling social justice follow these primary three and may be seen as consequences of them. The notions of discovering God in the life of the world and being formed through active engagement in reconciliation and justice are less salient features in this conceptualization of discipleship.

When the responses are analysed in relation to the churches to which respondents belong, despite some modest variations in the ranking the same pattern is broadly maintained: with the three top, two lowest and four middle scoring features remaining within their respective sections. In other words, across all the churches surveyed, the shape of the view of Christian maturity is the same. It is realized primarily in qualities closely linked to belief and church community, followed by personal application in home, work and witness to others; with a third layer being action in the wider issues of civic, national and international society. It is possible that the lower scoring features are seen as less important, or as growing from the higher order aspects of maturity. Either way, fewer view maturity as being formed and expressed through action in the world. Such involvement appears to be consequential upon, not formative of, Christ-likeness.

Reflections and Research Issues

There is no real sharp contradiction in these data between the views of church leaders and ordinary believers on the subject of discipleship. Indeed, from the evidence of this research there is much that is common. The reasons for this may be tentatively outlined. First, discipleship is a less formal area of theological dogma. Unlike, say, Christology, the distinctions between the various theological voices on the topic of discipleship are less clear, in particular between normative theology, espoused theology and operant theology (Cameron et al., 2010: 53–6). It may be that we can discover much about the ordinary theology of discipleship from the church leaders, who are themselves not schooled in the disputes and standards of past debates and formulations on discipleship, as they are in other credal elements.

Second, the data here are not comparing like with like. For the interviews with church leaders we are drawing on qualitative data over many hours of interviews. For the views of ordinary Christians we have used quantitative data from 691 questionnaires. Beginning from another place may reveal quite different conclusions. What is more, the sample may be atypical, and while the advantage of exploring notions of discipleship embedded within research about experience of small groups was set out above, its limitations are equally visible. There is a need to tackle ordinary discipleship more 'head on', and explore some of the questions about belief and practice with ordinary disciples at greater length and in greater depth.

Nevertheless, there is the beginning of useful material here. We have uncovered language and concepts that populate the field of ordinary discipleship. The four themes drawn from church leaders' conversations allow us to begin to describe the common discourse of discipleship across a range of churches. This may provide some benchmarks for dialogue with the findings from further research among ordinary believers. Moreover, whilst most church leaders could not be described as 'ordinary theologians' in most areas of belief (Astley, 2002: 56, 63–4), the field of discipleship may illustrate a spectrum rather than a sharp contrast of beliefs in this less formal category of theological discourse. Finally, we identified a pattern of describing (mature) Christian discipleship that is a little worrying, not so much for what it affirms as hallmarks of maturity but for what it seems to neglect. Both for leaders and believers, the formative power of engagement with the world and its, often hidden, promise of encounter with 'the other' is not promoted or sought. As a description of ordinary discipleship this may be accurate, but it may make some want to revisit the theology of an immanent God and the *missio Dei* in the midst of the life of the world.

References

Astley, Jeff (1994), *The Philosophy of Christian Religious Education*, London: SPCK.

Astley, Jeff (2002), *Ordinary Theology*, Aldershot: Ashgate.

Atkins, Martyn (2011) 'Contemporary Methodism: A Discipleship Movement Shaped for Mission', in *General Secretary's Report*, Methodist Conference.

Cameron, Helen, Deborah Bhatti, Catherine Duce, James Sweeney and Clare Watkins (2010), *Talking About God in Practice: Theological Action Research and Practical Theology*, London: SCM Press.

Dunn, James D.G. (2009), *Beginning from Jerusalem*, Grand Rapids, Mich.: Eerdmans.

Lave, Jean and Etienne Wenger (1991), *Situated Learning: Legitimate Peripheral Participation*, Cambridge: Cambridge University Press.

Ministry Division (2006), *Shaping the Future: New Patterns of Training for Lay and Ordained*, London: The Archbishops' Council.

Potter, Phil (2001), *The Challenge of Cell Church: Getting to Grips with Cell Church Values*, Oxford: Bible Reading Fellowship.

Walton, Roger L. (2012), 'Disciples Together: The Small Group as a Vehicle for Discipleship Formation', *Journal of Adult Theological Education*, 8, 2: 99–114.

Chapter 19
Sharing Friendship: God's Love in Ordinary Church Life

John B. Thomson

Many people imagine that faith and theology are about ideas. Yet for Christians, faith is a performance embedded and embodied in the practices of ordinary churches before it is an ideology. Without performance, faith and theology are abstractions. This chapter aims to explore the operant theology implicit in the performances of three congregations with a view to showing how they exhibit the love of God in ordinary church life (Cameron et al., 2010: 14 n.14, 54). It does this by listening to the way congregational members talk about their Christian practice, in order to pay attention to the way they understand Christian theology in their own language. In conclusion, I try to show how this relates to common theological themes and what their descriptions and emphases tell us about their ordinary theology.

Three congregations were selected from the Anglican Diocese of Sheffield, England, located in contexts typical of the predominantly urban working/lower middle class character of the diocese. A group from each congregation was interviewed using a common set of questions. The focus groups were all chosen as representative of their congregations, reflecting their gender, age and ethnic make-up. None of those taking part had any formal theological training.

St Peter's, Warmsworth, Doncaster

St Peter's parish is in an urban setting with a population of approximately 11,000. It is almost exclusively working class, although part of Warmsworth old village is more affluent. The north side of West Balby is poor, with social housing, and certain streets are reputedly 'bad areas', although the actual experience of the people who live there is positive. Most of the congregation live in the predominantly privately owned, modest housing on the south side of West Balby where the church is situated. There are two areas of social housing in this part of the parish which have historically been known to have drug and other social problems. Occasional office ministry, services for public remembrance, social events and openness to those on the fringes of society characterize St Peter's mission. In addition, a 'Scarecrow Saints' Parish Trail, Stations of the Cross in local shops, community carol singing in the park and pubs, and a parish-wide Passion Symbols initiative during Holy Week represent ways the gospel is shared with the community through art.

The reflection group comprised three women and one man; all were white British, in a predominantly white parish. Two of the women were pensioners, with the other woman and the man in employment, though all were over 55. All were committed, long-standing members of the congregation, with three being office-holders.

How Was Jesus Present in These Initiatives and Activities?

All four said they believed that Jesus was present in the inclusive welcome offered to those who come to worship, regularly or occasionally. They spoke of the iconic impact of the white building, which has an oriental appearance and connects the world and presence of Jesus with the parish. The inside is spaciousness and light and speaks of the accessibility of Jesus. A large crucifix behind the altar points to a Jesus who is present as a sacrifice and a symbol of the character of discipleship. The building is sacred space which draws people's attention. 'It's so different from mundane life.' This sets up a creative tension between the Jesus in the mundane and the challenge to be set apart for God. Jesus is the sign of God's love, the symbol of ultimate sacrifice and the one who invites us to share his holy ground. In this way Jesus' presence denies the regular congregation ownership of the space, since it belongs to Jesus and is inhabited by him and those he invites.

The church should therefore be a community imitating the love and hospitality of God in Jesus. Practically, this involves welcoming outsiders, refusing to be proprietorial about the building and finding ways of enabling people to participate. The group stressed the presence of Jesus in their sharing with the community, even though the connection between the church and the church community hall was not always made by the users (despite the upside-down cross of St Peter in the hall). The use of the hall for social outreach shows Jesus as a bridge-builder between congregation and parish. People meet Jesus in prayer and in community service. Those doing community service in the graveyard found the congregation's hospitality very moving: 'They like to come to St Peter's best of all … it's how the people are with them … we always give them a public acknowledgement and thanks.'

What Do They Tell Us About What God is Like?

Social engagement speaks of a welcoming God. God's judgement is one of love and embrace. 'Church is not just the building … it's the people, what they are and do … the love of Christ is in and through us wherever we are. We live it.' For many people in the parish the church represents a sort of sanctuary, a place of safety and comfort in hard times. Memorial Services were highlighted as occasions when people could offload their burdens onto God. The Mothers' Union Marriage Preparation Group likewise enabled couples to explore the dynamics of relationships in a safe and mature context. Yet alongside this was an ambivalence about parts of the Bible. One participant felt that listening to the Bible in worship must be very difficult for outsiders, since God could appear quite violent on many occasions. Another suggested that God might have changed through his relationship with his people. 'God is a growing reality', she said. Further, God was a more difficult reality to 'explain' compared with Jesus, who indicates the welcome, hospitality and loving character of God.

What Do They Tell Us About the Role of the Church in Today's Society?

The group felt that many occasional worshippers, and those reached out to, had little understanding of the meaning of the symbols and ceremony of Christian worship and practice. Sometimes there was confusion about whether St Peter's was a Catholic church, given its style of worship. Much was made of tradition as a link through occasional offices and of St Peter's as a sacred space where God was close. Baptism and marriage preparation and bereavement visits enabled the church to explore this faith. In particular, the story of Jesus helped them understand God better. 'God came in human form in Jesus in order to identify and understand us … and after the passion he didn't leave us … the Holy Spirit is a constant guide.' Nevertheless, the Bible is complex and challenging. God remains mysterious and can seem distant. People want more evidence. The church seeks to illuminate this story through its life but can't explain everything in detail. It tries to challenge assumptions about God, especially when people are very quick to blame rather than see God with us in life's experiences.

What Do They Tell Us About Mission and Evangelism?

'The role of the church is to go and meet people where they are.' Changes in church life over the years have made it a warmer and more welcoming community to those in the parish. 'It's very different to when I was young … it was very stuffy and starchy.' The geographical parish challenges the congregation to be outward-looking. Outreach activities 'demonstrate our willingness to show the church in us, all of us and them as well'. In all of this Jesus is present and God is seen as one who reaches out and engages people. The church is a porous community and the response of local people is often encouraging. 'How welcome we were in the pubs when singing carols at Christmas.' Mission and evangelism are about people seeing that churchgoers are normal people and that God's love is freely offered and received. It is 'about making visible the presence of God in the community … God working through us … it is doing what God commanded us to do.' Mission and evangelism therefore embody God's hospitality and friendship in practical ways which draw people nearer to the love of God. They involve accepting people where they are, sharing the faith in accessible ways and then letting people take things further in their own way and time. Mission is about going out. The word 'apostolic' was used.

Christ Church, Pitsmoor, Sheffield

Pitsmoor is a culturally rich but economically poor inner city area. Most people who live there are proud of its cultural diversity. Set just off Sheffield city centre, the parish is part of an area which has regularly received government money for regeneration. This is a place of multiple cultures and many different faiths. There are a large number of churches active in the area, as well as many mosques and a Sikh temple. There is a feeling that things are changing for the better, and there is an openness to the church as an agent of change in the area.

The group of reflectors comprised five females active in a befriending scheme and an outreach scheme to local women. The befriending scheme links local vulnerable and isolated people with volunteers in friendship. Referrals come through local GPs and the local district nursing team. The outreach project engages the vulnerable through regular street outreach and a weekly drop-in providing a meal, second-hand clothing and a craft activity. There are also opportunities to meet with individual women each week for coffee/lunch, social activities and various appointments. The project also seeks to support individuals when in hospital, and prison visits.

The focus group was middle-aged or older. Four were white British and one was black African, in a multi-ethnic parish where 50% of the population are white and 50% of other ethnic origin. They were all female, as the projects related primarily to women. Only one of those taking part was involved in the core organization of the congregation. Two were relatively new to the church and still somewhat on its fringes. One was the church cleaner. This represents the liminal character of their 'Fresh Expressions' initiative, which attracts those on the edge of church life and those of a practical rather than a verbal bent.

How Was Jesus Present in These Initiatives and Activities?

One person said she 'didn't know whether Jesus encouraged me to do this unbeknown to me'. Another said she tried to avoid it, but the Vicar encouraged her and she became part of things. 'Before he collared me, something was bugging me that I ought to do it.' One participant said, 'I do think Jesus was present.' The pull towards her deeper involvement included tragically discovering that one of those she befriended, who was later murdered, was actually related to her. For this person, what really mattered is that Jesus starts with us as we are and where we are. A non-judgemental approach reflects Jesus' way. Yet equally firm boundaries, such as 'no drink, no blokes and no drugs', express the love of Jesus.

What Do They Tell Us About What God is Like?

God is on the streets rather than safely locked away in church buildings. The group felt that their outreach was distinctively different from that offered by statutory bodies, since it was simply friendship without targets and funding-driven agendas.

It was about giving people time, which spoke about God's slow care for the little people of life. 'We've got to hang on in there.' Indeed, when a new vicar arrived one of the participants told him bluntly, 'If you're not prepared to accept the people and their language then you've no business to be here.' Giving and expecting respect were important and the women on the street acknowledged a moral code as they frequently apologized for swearing, etc. Yet they also got to see Christians 'warts and all'. As one member of the group said, 'when they see you, you're not perfect. We've all got us crosses to bear … I like a drink too … God loves everyone for who and what you are.' God is a cornerstone, a guide and someone to share with. They felt that God was present in all that they did, even though they didn't always present God in 'religious language'.

What Do They Tell Us About the Role of the Church in Today's Society?

'The church is trying to look out for people who are less fortunate.' This is just what Christians do, like footballers play football. 'The church is a support group which keeps the story of Jesus alive … a sense of togetherness, supporting each other.' 'The church is about relationships, making links and helping people to see another way to live.' The church is 'us going out there and spreading God's love, especially amongst those who don't feel worthy.' You 'go along with it and God is there with you … a sense of peace telling you that you are on the right track.' One observed that 'women tend to be more involved because they go through more in life than men.'

What Do They Tell Us About Mission and Evangelism?

Mission isn't in the church, 'it's going outside the church and should be done that way.' 'We are not just a church group but are open to others and have a wide range of volunteers.' It is about being a befriender rather than coming from 'the church'. 'As a Christian you should be expressing friendship.' The support, prayers and guardians of the church are necessary, however, since Christians need to be with others in worship, sharing and support. One said she had come back to church after many years away. Another felt she needed answers to life's challenges, and that getting a good sermon each week helped her to think out her faith and life. 'It was like an energy drink.' The key thing was to be linked to the church. The Vicar helped one person dealing with the fear brought by occult practices. His prayers brought peace. For another, it was friendship in the church and its welcome that made the difference. When the word 'evangelism' was mentioned one person said, 'I just see Billy Graham.' Another said, 'it's sharing good news about Jesus.' Another understood this to be about 'giving people stuff to read about God'. Another asserted that it is 'not really proclaiming God … but us being present and sharing with them … they see God through us … just by your actions.'

St Mary's, Stainforth

Stainforth is a mining village about ten miles north-east of Doncaster. The congregation is small, with 60 on the roll and a Sunday attendance of 52 adults, although there are relatively high numbers of occasional offices. The present vicar arrived in 2002 and since then a number of major initiatives have taken place including vicarage meals cooked with local children (under appropriate safeguarding arrangements), the setting up of a local cinema in the church and the establishment of an indoor bowling club in the nave. Funding has been attracted to add a community centre to the church building. There have been street suppers, a child contact centre, a luncheon club and an Oasis listening project. In 2009 the church was involved with others in the memorial events recalling the twenty-fifth anniversary of the Miners' Strike and the seventieth anniversary of the Cage Crash Disaster at the pit.

Three female members of the congregation took part in the conversation: all where white, two were pensioners and one was in employment. All currently held office within the church and had been part of the congregation for over a decade.

How was Jesus Present in These Initiatives and Activities?

Meals with children at the vicarage were evidently a lively and sometimes challenging experience. While there was some conversation about matters of faith, most of the communication happened while creating the meal, setting the table, eating together around a table, saying grace and playing games afterwards. 'Telling the story of Jesus by words was limited … there was very little conversation … we tried to teach them how to eat a meal at table, which was unusual for them, but they always held hands and said grace even if they didn't know the words.' Yet this sharing together established relationships so that in the streets children and young people still call out, 'Annie, what are you doing today?' The group believed that Jesus was present 'through our example more than our words'. The children saw that 'a friend of Jesus is an ordinary person not a fuddy-duddy.' It was about 'showing care and interest in people … that they matter … just being there'. Sometimes it felt like casting bread on the waters, but it was about sharing Jesus' friendship and hospitality. Although the attention span of the youngsters was short, these meals embedded a practical memory in the children about the church and what it stands for.

What Do They Tell Us About What God is Like?

A similar emphasis upon the practicality of faith, Jesus in our deeds, was evident in their understanding of the cinema, street suppers, luncheon club and community centre. These were about 'showing God's love and care for others'. When the church did street suppers for alcohol and drug addicts, surprising and unexpected conversations about matters of faith took place. Similarly, 'loads of people come to the memorial services' who believe but are reserved about belonging. When thinking about their own vision, the women drew on Bible stories such as the feeding of the five thousand since, 'like Jesus, we don't know how many people will turn up!' and, like Jesus, feeding is a way of sharing that is central to their faith.

What Do They Tell Us About the Role of the Church in Today's Society?

The church is an outward-facing, giving community rather than a holy huddle. One contributor paraphrased Archbishop Temple by saying that the church is 'here for the people who don't come yet and to spread God's word. It is not a club.' Giving is very wearing but the spin-offs were fellowship, friendship and the sense of making a difference. In addition, those involved were more aware of the sustenance of worship and fellowship, and drew on Bible passages which spoke about being connected into God's resources, such as the vine in John 15 and Psalm 121. The 'key is sharing together in our need'. As one of the group commented, 'I was put here for a purpose. I found my purpose catering [for the luncheon club] which brings people together. They have different views about the church and ask questions and want to know what is going off in church. Different ones will come for different things, though getting them to services is difficult. Sometimes I just take them into church for prayer.' All agreed that the church needed to look at service times, etc., and respond to the reality of most people's struggles with time, now that Sunday is no longer a special day.

What Do They Tell Us About Mission and Evangelism?

It is very hard to get people to become regular members of the church. 'There are lots of believers but they won't step over the doorway.' They are happy to know about it and to support it in a semi-detached sort of way, but commitment is fragile. People join through personal invitation and accompaniment, as happened to one of the interviewees. However, the three agreed that the mission of the church is 'first to worship and serve God … other stuff follows from this'. Equally, the church is to treat people as Jesus treats us and how he expects us to treat others. It is about 'respect for others' and 'meeting people on their level'.

Reflection: A Theology of Practical Friendship

The way the participants in this exercise describe their theology is in practical, down-to-earth terms, with little time for abstract ideas. It is a theology of engagement, caring and reaching out. In popular discourse they walk with God, and are thereby discovering a way of talking about and witnessing to God and God's love as they go. This is reflected in the imaginative initiatives they have been part of in quite unexpected contexts. Certainly the clergy have influenced their congregations. Yet mission has been argued about and owned by ordinary disciples. Indeed, in some sense they are themselves a language or dialect of God, rendering intelligible the sounds of God's presence in life to those in their communities (Thomson, 2004: 15–26; 2010: 14–15, 120). They speak of an immanent rather than a transcendent view of God, who as Immanuel actively reaches out to those who appear lost and vulnerable. It is a theology of love and gift rather than of reason and calculation, a theology embodied in the selfless, other-focused practical love seen in Jesus. The Stainforth group contrasted their work with the verbal outreach of mission teams of ordinands organized by a previous incumbent, which they felt disempowered them. Instead of being relatively passive and supportive, local people were now the key agents expressing the gospel in culturally appropriate ways through their own actions and conversations. This is dispersed mission, owned by local people on the ground, rather than specialist mission imported from elsewhere; and it embeds a memory, particularly in the young, of churches whose actions and words speak of compassion, commitment to the wellbeing of others and a selfless giving.

For these ordinary disciples, faith is less a package of ideas and more a series of practices through which a deeper understanding of God's ways with the world is discovered. It was interesting to note how diffident all were about articulating a coherent faith. While some of this was deference to trained ministers, I wondered whether it was also because thinking and talking about faith is less important to them than performing their faith. In the words of Brad Kallenberg, they were engaged in embodied apologetics rather than rhetorical apologetics (Kallenberg, 2001: 156). They expected God to make a practical difference in life and this involved cooperating with God in their contexts. Indeed, the group from Pitsmoor felt they needed to induct their vicar into contextual mission.

All this reminds clergy that ordinary Christians privilege practical discipleship and practical theology above abstract theology. 'God with us' is a major theme, and prayer focuses on resources for transformation rather than on contemplation. God is an active agent in the world rather than a distant monarch. The Spirit webs people together to serve God in the world and inspires them to keep going even when they feel exploited and exhausted. Mission is about the expression of God's practical love and friendship rather than a way of conveying information about God to others. It is about embodying the hospitality of God, which makes space for those who are different from us. This can involve food, as at Stainforth; welcoming marginal people into the community, as at Warmsworth, going into the world of others and offering help, as at Pitsmoor. Together these are fragile signs of hope pointing to another way of living, another world which those they encounter are invited to be part of.

This situated, hospitable and dispersed approach to mission coheres with the mission narratives of Matthew chapter 10 and Luke chapter 9, where the host community's response to the evangelists indicates their response to God. The Christian community is a sign of God's faithful presence which invites a response from its host society (Hunter, 2010: 235). The church cannot control mission. Instead, it must simply be faithful to God's call to embody and share the gospel faithfully among particular communities and societies. Further, engagement at ground level with those most marginal to church and society reflects the liberating themes of Luke chapter 4. Sharing divine friendship with deeply wounded and vulnerable people integrates worship and mission. Worship is mission since worship trains Christian communities to see others in the love and friendship of God, and to share with them in appropriate ways. It expresses the hospitable, generous and dispersed friendship of God embodied in Jesus and witnessed to by local Christian communities such as these. It is God's love in ordinary church life.

References

Cameron, Helen, Deborah Bhatti, Catherine Duce, James Sweeney and Clare Watkins, (2010), *Talking About God in Practice: Theological Action Research and Practical Theology*, London: SCM Press.

Hunter, James Davison (2010), *To Change the World: The Irony, Tragedy and Possibility of Christianity in the Late Modern World*, Oxford: Oxford University Press.

Kallenberg, Brad J. (2001), *Ethics as Grammar: Changing the Postmodern Subject*, Notre Dame Ind.: University of Notre Dame Press.

Thomson, John B. (2004), *Church on Edge? Practising Ministry Today*, London: Darton, Longman and Todd.

Thomson, John B. (2010), *Living Holiness: Stanley Hauerwas and the Church*, London: Epworth.

Chapter 20
Ordinary Learning

Helen Savage

On a bleak January morning in County Durham, seven women and their minister met to learn and pray. They gathered in the warmth of one of their homes, and fortified themselves with steaming tea and home-made cake. One of the women took responsibility for starting the discussion, based on the study guide, *God's Amazing Gifts*. Her friends joined in cheerfully. They read the prescribed Bible passages aloud and did their best to engage with the suggested questions. The conversation was animated and involving and it often shot off at a tangent. Their minister, content at first to listen, then joined in as an equal member of the group. Like the others, he asked other questions and told his own stories. Stories dominated.

The Receptive Ecumenism Survey of Adult Learning and Formation

The group was typical of many we encountered during a study carried out between 2009 and 2011 as part of the Receptive Ecumenism and the Local Church Project, sponsored by the Centre for Catholic Studies of the Department of Theology and Religion, Durham University. Its aim was to listen attentively to adult learning and formation groups in north-east England, to describe their character, activities and concerns, and to begin to draw attention to some of the educational, theological and ecclesial issues that arose from these.

Marcus Pound and I gathered evidence from groups in 51 localities, through 15 visits to groups and significant providers of learning and formation in the Anglican Dioceses of Durham and Newcastle, eight in the Northern Baptist Federation, six in the Methodist Districts of Darlington and Newcastle, one in a Methodist/URC Local Educational Partnership, seven in the Roman Catholic Diocese of Hexham and Newcastle, four in the Northern Division of the Salvation Army and nine in the Northern Province of the United Reformed Church. Evidence also came from one wholly ecumenical group.

The study was, by and large, an investigation of those places where groups meet *and* where something interesting was thought to be happening. Many groups were selected or suggested by colleagues with some responsibility for adult learning within their denomination. Although by no means a representative survey, therefore, it was a significant study of the attitudes and activities of those who participate in learning and formation within the churches.

The methodology was simple: in the course of each listening exercise we sought answers to a number of questions derived from an earlier, unpublished study of around two dozen adult learning groups that I carried out on behalf of the Anglican Diocese of Newcastle in 2006. The questions formed a checklist rather than a rigid framework, for the groups themselves often generated other questions and issues. But, as a starting point, we sought to discover:

- what adult learning/formation takes place;
- who articulated a need for such learning;
- how that need was articulated;
- who responds/takes responsibility for that learning;
- what has worked well – and why;
- what hasn't worked so well – and why.

Each case study either took the form of an 'appreciative enquiry', an exercise in listening that normally lasted about an hour; or we attended and observed a learning session (as on that January morning in County Durham) and then asked somewhat briefer questions. Our findings did not differ significantly whether we asked questions throughout the session or spent most of our time listening: indeed the opportunity to watch and listen to learning in progress proved an effective way to check, corroborate and amplify the points made in the course of the appreciative enquiries.

What the groups did and how this was described by the group members was enormously varied. Many were engaged in Bible study, many others took a published course, DVD or book as a starting point for their discussion; and most were keen to stress that they adapt these materials to their own needs. Just as many groups that met primarily to learn included some elements of worship, so those groups that met primarily for prayer or worship included some element of learning – such as, for example, experiments with 'café church'. Other groups were even less formal. One example was a walking group: which, as the leader said, 'gives folk an opportunity to talk about things'.

Whatever groups did, it soon became clear that, right across the Christian traditions, a pattern was emerging: the factors that enabled most people to learn effectively, the context of that learning and its very nature displayed many strong similarities. I have chosen to describe this as 'ordinary learning' and suggest that it has much in common with ordinary theology, which is typically the subject and product of this learning.

Why Adults Learn

Most textbooks about adult learning emphasize that adults typically engage in learning in order to address a need, and that this is the way they learn best. Obvious examples would be the need to learn how to mend a leaking tap in order to avoid a huge bill from a plumber, or to learn at least a few words of a foreign language in order to make the most of a holiday abroad.

But learning is not always governed by such obvious needs. People are inquisitive. We like to learn about other people and other places partly because this may offer us an opportunity to escape from our own situation and to engage our imagination, as we might enjoy a novel or a television drama, and partly because the stories of other lives help us to understand better the contexts of our own lives. And some learning is otherwise pointless – the acquisition of knowledge for knowledge's sake. Knowing who won the English Football Association Cup in 1914 or which grape variety is used to make Chablis may serve no more useful purpose than to win a pub quiz, but the popularity of television and radio quiz shows is testament to the seductiveness of this kind of trivial knowledge.

Our study revealed little evidence that the rich variety of learning opportunities afforded by the churches is offered in response to learners' needs. For example, although we found that some Bible study groups may have first formed in response to a real, expressed desire to understand the Bible better, most continue to meet out of a rather ill-defined sense of duty. Studying the Bible is what Christians are supposed to do. The evidence indicates that many people join church learning groups simply because they are joiners. They value being with other people and, above all, they enjoy the opportunity to learn about other people and their experiences. They are inquisitive and want to be reassured that others share their concerns and experiences.

The learning that is integral to this is predominantly ordinary learning. Its genesis is a thoroughly human activity, and not essentially religious. It's what we do all the time without really thinking about it: listening to one another, sharing stories, and learning by and through reflecting on these, individually and together. It might be said to be the kind of learning that takes place at a conference bar over a drink, rather than during the organized seminars.

Ordinary Learning is Relational and Conversational

We found that, in the context of church learning groups, ordinary learning is founded on conversation and the quality of relationships. We observed that people value the opportunity to share their experiences and to listen to the stories of others, but that this can only be achieved where there is a feeling of trust, acceptance and mutual respect. It was also plain that many people worry that their feelings, thoughts and experiences may *not* be shared by others; and that their faith, such as it is, may be unorthodox. They are then hugely relieved to discover that many other people share such worries and misgivings. Time and again we heard comments such as:

> The discussion is best: it's informal and I don't feel quite as stupid as before. It's marvellous what I learn.

> [The course] gave a feeling of acceptance and an opportunity to talk about God, and not feel embarrassed to have doubts or issues.

> It's very free and easy. People feel free to express opinions; it might be unorthodox, but I value that.

> You can ask daft questions and feel safe; it's comforting and comfortable.

The dominant characteristic of this process of learning is that it is relational and conversational. It is not a learning of propositions, but an appreciation and endorsement that to be religious is about engagement in a way of life. Insofar as this is more about the process of faith than the content of belief, it is essentially tentative and sometimes hesitant. It recognizes the necessity of struggling with conflicting ideas and with serious doubt, but it does so in a way that is typically engaged, passionate and committed. To this extent, the religious form of ordinary learning may go beyond the very human process of learning through conversation and reflection. But its outcomes are wholly consonant with this. Overwhelmingly they describe deepened relationships:

> The beauty of house groups is that I've learned something about you tonight even though I've known you for years – it allows you to talk at a deeper level.

> In groups like this we build up trust and a relationship and friendship.

> It's so much more helpful to learn … from others in a down-to-earth way.

> The content of the course enabled the sharing of stories that helped to deepen relationships.

If and when God is mentioned explicitly, this kind of outcome does not change. For example:

> People are relaxed with one another and ask questions about their faith. It is quite amazing what comes out.

> As I get older, I'm more willing to question and to say I don't understand this, God; but oddly, my faith seems deeper too.

Ordinary Learning is Tentative and Embraces Diversity

Such ordinary learning, characterized by conversation and informality, is subtle and provisional. It delights in a rich variety of different perspectives and points of view (and is thus distinctively adult). It values and affirms the individual person, and is both reflective and self-critical.

We discovered that Bible study often provided a particularly fascinating illustration of how the significance of tentativeness, combined with an openness to and embracing of different perspectives, may function.

First, it is important to note that Bible study can be daunting. We found that many learners in these churches are reluctant to engage in Bible study for a variety of reasons. One person, for example, said that 'people need to see why they should do Bible study. They won't do Bible study for Bible study's sake. Even the name "Bible study" could be a barrier. The Bible is to be believed, not studied.' Another added, 'I think the Bible tends to put people off: they think it frightfully serious.' Others were reluctant to engage with Bible study lest they were shown to be ignorant. This was one of the main factors that prevented people from joining any kind of church group: 'I might feel frightened if my question was a bit silly – the fear of being shown up', 'People can be put off because they think they know less than others', 'I'm frightened that if I go to a class I won't understand.'

When, however, these barriers are breached and a group is given permission, opportunity and encouragement to open the Bible and ask questions of it – in an atmosphere of trust, confidence and acceptance – we were told that the results could be startling, even (as one young woman remarked) 'an amazing eye-opener'.

Even in conservative evangelical groups, we found that this view went hand in hand with a process that typically allowed several different hermeneutics to operate within a discussion, not only with little apparent discomfort or conflict, but with a ready acceptance that a range of positions might significantly enrich the discussion, and function as a gateway to truth. At its simplest level, we heard comments such as 'different translations may help'; but at a deeper level, as one person said, 'Others' views help [me] to understand the written word. It's not always easy to take in.' Or again, 'We like different perspectives; we think differently on things, we can get different insights.' This typically sophisticated, subtle and adult process was not narrowly relativist. It did not mean that learners necessarily held that one view was as good as another; but it recognized that complexities articulated by individuals enabled the whole group to grasp a more real and complete appreciation of the truths revealed in and through the process of grappling with scripture.

We also discovered a striking example of the way in which this subtle process, nurtured by trust and a proper tentativeness, can so easily be compromised. A young woman turned up in three different Bible study groups, each in a different denominational setting. She had a formidable ability to quote biblical texts and was determined to use this knowledge to contribute to each group, but her interventions seldom proved helpful. Her persistence in offering the 'right answer' was consistently effective in stifling discussion. This provided a rather stark illustration of the way in which the employment of a more obviously pietistic, formal and sometimes academic theology can consistently miss the point of a discussion – and also lack the grace and sensitivity to engage with the more dynamic, personal theologies that are the stuff of ordinary learning.

A recent study of adult Roman Catholics in north-east England (Moran, 2010) investigated the 'results of a policy of investing heavily in the education and formation of the young, while virtually neglecting the ongoing formation of adults.' It concluded that many of those interviewed could be said to have an 'adult' faith that is, in part at least, the product of an ecclesial hierarchy that fears diversity and dissent. If Patricia Moran is right, this would seem to be another, and perhaps more seriously worrying example, of the stifling of ordinary learning. Counter to this, however, our research also showed that, given the opportunity to engage with the Bible in an atmosphere of trust and acceptance, Roman Catholic groups were perfectly adept at engaging in ordinary learning and took no less delight in diversity that did those from any other tradition. Ordinary learning is not easily suppressed.

The Role of Story in Ordinary Learning

One of the reasons why this is so, and why ordinary learning may remain hidden from even some of the most careful studies, is that it is essentially a spoken rather than a written process. Similarly, ordinary theology, which is the tentative product of ordinary learning, typically not only resists being written down but is also fundamentally compromised by any attempt to do so.

Ordinary learning is dependent on story. A good example of this role of story that emerged from our survey was the use of film by a number of the groups. One film that engaged the imagination of several groups from different Christian traditions was *Chocolat*.[1] An engaging, but rather improbable and slightly saccharine romance, it makes its own point. Rather like a parable told by Jesus, it invites those who pay it attention to explore and play with their own values and experiences. Is it not significant that when Jesus was confronted with a problem his default position seems to have been to adopt the typically Jewish response of telling a story? The telling and sharing of stories is not a descent into gossip, nor an excuse for self-indulgent introspection, but offers rich and rewarding possibilities for learning that help us take stock of our situation, and free our imaginations to consider radical new possibilities.

Is Ordinary Learning Distinctively Feminine?

Nicola Slee argues that the sharing of stories, as part of a spirituality in which relationship, dialogue and conversation are also highly significant, characterizes a

---

[1] *Chocolat* (2000) was directed by Lasse Hallström, and was based on the novel of the same name by Joanne Harris.

typically feminine way of learning (Slee, 2004). As the shape of ordinary learning is wholly consistent with this, and as the gender balance of the groups we surveyed were typically dominated by women, it may be that this account of ordinary learning primarily describes how women learn best. Slee, following Belenky and others, calls for the creation of 'relational and conversational settings' in which (in 'contrast to the traditions of academia') a 'midwife teacher' may enable learners to give birth to their own ideas. She argues: 'Midwife teachers provide a culture for growth by encouraging genuine dialogue, marked by the collaborate pursuit of understanding, permission for uncertainty and tentativeness, the embrace of diversity and the connection of the student's subjective experience with the objective knowledge provided by scholars' (Slee, 2004: 170–71). Ellen Clark-King has also described the deep significance of 'relationality', earthed primarily in family and community, in the God-talk of women in urban Newcastle upon Tyne (Clark-King, 2004).

This describes, almost exactly, the process of ordinary learning as we witnessed it. But it was clear from our research that some men also welcomed this intimate, feminine dynamic of learning. More work is needed to explore the relationship between gender and learning styles in Christian formation, and the extent to which the processes of ordinary theology may perhaps sit more comfortably with feminine ways of holding faith than with masculine ones (cf. Astley, 2002: 50–51, 77–82).

Ordinary Learning as Lay, Adult Learning

As I have often suggested above, another essential aspect of the ordinary learning that this project discovered is that, like ordinary theology, it is typically lay and adult. The split described by Edward Farley between formal theological education and 'church education' leaves clergy ill-equipped to reflect theologically on their own experience and practice, and that of their congregations (Farley, 1983: 130–31; cf. Astley, 2002: 62–4). But ordinary learning, as we encountered it, is not quite like this. It is indeed a form of 'church education', but one in which the clergy may be accepted as equals, enabled to find new meaning and significance and to make a valid connection with their own religious experience and practice. In such contexts, clergy are also permitted to be tentative, to express doubt and to receive acceptance in a way that enhances rather than diminishes their role as local leaders, *precisely* because they commit themselves to a common task of honest exploration with the people they are called to lead.

Of course, not all ministers are prepared to risk such vulnerability. Some are sufficiently scared by the prospect that they prefer to retreat into the remembered husk of their theological studies – lest they are forced to place their own fragile, dying faith on the line. I well remember one such man who admitted that he had retreated into preaching a narrow interpretation of the Gospels because if he were to face his doubts he could not possibly continue in ministry, and felt he had no other prospect of employment. One of the risks of ordinary learning for the clergy is that it ties them more deeply and personally into the life of the community they serve, and may undermine any wish to maintain a professional detachment. They get to know other people better, but in so doing become better known themselves.

In this sample, the groups' ordinary learning, like their ordinary theology, was distinctively adult. This is hardly surprising, perhaps, given that the vast majority of the learners we encountered were aged over 50, with many over 70. Their way of holding faith fits fairly neatly with the stage of 'conjunctive faith' described by James Fowler, which becomes more common from mid-life onwards. It is characterized by a kind of 'second naïveté' that allows a genuine openness combined with committed belief, while recognizing that truth is complex and being willing to hold together the tensions of polar opposite insights (Fowler, 1984: 64–7). The evidence for this way of being in faith is to be found in statements such as: 'People are relaxed with one another and ask questions about their faith. It is quite amazing what comes out'; 'people feel more confident after the experience of learning together – and we learn to respect each other's temperaments (that's real maturity)'; and, in the comment quoted earlier, 'as I get older I'm more willing to question and to say I don't understand this, God; but oddly, my faith seems deeper too.'

The nature of such an adult way of holding and expressing faith may also help explain why the earnest young woman who was so anxious to demonstrate her extraordinarily detailed knowledge of the Bible only served to silence the groups she attended. Her failure went beyond that of one who served up second-hand theology culled from the academy; she was just not on the same wavelength as the rest of the group and did not appear to understand this. However, there were also clear instances of intergenerational learning, provoking comments of appreciation such as: 'Older people learn from younger ones. Sometimes children ask the obvious questions that the adults would like to ask.'

Ordinary Learning and Academic Theology

Ordinary learning as described here is typically a group activity, but it is fed by a wide range of other resources and learning opportunities. There was little enthusiasm for Bible study notes, and even fewer people admitted to reading a theological book – academic or popular. But we found, for example, that many learners resort to the Internet to expand and reinforce their learning: though, significantly, they also often commented that they were unsure how trustworthy such resources might be. As one woman remarked, 'We need wisdom and discernment when we look as the Net, it's so big.' Learners look to the group for that discernment. It is in the group, too, that concepts from academic theology may be sifted and assessed.

It was significant that we heard evidence of a group of distinguished professional theologians who welcomed the opportunity (as a house group) to paint, embroider, listen to music or make things – and then reflect on that process. They were prepared to recognize that neither ordinary learning nor ordinary theology was antithetical to academic learning and theology. Each could shed light on the other.

It was, however, fascinating to note that no ordinary learning group that we encountered was concerned to discuss the 'big' issues that so exercise senior church leaders and councils. There was, for example, no interest shown in matters of human sexuality and how that might relate (or not) to the church's ministerial organization; and no discussion of future patterns of ministerial deployment. The concerns of ordinary learning, as of ordinary theology, were overwhelmingly to do with shared lives and everyday decisions – and what the faith tradition might have to say to these truly serious matters.

Conclusion

It would appcar that ordinary learning is the preferred learning style of many Christians in north-east England, especially women and those of both genders who are prepared to come together in groups. It is a distinctively group activity. Insofar as the outcome of ordinary learning is ordinary theology, this qualifies somewhat the assertion that ordinary theology is a 'personal thing', if that were to be taken too individualistically; but it affirms Astley's comment that 'the first mode of religious learning is a product of social formation' (Astley, 2002: 34).

Ordinary learning is sophisticated and subtle. It is prepared to take risks and thus create ordinary theologies that give hope and sustenance to the Christian community. And the sheer liveliness and faithfulness of the groups we experienced suggest that, despite many outward signs of institutional decline, new life *is* blowing through the churches of this region – and surely others, too.

References

Astley, Jeff (2002), *Ordinary Theology: Looking, Listening and Learning in Theology*, Aldershot: Ashgate.

Clark-King, Ellen (2004), *Theology by Heart: Women, the Church and God*, Peterborough: Epworth.

Farley, Edward (1983), *Theologia: The Fragmentation and Unity of Theological Education*, Philadelphia: Fortress.

Fowler, James W. (1984), *Becoming Adult, Becoming Christian: Adult Development and Christian Faith*, San Francisco: Harper & Row.

Moran, Patricia (2010), 'Voices from the Pew: The Experience of Religious Formation as Reported by Adult Roman Catholics in the Diocese of Hexham and Newcastle', PhD thesis, University of Newcastle upon Tyne.

Slee, Nicola (2004), *Women's Faith Development: Patterns and Processes*, Aldershot: Ashgate.

Chapter 21

Ordinary Theology as Process: A Phenomenographic Approach

Grant Barclay

Introduction

The category of ordinary theology covers not only the content of the beliefs of those who have not received a 'scholarly, academic or systematic' theological education (Astley, 2002a: 56), but also the 'processes of ordinary people's articulation of their religious understanding' (Astley, 2002b: 26), while recognizing that connections exist between content and process and that the outcome of learning is 'profoundly affected' by its form (ibid.: 22). Examining the processes whereby ordinary theologians articulate and share their views may offer insights that support Christian learning (see Barclay, 2009: 13).

Ordinary theologians often share views concerning faith through small group discussions (Astley and Christie, 2007: 22; Hull 1985: 17), but the extent to which such settings support the articulation and sharing of their beliefs may be limited. Contributing may be perceived as difficult by some, requiring rapid reflection and response or familiarity with a specialized vocabulary, and participants may be daunted by being expected to contribute rather than remain silent.

Prior subject knowledge and some awareness of patterns of discussion ('how the game is played') may be helpful. Preparatory readings can enhance subject knowledge; but unfamiliarity with process may inhibit participation, thus hindering the very involvement that fosters knowledge, skill and confidence.

Social Learning

Lectures or sermons may support reflection on faith-related issues, but they offer only a limited opportunity for the mutual articulation of views. Social learning emphasizes the pedagogical value of participating in social practice (Jones, 2008: 619) and indicates that learning may be encouraged by learners' mutual engagement. Drane implicitly advocates social learning within church congregations, suggesting that Christian learning that is largely confined to listening encourages attitudes of consumption rather than creation, leading to the disempowerment of hearers (Drane, 2008: 111). Differentiating those who proffer wisdom from its recipients has been described as an 'unhealed wound' (Pickard, 2006: 82), which needs to be addressed by recognizing various ministries (97).

Lave and Wenger (1991) emphasize involvement within a community as an aspect of learning, contending that those who seek to learn require 'access to practice as resource for learning, rather than to instruction' and that 'language is part of practice, and it is in practice that people learn' (85). Discourse within a community is, then, an influential and transforming activity. Wenger (1998) describes the outcomes of such learning as 'chang[ing] who we are by changing our ability to participate … And this ability is configured socially with respect to practices, communities, and economies of meaning where it shapes our identities' (226).

Vicarious Learning

Can listening be temporarily decoupled from contributing? This is achieved in vicarious learning, a process that is of pedagogic value in permitting learners to observe others describing their thoughts without any possibility of the observer contributing. 'A learner's approach to learning something is shaped by the observation of others attempting to learn it' (Mayes et al., 2002: 213).

Several reasons have been advanced for this. The lower cognitive and emotional load of watching without being required to frame a contribution allows learners to devote more resources to considering an issue (McKendree et al., 1998b: 114). Observing also makes approaches, strategies and processes connected with learning more explicit (Mayes et al., 2002: 213), and may be affectively helpful in 'drawing learners in' to a discussion (McKendree et al., 1998b: 117).

Vicarious learning has been applied to faith issues through observational spiritual learning. This suggests that individuals develop perspectives connected with faith by looking to the examples of others, principally how they have considered and lived out their faith. Oman and Thoresen (2003a, 2003b) have identified this learning through observation across a range of religions and within several Christian denominations, though investigating roles for observational spiritual learning in spiritual development has received little attention (Oman and Thoresen, 2003a: 151, 154). Bandura (2003: 171) supports the contention that spiritual modelling is influential in the development of faith. Learning gains may result from being exposed to others' developing views as well as to expert opinions. Oman and Thoresen suggest a programme for supporting religious development by providing access to helpful models through groups, texts and 'live observation' by making specific types of media available to learners (Oman and Thoresen, 2003a: 158).

The Investigation

Ordinary theology is frequently articulated conversationally in dialogue. Learning may be encouraged through activities that promote such participation. Coupling too closely the opportunity to listen to others with the requirement to contribute oneself may be unhelpful, however, particularly in the early stages of considering an issue. Hearing other people's ordinary theologies *in advance* of articulating one's own may be more useful, but is unusual in a small group setting.

To facilitate this, the dialogues of other ordinary theologians needed to be captured and made available on demand in straightforward and economically feasible ways (Mayes et al., 2002: 213), which learners can access and use directly (Strom, 2002: 5). In this investigation, video recordings of ordinary theologians offering their views on issues initially introduced in a printed text were shared among others in advance of a group discussion. This approach combined text, live observation and group discussion, but permitted the observing of video clips to be decoupled from contributing to the discussion. The video clips were available on demand for participants at times and locations, and for durations, convenient to them.[1]

This adult Christian learning programme, set in a Church of Scotland congregation, provided resource materials and opportunities for individual comment and group discussion. Each participant, having read a relevant article or excerpt and having watched video clips of their peers' views, offered their spoken views in video recorded conversations. All video clips showed the researcher-producer in conversation with one contributor; there were no single 'talking heads'. As learners sometimes require support, or reasons to speak or engage in discourse (McKendree et al., 1998a: 3), 15 activities or open questions based on Ohlsson's (1995) epistemic tasks for generating discourse on abstract concepts were provided to the contributors. These included: 'What have you come across here that's most different to what you think about this subject?', 'Can you explain how you went about reading this, and understanding it, and making connections with what you think or how you live?' and 'What are the two or three most important things for you in this – and why are they important to you?'

Video recording offers the possibility of re-recording contributions to allow a clearer articulation of views. While there is less need for an ongoing flow of discussion whose pace has to be maintained, the need to offer an articulated view requires contributors to consider the subject in sufficient depth. Articulating one's ideas is often a useful part of refining them (Astley, 2002a: 119). Doing so in conversation with one other person, with little pressure immediately to defend or justify one's views, might offer an appropriate rehearsal opportunity.

---

[1] The material was originally envisaged as documents and video clips viewed on a computer, but DVDs viewed on domestic televisions were added to include those who had no computer access.

These recorded contributions were edited and then made available as video clips to subsequent contributors, in addition to the printed text, prior to their own conversations which were also recorded. In this way the number of clips available to each subsequent contributor increased. The final resource, consisting of the text and all the video clips, was distributed either on a CD or DVD to encourage further face-to-face group discussions on the topic (which were not recorded).

Ordinary theology informed the decision to share the churchgoers' views and the methods used to capture and analyse participants' experiences (achieved using an approach from phenomenography, described below). The recorded and transcribed research conversations of 32 informants were repeatedly read, analysed and categorized in an outcome space: that is, a set of interrelated but distinct categories into which the descriptions could be organized. This provided an interpreted summary of the experiences of participating in adult Christian education activities that involved printed and video clip resources and provided opportunities for people to speak both as individuals and in groups.

Phenomenography is an empirical approach allowing insight to be gained into the range of ways that a phenomenon such as a text or a situation is understood from the perspective of those who experience it (Marton and Säljö, 1976). It provides empirical evidence as to how learners experience aspects of the processes of learning (Laurillard, 2002: 69), classified in a limited number of qualitatively different categories that are related to one another in a logical and hierarchical manner in an outcome space, and allows large quantities of data to be analysed in highly interpreted and relatively sparse forms (Jones, 2004: 108-9). Phenomenographic approaches have been employed in educational research and within Christian education (Hella and Wright, 2009).

Learners are encouraged to reflect in a self-aware manner on their experiences (Marton and Booth, 1997: 34), foregrounding people's experience of a phenomenon and leading to an understanding of learning as a developing relationship between the world and the world as it is experienced in a range of ways by a number of individuals, whose described experiences are aggregated and distinguished in the analysis. The resulting outcome space categorizes classes of described experiences, permitting discovery of the range of learning by analysing a number of learners' descriptions (ibid.: 13).

Ordinary theology supports methodologies that place the experiences of ordinary theologians at the centre of research endeavours (Astley, 2002a: 2). Here, informants' descriptions, from individual comments and discussion in groups, supply an empirical basis for understanding their experience of using resources, allowing differences in experiences to be identified.

Findings

Distinguishing and relating informants' accounts of experiencing the resources and discussions, by means of a phenomenographic analysis of transcripts, produced an outcome space describing various experiences of participating in these activities. A separate, though similar, analysis led to additional outcome spaces concerning the influence of reading the text, watching others' video clips, articulating one's own view and group discussion.

The outcome space indicating experiences of participating may be represented in four quadrants, as shown in Figure 21.1. Descriptions of experiences could be located within one of four categories, related to one another by the theme of participation and forming a hierarchy such that higher categories included lower ones. For example, the most inclusive Category A involved influencing lifestyle through cognitive participation (Category B) which also included an identity of participation (Category C).

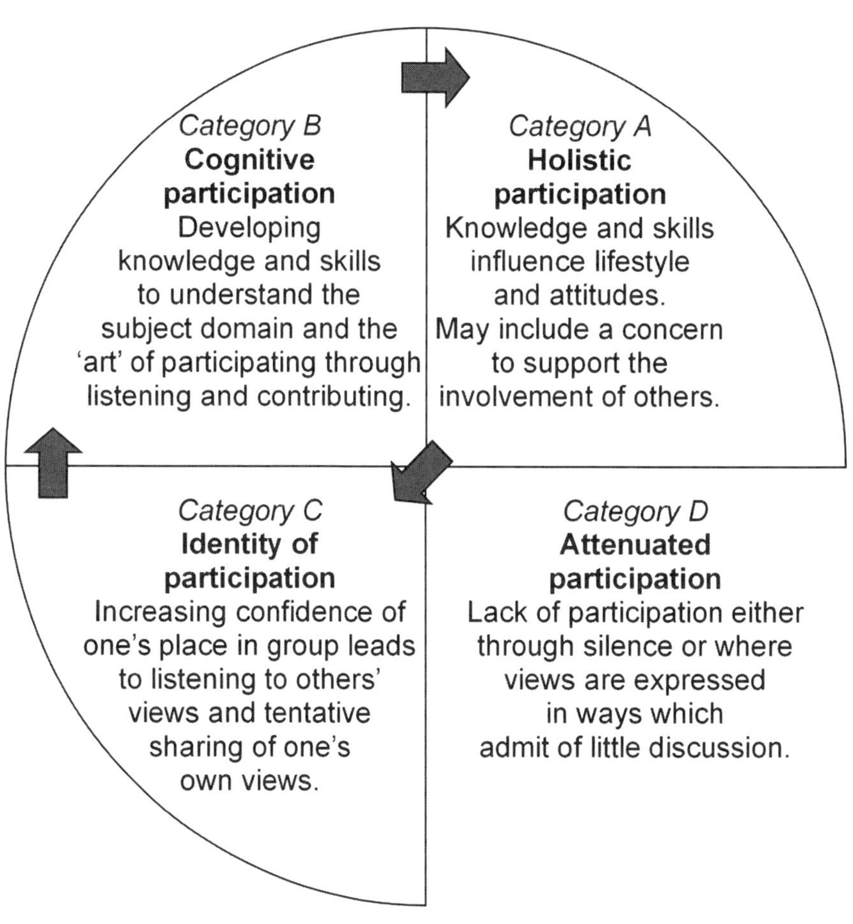

Figure 21.1 Outcome space indicating experiences of participating

In D, the least inclusive category, attenuated participation with others was evidenced where group members reported feeling unable to contribute or they anticipated little positive sense of participating:

> I think you can tell when somebody's got a viewpoint and they're not going to change from it.
>
> *Is that not as helpful?*
>
> Absolutely not.
>
> *Why not to you?*
>
> I think because, you know, people have switched off. You can tell that they've decided that's what the case is and that there's not going to be a discussion and you think that any discussion will feel like a personal attack. (AP: para. 2.176)

A development of one's ability to participate, based on a self-perception of belonging within a group, was discerned in Category C. This sense of membership, including the perception of being valued, encouraged people to listen to others' views and to offer, sometimes tentatively, their personal views:

> The fact that although we're all sitting there with the same background in regards to the church, nobody can turn round and say, 'You can't say that,' or 'your views aren't relevant.' I feel that by [participating in a discussion] some people are taking notice of what I say with regards to church life. (CM: para. 2.152)

Such awareness of belonging was further developed in Category B to allow exploration of ideas and develop skills in participating in discussions, while also including a greater freedom to admit that one's knowledge was incomplete. The views of others assisted in enlarging one's own understanding:

> I like to read something for myself and get my own views and thoughts on it and I liked the DVD because it gave other people's views and thoughts on the same thing so it made me, made me, think more. … I think listening to other people and their views helped my understanding of what I had read. (CS: para. 1.23, 25)

In the most inclusive Category A, increased knowledge and reflective skills influenced individuals' attitudes and lifestyles, evidenced by a described intent to apply the insights resulting from reflecting on the resources and discussion to life situations: 'it was more what … I had learned about my life from it, not what I had learned about the Lord's Prayer' (AJ: para. 2.32). In a few cases, this development of attitude included a concern to ensure that others were enabled to participate to a greater extent in the community's discussion and reflection activities: 'I think I was hoping I was helping other people in the group by introducing my contribution and, I suppose, I had a little bit of a background I could bring to it' (AH: para. 1.96).

Participation comes partly through contributing to discussions, which develops an 'identity of participation' – both contributing and being self-aware of a right and ability so to do:

> We function best when the depth of our knowing is steeped in an identity of participation, that is, when we can contribute to shaping the communities that define us as knowers … honouring the meaningfulness of their participation and valuing their membership as a key to their ability to contribute to the competence of the organisation. (Wenger, 1998: 253)

This has three parts. The first is an identity connected with perceiving a right to participate which is not entirely dependent on the content of one's contributions. The second is possessing sufficient skills to engage with the Christian tradition, transmitted both in texts and through dialogue. Participating in discussion requires combined skills, including reading, listening, assessing, interpreting and responding quickly in conversation. Motivation to participate is the third element, grounded in an understanding of a community which fosters faith growth, but which is also valued by members and is dependent on their participation for its continued life.

Some informants found the printed text provided a helpful structure for considering the issue, though it was occasionally perceived as an authoritative contribution that inhibited their offering and developing their own views, which they perceived as greatly inferior to those of experts.

Others, who found the text's demands almost insurmountable, reported that video clips of other participants offered an accessible range of views, which were spoken conversationally, possibly in simpler language and accompanied by gesture, and which assisted their comprehension and encouraged perseverance in considering difficult subjects. This was true both cognitively and affectively, illustrated in this extract from informant CP who was presented with new and challenging views addressed both in the text and by a clergy contributor, Helen:

> I'd read, and then I was like, 'I just don't like this man [Schweitzer] at all.' [Laughs] … The things he was saying about how God had abandoned him [Jesus] and all of that. I was like, that's so wrong, em, and then, when I watched the DVD and Helen said that she disagreed … so I thought, right, so that means I've kinda disagreed, so I'm kinda right. I'll give it a … I will read it again. And after I'd read it again, I understood well there is some things they're saying that I still disagree with, but there are things that I do agree with. (CP: para. 1.138–49)

The range of views in video clips permitted opportunities for reflection through comparing and contrasting contributions. Watching fellow church members who were familiar to them encouraged some to perceive the apparently daunting task of articulating their own views as achievable:

> *Did seeing videos of others help you speak about the text in your video?*
>
> It did. I think it gives you confidence when you see other people taking part, people that you know. If you see people that you know doing it, you think that's fine, I'll be able to do it as well. (AS: para. 3.70–71)

Being asked to contribute a view encouraged some informants to perceive their valued role within the community:

> What really is at the back of my mind is that [the text's author] studied theology for years and years and here's me, Joe Soap, and you interviewed me and I don't know one per cent of what he knew. It may not matter but there's something in the back of your mind … the fact that you're reading the text written by some expert.
>
> *So the fact that the video clips are made by people who are not any more expert than we are – doesn't that make them valueless?*
>
> No. That helps. The fact that we're learning from each other … I think the fact that you know the people on the video. That matters. I think it gives you a better insight into what they're thinking. (CM: para 2.114–16)

Recorded conversations were informal, though the requirement to articulate views was considered helpfully challenging:

> *Having all this [process of recording a conversation] helps you understand this?*
>
> Yes, because as soon as you start to speak you get whether you have really thought about this at all, and I'm way all over the place in my thinking, so I think it helps you to clarify your thinking … It's almost a kind of process of thinking through what your thoughts are. (DE: para. 3.52–4)

Editing recorded conversations enabled comments to be repeated, or digressions and hesitancies to be excluded, leading to a clearer presentation of views.

Reflection

Video clips of the articulations of churchgoers make ordinary theology more visible, while sharing those articulations demonstrates the processes of ordinary theology within a congregation-based learning setting.

Recorded articulations of ordinary theology differ from group discussions in being discrete rather than sequential, available for longer periods and at times that are more convenient to viewers, and offering opportunities for reflection without demanding any immediate response. Positively, this may encourage continued consideration and remove the possibly daunting demands of speaking in a group. Negatively, the lack of immediate interaction may be frustrating. The challenge of being recorded on video seemed not to preclude involvement, particularly where peers were observed to have succeeded in the task. It may have provided both a reason to consider the issue and an early opportunity to articulate views. This affirmed the value of the ordinary theologians' contributions, a process described by one informant as engendering a greater engagement, both with the subject and with those who were also literally seen to be reflecting on it, as companions in a joint activity of theological reflection.

The reported experiences evidenced a range of senses of participating, suggesting that a real pedagogical benefit is derived from enabling learners to hear other ordinary theologians' views and to articulate their own. This deepens subject knowledge and increases awareness of participating in a community of enquiry. Sharing ordinary theologies offers opportunities to encourage such participation.

The theological discourse investigated here is spoken, and thus distinguishable from academic or professional theology, which is generally written. The value of spoken discourse – which has a long-standing Christian heritage (Botha, 1993: 414) – should be noted. Spoken contributions may now readily be captured, stored and accessed. (The technical requirements for this investigation were modest and are becoming increasingly widespread via a range of television, computer and Internet-based technologies.) The emphasis on spoken theology exemplifies a new type of interaction between the processes of communication and their content. This approach may be contrasted with that of viewing pedagogic strategies in instrumental terms, which risks omitting wider aspects of learning.

Phenomenography as an empirical research methodology foregrounds ordinary theologians' views by analysing and interpreting research conversations. While limited in scope, the emphasis on process aspects of ordinary theology in this study suggests that investigating the contexts and processes of Christian learning may furnish not only academic insights, but also practical benefits by assisting reflection on and discussion of issues of faith. It is offered here as a contribution towards developing the study of ordinary theology.

References

Astley, J. (2002a), *Ordinary Theology: Looking, Listening and Learning in Theology*, Aldershot: Ashgate.

Astley, J. (2002b), 'In Defence of Ordinary Theology', *British Journal of Theological Education*, 13, 1: 21–35.

Astley, J. and A. Christie (2007), *Taking Ordinary Theology Seriously*, Cambridge: Grove Books.

Bandura, A. (2003), 'On the Psychosocial Impact and Mechanisms of Spiritual Modeling', *International Journal for the Psychology of Religion*, 13, 3: 167–73.

Barclay, G. (2009), 'Participation in Adult Christian Education: An Investigation into a Role for Multimedia Resources', PhD thesis, Lancaster University.

Botha, P.J.J. (1993), 'The Verbal Art of the Pauline Letters: Rhetoric, Performance and Presence', in S.E. Porter and T.H. Olbricht (eds), *Rhetoric and the New Testament: Essays from the 1992 Heidelberg Conference*, Sheffield: JSOT Press, pp. 409–28.

Drane, J. (2008), *After McDonaldization*, London: Darton, Longman and Todd.

Hella, E. and A. Wright (2009), 'Learning "About" and "From" Religion: Phenomenography, the Variation Theory of Learning and Religious Education in Finland and the UK', *British Journal of Religious Education*, 31, 1: 53–64.

Hull, J.M. (1985), *What Prevents Christian Adults from Learning?* London: SCM Press.

Jones, C.R. (2004), 'Quantitative and Qualitative Research: Conflicting Paradigms or Perfect Partners?', in S. Banks, P. Goodyear, V. Hodgson, C. Jones, V. Lally, D. McConnell and C. Steeples (eds), *Proceedings of the Fourth International Conference on Networked Learning*, Lancaster: Lancaster University and University of Sheffield, pp. 106–13.

Jones, C. (2008), 'What do we Mean by Networked Learning?', *Proceedings of 6th International Conference on Networked Learning*, Halkidiki, Greece, 5–6 May 2008, pp. 616–23.

Laurillard, D. (2002), *Rethinking University Teaching*, London: Routledge.

Lave, J. and E. Wenger (1991), *Situated Learning: Legitimate Peripheral Participation*, Cambridge: Cambridge University Press.

McKendree, J., J. Lee, F. Dineen and T. Mayes (1998a), 'The Vicarious Learner: Helping Students "Listen in" to Learn', *Distance Learning 1998: Proceedings of the Annual Conference on Distance Teaching and Learning*, Madison, Wis., 5–7 August 1998.

McKendree, J., K. Stenning, T. Mayes, J. Lee and R. Cox (1998b), 'Why Observing a Dialogue may Benefit Learning: The Vicarious Learner', *Journal of Computer Assisted Learning*, 14, 2: 110–19.

Marton, F. and S. Booth (1997), *Learning and Awareness*, Mahwah, NJ: Lawrence Erlbaum Associates.

Marton, F. and R. Säljö (1976), 'On Qualitative Differences in Learning: I – Outcome and Process', *British Journal of Educational Psychology*, 46: 4–11.

Mayes, T., F. Dineen, J. McKendree and J. Lee (2002), 'Learning from Watching Others Learn', in C. Steeples and C. Jones (eds), *Networked Learning: Perspectives and Issues*, London: Springer-Verlag, pp. 213–27.

Ohlsson, S. (1995), 'Learning to Do and Learning to Understand: A Lesson and a Challenge for Cognitive Modelling', in P. Reimann and H. Spada (eds),

Learning in Humans and Machines: Toward an Interdisciplinary Learning Science, London: Pergamon, pp. 37–62.

Oman, D. and C.E. Thoresen (2003a), 'Spiritual Modeling: A Key to Spiritual and Religious Growth?', *International Journal for the Psychology of Religion*, 13, 3: 149–66.

Oman, D. and C.E. Thoresen (2003b), 'The Many Frontiers of Spiritual Modeling', *International Journal for the Psychology of Religion*, 13, 3: 197–213.

Pickard, S. (2006), 'Healing the Wound of Ministry: A New Paradigm', *Ecclesiology*, 3, 1: 81–101.

Strom, J. (2002), 'Streaming Video: Overcoming Barriers for Teaching and Learning', International Symposium on Educational Conferencing 2002, Banff, Canada, http://cde.athabascau.ca/ISEC2002/papers/strom.pdf [accessed 13 August 2008].

Wenger, E. (1998), *Communities of Practice: Learning, Meaning, and Identity*, Cambridge: Cambridge University Press.

Index of Names

Index of Subjects